FROM LONELINESS
TO *LOVE*

FROM LONELINESS TO LOVE

My Miraculous Transformation

CYNTHIA D. JOHNSON

Order this book online at www.trafford.com
or email orders@trafford.com

Most Trafford titles are also available at major online book retailers.

Printed in the United States of America.

ISBN: 978-1-4669-7466-1 (sc)
ISBN: 978-1-4669-7465-4 (e)

Trafford rev. 01/10/2013

 www.trafford.com

North America & international
toll-free: 1 888 232 4444 (USA & Canada)
fax: 812 355 4082

CONTENTS

FOREWORD

It's one thing to hear, and maybe even read, about one's exhausting hands-on experience with the very gutter of life's un-wanted dilemmas. From Loneliness to Love, is an amazing shameless master-piece that is sure to grip the hearts of all who dare to release the shame of their past, and use their past as the bridge to triumph. Life's ups and downs are the proof that one needs to connect their own personal pieces of their life's puzzle . . .

I am extremely elated to have been privileged this wonderful opportunity to endorse this awesome book that depicts surviving adversity. Author Johnson, very uniquely shares her story with a timeline that gives struggle after struggle in their proper timing. I'm excited to read this story, because it signifies that just because you may go through rough times, your strength is a byproduct of issues. Although, you may find yourself troubled due to seemingly unavoidable situations, it's all about enduring which is the mere thing that allows you to overcome.

Johnson states that she never thought about writing a book before . . . sometimes, it takes our brick walls to open our eyes, and cause a revolution with inner purpose. This work is indeed a miraculous transformation symbolizing that endurance is one of the major factors in survival. It took everything that this author went through to mold and shape her into the mentally developed motivator that she is today. I commend her as she brazenly shares her story to help encourage those who are in need of encouragement.

Normally Foreward's are lengthy, but due to the forthcoming text; I rest my case to allow this outstanding work speak for itself. Thank you author Johnson, for bravely sharing your story . . . . From Loneness to Love.

Eric Maurice Clark

INTRODUCTION

I must start by letting you know that before now, I've never had any aspirations to be an author. In fact, I didn't even know I was writing this book when God had me start. Funny story, I had finally reached the point in my life where I was willing to let God in. I was actually willing to listen to Him and follow His lead no matter what. He had let me work myself so deep into a hole that I finally realized that HE was my only way out. You see, I am a very stubborn and self-sufficient person. I had been so hurt during the course of my life to that point that I didn't want to need anyone else's help. I had too many terrible experiences where I accepted someone's help, and then they expected things of me that I either could not or should not have given in return. God doesn't work that way though. When we decide to truly let Him into our lives, He simply loves us through the hard times and restores us to a better position than we've ever been in before.

When God started dealing with my heart in tremendous ways, He laid it on my heart to start journaling my daily walk through a couple of social media pages and in my own private personal journal. At the time, I had no idea that He would later ask me to go back and retrieve all of this data, all of the information that composes this spiritual journal that you are about to read, and compile it into a book. This book starts in December 2010 when I spent that magnificent New Year's Eve with my Heavenly Father. New Year's Eve has traditionally been a heartbreaking holiday for me, but this particular New Year's Eve was different. God laid it on my heart to turn down all of the social invitations that would be extended to me and simply spend the evening with HIM. I can't tell you how glad I am that I did just that. This amazing New Year's Eve would be the beginning of a magnificent, overwhelming, and miraculous healing season for me. At times, the pain was, in my mind, too much to bear; but the Lord is always faithful, and He never left my side. He stayed with me through all of the anger, pain, tears, rebellion, repeated trips and falls; all of the exhaustion, loneliness, and deeper pain than I thought I could ever bear. HE healed it all!

What you will find in these pages is my spiritual journal, what the Lord gave me every single day as He and I walked through this amazing, heart-wrenching healing process together. (NOTE: I have purposely kept the journal entries in their raw form; I didn't "pretty them up" so they could be read easier. I wanted to pass this information along to you exactly as it appeared in my journal.) When He showed me what He wanted me to do with this journal—write a book and tell my story—at first, I was scared to death. Then after He calmed my nerves, He showed me that if I would just be faithful to Him to get my story out there, He would bless many others through it. If anyone at all, even just one person, can realize how much God loves them, how much they are Truly worth to HIM; if anyone can see past the expectations and social norms of this world and really **get it** that **He loves** them more than anyone else possibly can; that they are not expendable, they are not worthless, they are not a waste of space, then the whole process has been well worth the journey. I need to let the world know that God has taken me from the pit of despair, a place where I felt totally and utterly worthless, a place where I was convinced that no one in the world would possibly ever love me, to a place where *I know* my worth is found in Him. I *know* that I am a priceless daughter of the Most-High King and that He has a *magnificent* plan for my life that I cannot even comprehend right now. If I can share this with just one person, if my story can encourage anyone to let the Lord bring them out of that horrible place, then all the pain has been more than worth it. God *loves* each and every one of us more than we can possibly dream or imagine. Please come along with me, and let me share my journey of heart-healing with you.

To give you just a little bit of background about me, I have been a single mother of a biracial child for nearly seventeen years now as I sit here typing this note to you. I had let the world, my situation, and my attitude put me in a very poor position in life. I let the enemy convince me that I was worth nothing and that no good man would ever want me. A lot of my pain revolved around the fact that

I felt completely and utterly unloved. This manifested itself with me trying to feel loved through human relationships (wrong relationships because they were all based on worldly standards instead of God's standards). Anytime any of these relationships didn't work out (and none of them ever worked out well at all), I would be completely and utterly devastated, sometimes to the point of not being able to get out of bed. I had actually called in to work sick before because some guy had walked out of my life, and I was so distraught that I could not function as I needed to for the next few days. I was so distraught about these things because I was gauging my personal worth through my relationships instead of looking to the true source of my worth—my Heavenly Father.

No matter what your pain revolves around, I am convinced that once we all realize how much we are loved by our Heavenly Father, only then can He completely heal our hearts and restore our lives. Your pain most likely comes from a different source than mine did, but at the core, pain is pain. God can and will heal *all* pain if we let Him. He doesn't just barge in and take control without our permission though. We must make the decision to let Him deal with our hearts and work in our lives every single day. We must be willing to be obedient to His will and His ways. In order to find out what His will and ways are, we must be in constant communication with Him through prayer, the reading of His word, and fellowship with other true Christians (Christ followers, not just pew warmers in the church building, but people who do His work and will in their daily lives, people who show Christ's love through their actions and caring for others). I learned quickly there is a huge difference between true Christ followers and those who darken the door of the church building once a week just to get "credit" for being there. I can honestly tell you that the people who made a real difference in my life when I was in my darkest places were people in whom I could see Christ's love. I didn't know what it was at the time, but I could tell that these people actually cared for me, even though they didn't know me. They didn't seem to judge me for my situation as so many others did . . . I wanted to find out more about these people and why they genuinely seemed to care. I had seen so little real true love in my life that they stuck out to me like a sore thumb. Who were these people, and why in the world did they care about me? When God catches your attention, He really catches it! This is my story of how my Jesus found and healed me.

The past few years of my life have been the most spectacular years yet! More than anything, I want to share what I've learned over these past few years with as many people who will listen. God has completely changed my perspective and my life! I never thought I would have a whole and complete life, especially without a husband, but God has shown me fullness in Him. For many years, I walked in loneliness, pain, suffering, self-condemnation, low self-esteem (well, to be honest, NO self-esteem), and woundedness from past heartache and past physical abuse. In short, I was convinced that I had messed up my life beyond repair. I had let other people convince me that I was worth nothing and had absolutely nothing to contribute to society. More than that, I was convinced that I would never be able to take care of myself, much less raise my daughter in any kind of constructive way. I was just another statistic to *everybody*, including myself. But what I didn't realize is that God never saw me as a statistic. He loves me more than I can even fathom, He pursued me like no other, He never gave up on me, and He brought me out of the pit of despair and saved me. Now I am completely and victoriously walking in the Light of His will for my life and am complete in Him.

For those that are wondering, no, I am not yet married. I still desire to be married, but it is no longer the reason I get up in the morning. It is no longer a tragedy when some man decides to leave my life. I am completely grounded in God's love for me and know, beyond all doubt, that He will bring my husband into my life when the time is right. You can live gloriously too, *regardless* of your marital situation or any other heartbreaking circumstance in your life. God loves each and every one of us more than we can even comprehend. I have been so tremendously blessed by what Jesus has shown me! In these pages, you will find His revelations to me as they happened. My hope and prayer is that they may bless you just as much as they have blessed me. God has used these revealed truths to completely change my life! I no longer walk in hopelessness, loneliness, and condemnation. I walk in His glory and know my worth in Him.

Please pray before reading the following that God will use the content to speak to you, bless you, and encourage you in your walk with Him. Our God is such a magnificent God. HE will speak to you and bless you . . . Just trust in Him and let Him transform your heart and, thereby, your life. Blessings to you forever in the Father.

December 2010

At this point in my life, I had been a single mother for fifteen years and had attained my paralegal certificate, associate's degree, bachelor's degree, and master's degree. I had done this all on my own with very little help from anyone else. I had locked down a good job in the energy industry, making a respectable amount of money, had a healthy child who was well provided for, and had a family that cared for me (relationships had been steadily healing for many years at this point). From the outside, it seemed I had it all together. I'd even had men walk out of my life because they were sure I was too good for them. Truth be told, I was miserable! I was still looking for love in all the *wrong* places. I felt empty inside, I felt like I would never be complete. Enough was never enough! There was always this terrible empty feeling inside of me that would just not go away. I knew no one truly loved me and always settled for wrong relationships because that's all I thought I would ever deserve. Lord knows, no *real* man would ever want to be with me—not with my past, the things I'd done, the people I'd allowed in my life before. I knew I wasn't worth anything regardless of what I'd achieved academically, and I was sure my daughter only loved me because I was all she'd ever known. After all, she is my daughter. She *has* to love me, right? Especially when her dad has never been in the picture, I am literally all she has ever known. Now don't get me wrong, my family loves her tremendously; but as far as living arrangements, we lived with my mom and dad for a couple of years after I got out of the military, and there were a couple of years when we had a roommate of some sort. But other than that, it has always been just her and me in the house.

I had done everything humanly possible to achieve success, and my main motivation for these achievements was anger and pain. I was told, after I had my daughter, as she is biracial, that I had completely messed up my life beyond repair, that I would not amount to anything ever, and that I would be lucky if I wasn't on welfare the rest of my life. I was told that no respectable man would ever love me with all of the trash in my past, that I should just resign myself to the fact that I had messed everything up permanently, and that I could never achieve anything of worth. The sad part is I believed them. I strived to prove them wrong because I was so mad and hurt beyond words, but at the core, I completely believed them and carried around a lot of pain, bitterness, regret, and anger for *many* years.

Now here comes the miraculous part. Given all of this, given that my heart had been completely torn up, my spirit murdered, my emotions completely shut off at this point, my body and mind numbed to the wickedness and harshness of this life—God saved me anyway! HE healed my heart and opened my eyes to His love. HE never stopped pursuing me. He *never* gave up on me! HE is the lover of my soul, my salvation, my *one* True Love! Please come with me on the journey He has taken me through for the past couple of years. I can honestly tell you that this journey has completely and permanently changed my life.

To show you where I was at this point, I started with the entry the day before I spent New Year's Eve with my Heavenly Father. This is where my transformation began. I was completely relying on myself to forge my own path. I was still trying to do everything in my own power. I realized that I needed to rely on Jesus and wanted to, but had no idea how to really put it into practice. No worries though, Jesus took a hold of my willing hand and led me blindly through. As He healed me, He gradually opened my eyes to His love and grace. What a wonderful God we serve! What you are about to read is essentially my spiritual journal for a period in my life when God miraculously transformed my heart from "totaled" to completely and utterly restored and overflowing with His love and purpose. I wouldn't believe it myself had I not lived it every single second from then until now. I look back on where I was and where I am now and am still flabbergasted at how He has guided me through it all. To get the full impact of my story, please understand that until I started a reading program with the church I attended at the time to read the Bible for ninety days (you'll see later in the book),

I was not reading the Bible with any structure at all. I would open it and struggle with where to start or what to read. I couldn't stay focused on the Word for long, and when I was able to focus, I didn't understand much of what I read. God was so very patient though; He walked me through it, gradually giving me more understanding as I was able to soak it in. He gave me so much through songs and tidbits that my friends posted in social media sites. He met me right exactly where I was, not judging me, but loving me dearly enough to be patient with me through all of my anger, bitterness, pain, and rebellion; patient enough to walk me through healing simply because I was finally willing to listen to Him and follow His guidance to the best of my flawed ability. The journey began as follows:

December 29
- Be true to yourself. Don't just do what you think others expect of you. Forge your own path.

December 31
- Patience: The best things in life truly are Worth waiting for.
  "For I know the plans I have for you, declares the LORD, plans to prosper you and not to harm you, plans to give you hope and a future." Jeremiah 29:11
- Regardless of what you see or what you feel, God is in full control of your situation. Don't let impatience rob you of the life God wants to bless you with. God knows what is best for you. His timing is perfect, and He will take care of you.
- (NOTE: Jesus was getting His message to my heart through song lyrics this New Year's Eve. I have all of the song titles and artists listed in the back of the book by the date they appear in the book in the Song Appendix for your convenience.)
- Song: "You Are More" by Tenth Avenue North
- Song: "Stand in the Rain" by Superchick
- Song: "Faithful" by LeCrae

- Song: "Don't Waste Your Life" by LeCrae (feat Cam and Dwayne Tryumf)[Hook: Cam]
- Song: "Take Me as I Am" by LeCrae
- Encouragement from a friend: "Healing may not be so much about getting better, as about letting go of everything that isn't you—all of the expectations, all of the beliefs—and becoming who you are."

January 2011

As I read over these journal entries again, I realize how the good Lord was always giving me exactly what I needed to hear. He had me journaling about how everything would turn out exactly how it was supposed to if I would just have faith and rely on Him. Many times, when I wrote these kinds of things, I was struggling to believe them, struggling to do them in my own life. Many people get the impression that when you know the right path that you are obviously living it. Wrong! I was struggling with deep core issues and struggling hard to do the right things and live the right way; all the time, making just as many mistakes as the next person, trying to recover from them, make progress, and not let anyone else be the wiser.

While I was receiving encouragement to trust the Lord, I was also receiving the message that I needed to stop judging other people. I had been hurt by so many people in my life that I didn't trust anyone for anything. In my healing process, God was trying to show me that until I could stop judging myself and stop judging others, my process would not be complete. You see, my judgmental attitude came from being judged and treated harshly. Until I could learn to see other people, especially those who had hurt me, the way HE sees them, I would not be healed. I had to get used to the idea that I had to not only stop judging other people and stop judging myself, but I also had to embrace forgiveness. Fortunately, God knew that this process was going to be slow and very difficult for me, so He gently planted the seed in many, many ways and continued to water it in my life. He knew it would take years for me to go through this process and gave me exactly what I needed, when I needed it in order to grow closer to Him. It was very uncomfortable most of the time but so very worth it.

So many times, we walk through our own personal struggles, trying so hard not to let anyone else know what we're going through, so we don't look bad or air our dirty laundry. However, we fail to realize that many others are also going through their deep personal struggles. Many times, if we would simply put our pride to the side and open up to those around us, we could mutually encourage each other and help carry each other's burdens. God is patient with us all, nonetheless . . . HE has certainly been patient with me, and I am one of THE most stubborn individuals I know!

We should try to let others walk with us in our journeys though. My trust issues stopped me from embracing others' help or encouragement for many years, and God walked with me anyway. I would highly encourage all those who are able to confide in a trusted confidant and let them walk with you; it makes the journey a bit less overwhelming. Lucky for me, I have the best best friend in the entire world! Even when I pushed her away, she never stopped praying for me, listening to me, and encouraging me; even though I know for a fact that she was thoroughly frustrated with me more than a couple of times! I thank God for her every day.

January 3
- Don't let fear get the best of you. Give people a real chance before assuming the worst. They may just surprise you ☺

January 4
- Thought: Just because someone appears to have it all together with no worries doesn't mean that they actually have it all together. They just manage to hide it a bit better than the rest of us. No one is perfect. We all need each other more than we would like to admit. ☺

January 6
- You know you're going in the right direction when things keep getting thrown in your path to distract ya. Just stay focused and you will attain the prize. ☺
- Encouragement from a friend: If we knew every outcome and every answer, we wouldn't need faith! But because we don't, we LIVE by faith.

January 11
- What you have is not yours. It's God's. Trust Him when He directs your steps. He loves you and knows what is best for you.
- Encouragement from a friend: To accomplish great things, we must dream as well as act, so today, make moves that will move you closer to what you desire.

January 13
- Live and LEARN. It's the Learning that makes life better, and ya gotta be open-minded to learn. ☺
- Song: "God Is Enough" by LeCrae (see Song Appendix for lyrics)

January 14
- You will face adversity and condemnation. Don't let others derail you. Stay on track. God will see you through.
- God, please give me the strength to give You everything that is Yours and to keep my hands off . . .

January 18
- "If I have all faith . . . but have not love, I am nothing . . . Love is: patient, kind, rejoices in truth, bears believes hopes and endures all things, never ends. Is Not: arrogant, boastful, envious, rude, self-serving, irritable, resentful, does not rejoice in wrongdoing . . . Faith, hope, and love abide, these three; but the greatest of these is love." 1 Corinthians 13:2, 4-8, 13

January 21
- Encouragement from a friend: God doesn't call us to be comfortable. He calls us to trust Him so completely that we are unafraid to put ourselves in situations where we will be in trouble if He doesn't come through.

January 23
- Only God can heal all the hurt and pain in this world, yet we are called to be His hands and feet. What an Overwhelming call. What can we do today to help someone who is hurting or in need?
- Things are almost Never how they appear. Never assume anything, good or bad.

January 24
- Truth: Time Always tells the truth . . .

January 26
- When people listen to the Word of the Lord, it affects families, which in turn affect societies, which in turn affect nations, which in turn can affect the world. Powerful thought!

January 27
- I am very grateful for all of the Wonderful people in my life! ☺ I am blessed indeed!

January 28
- Encouragement from a friend: You don't realize Jesus is all you need until Jesus is all you have.
  My thought: The SWEET thing is He (Jesus) wants to bless us with so much more!

January 30
- Embrace who you are. You are one of a kind, made for a higher purpose. You are truly and fiercely loved!
- Song: "The Best in Me" by Marvin Sapp (see Song Appendix for lyrics)
- Song: "Never Would Have Made It" by Marvin Sapp (see Song Appendix for lyrics)
- Song: "I'm Not Perfect" by J Moss (see Song Appendix for lyrics)

FEBRUARY 2011

February 2
- "But as for you, be strong and do not give up, for your work will be rewarded." 2 Chronicles 15:7

February 5
- Self-preservation: not everyone will hurt you like those in your past have. There are still Good people out there. If you never take a real chance, you will never get the real reward. Just a thought.
- It is hard to be patient, even when you know, Without a doubt, that it will be worth it.

February 7
- Gaining knowledge is not growth. Growth is when what you learn changes how you live.

February 8
- Don't just face your fears, stand up to them!

February 9
- I am thankful for the people closest to me who gently remind me to take all my worries to God. Sometimes it is hard to look up in the midst of the storm.

February 10
- I am so very thankful that, every time I need rest, I can take everything to God. He Always fills me up to overflowing and gives me peace.
- What a wonderful God we serve! ☺

February 12
- It is absolutely Amazing how God heals hearts, minds, and renews lives. It mesmerizes me that I am privileged enough to observe His handiwork!
- Encouragement from a friend: It's not about "them" versus "us." Everyone needs grace. Stop being partial.

February 13
- Song: "Note to God" by Charice (see Song Appendix for lyrics)
  Comment on song: Wow . . . What an Amazing performance . . . Powerful song!
- People and things are a poor substitute for God. Only He can heal and comfort beyond all understanding.

February 15
- Waiting for the best is Always worth it.
- "For God did not give us a spirit of timidity, but a spirit of power, of love, and of self-discipline." 2 Timothy 7

February 17
- When things seem all upside down, look up and surrender ALL. God works all things for good for those who love Him with their whole heart.
- Not my will but Yours be done, Lord . . .

February 18
- Flattered: It is beyond flattering to realize that God is indeed a jealous God and wants our FULL attention to do His work. He will supply all our needs in His time.

February 19
- Song: "Crazy Love" by Hawk Nelson (see Song Appendix for lyrics)
- Song: "You Can Have Me" by Sidewalk Prophets (see Song Appendix for lyrics)

- Encouragement from a friend: Never be afraid to trust an unknown future to a known God.

February 25
- God specializes in accomplishing the "impossible" for His glory.
- Women: Amazing benefit of faith! More faith equals less stress. Less stress equals less cortisol. Less cortisol equals less body fat in thighs and stomach. More faith equals more fit! Who knew? ☺
- Song: "This Is the Stuff" by Francesca Battistelli (see Song Appendix for lyrics)
- "Like a city whose walls are broken down is a man [or woman] who lacks self-control." Proverbs 25:28

February 26
- The answer you're seeking may be nearer than you think. The distance between standing up and kneeling down is only fifteen or so inches.
- Encouragement from a friend: To the single ladies, please don't settle because you want to be married. It's worth waiting for a man who can lead you spiritually—My Wife!—AMEN! Thank you. ☺

February 27
- God calls us to do the "impossible" through Him so we will depend on Him, so all will know that He is God for His Glory.
- As a mother, it pains me deeply to let my child receive the sometimes harsh consequences for her actions, or lack thereof. I can only imagine how much more it pains our Heavenly Father when His children are disobedient.
- I am a weak woman with a strong God.

February 28
- Place your trust in God not men.

MARCH 2011

March 1

- "Seek His will in all you do, and He will show you which path to take." Proverbs 3:6

March 2

- When it appears you can't, God can.
- Encouragement from a friend: God's blessing is on you. No matter what's happening in your life, above all else, remember today that God loves you! He is with you, for you, and He has abundant blessings and favor in store.
- Encouragement from a friend: Faith never knows where it is being led, or it would not be faith. True faith is content to travel under sealed orders.
- Encouragement from a friend: God knows our limitations and, usually, will place us in situations that stretch our faith far beyond what we think we can bear. God wants to develop our faith, and in order to do this, our faith must be tested.

March 3

- God uses my trials to Refine me, NOT define me.

March 4

- Encouragement: When you're headed in the right direction, you will constantly come under attack. Do not lose heart, God will see you through, and refine you in the process.

March 5

- "Praise be to God . . . the Father of compassion . . . who comforts us in all our troubles, so that we can comfort those in any trouble with the comfort we ourselves have received from God." 2 Corinthians 1:3-4

March 6

- Encouragement from a friend: True bravery is facing your fears together with the Lord and walking with Him beyond them. Don't mask your fears or avoid your anxieties; face them in the Lord and say, "God, I don't care what they say. I'm not following 'they.' I'm following 'Thee.'"
- Be still and know that I am God.
- His will is always accompanied by His power.

March 7

- A friend of mine and fellow singles group coleader passed away last night, leaving two precious children. Please keep her entire family in your prayers. Kathryn, you were loved more than you know and will be dearly missed! God keep you until we meet again . . .
  NOTE: My dear friend Kathryn shared a very compelling story with me that I will never forget. You see, she got married a little later in life and did so because she was tired of being single. As I accompanied her on a three-and-a-half-hour trip to get her son (who was in a group home for troubled children as he had autism, had just undergone some very tragic life circumstances, and due to his autism was not able to deal with things very well) to bring him home to live again with her and her daughter, she shared with me. She told me, "Cynthia, NEVER get married just because you are tired of being single. I can see that you are tired of being single, but God has a plan for you." She went on to tell me that her late husband (who had committed suicide, leaving her and her children) tried to kill her and her children before he took his own life. God had sent an angel and spared her and her children. Her story never left me. She made an impact on my heart that I will NEVER

forget. I've often thought of her story since then, and it has given me strength to hold on a while longer and invest my trust in Jesus, to know beyond a doubt that God does in fact have a wonderful plan for my life. You see, Kathryn trusted the Lord, and He spared her life a little while longer to be with her children. She passed at a very young age, in her forties, but I know she went to be with Jesus. God has provided for her children after her passing, as they are with family, very dearly loved, and well provided for. I may not understand why she had to be taken from her children at such an early age, but I do know that through her testimony to me, God has impacted my heart in a HUGE way. I must believe that her story, her life, and the lives of her children have impacted many, many others for HIM. I will never forget the lesson she taught me simply by sharing her story with me. It is one of the things that have inspired me to write my story. If I can impact just one person, let just ONE person know just how very much Jesus LOVES THEM, it will all be worth it.

- Song: "Tonight" by Toby Mac (see Song Appendix for lyrics)
- Song: "Lose My Soul" by Toby Mac (see Song Appendix for lyrics)

March 8

- Encouragement from a friend: We don't need a new marketing strategy for Christianity. We need real compassion and faith people can see.—Amen!
- I don't know if I'll ever get it right, but I'll never stop trying.
- God is working things out in the midst of those very parts of His will we do not want (the hard parts). He is crafting, shaping, and planning at a deeper level than we can see. Our vision is sooo limited.

- Myth: God will never give you more than you can handle. Fact: God will never give you more than HE can handle. No one can do it alone. We need Him.

March 9

- Encouragement from a friend: Red Sea Rule no. 2: Be more concerned with God's glory than with your relief.

March 10

- Song: "Blessings" by Laura Story (see Song Appendix for lyrics)
- The world tells us if you're single, there is something wrong with you. You're only living half a life. God tells us, "My grace is sufficient for you, bring all your worries to Me, and I will make you whole."
- The boat is rockin' and rollin', and the waves are high, yet I have peace in the midst of the storm because I know my God is bigger than it all!

March 11

- Encouragement from a friend: Relationship Thought: If you limit your choices only to what seems possible or reasonable, you disconnect yourself from what you truly want, and all that is left is a compromise. Say it with me, compromise isn't an option.
- I do not understand why some are called to go home with Father God well before it seems their work here is done. God, please give us Your peace and the strength to do what we should for those who have been left behind . . .
- A lesson I learned from my dear friend, Kate: Never settle for less than God's best for you. The consequences of settling are too severe. God wants to give you His best. Wait for it. Thank you, Kate. I will always remember how you touched my life.

March 12
- It is a new day. Take yesterday's lessons and put them into practice today, improve and move forward.
- CAUTION: God's word is habit forming. Regular use can cause loss of anxiety, decreased appetite for lying, cheating, stealing, and hating. Side effects can include increased sensations of love, joy, peace, and compassion.

March 13
- Song: "He Has His Hands on You" by Marvin Sapp (see Song Appendix for lyrics)

March 14
- Encouragement from a friend: God creates and rests satisfied in His work. We will never be satisfied in our work, so find rest/satisfaction in Him.
- "Take captive every thought to make it obedient to Christ." 2 Corinthians 10:5

March 15
- Admit it, quit it, and forget it. Let God take care of the rest.
- Things of the world: stress, worry, chaos, sickness, jealousy, hatred. Things of God: peace, contentment, order, healing, discernment, love.

March 16
- Breathe in . . . Breathe out . . . It will be okay . . .
- Forgiving someone does not mean you trust them and does not demand they get another chance. It simply means you have forgiven them for the past.
- Encouragement from a friend: God hears our requests. But his answer isn't always what we'd like. Why? Because He knows more about life than we do.—"So very true!"

- Funny thing, God always provides just the right Word, song, saying, or snippet right when I need it most and in the most unexpected ways. God is sooo good!

March 17

- Being a single parent must be the most challenging and rewarding job on the planet. Without God's grace and guidance, I'd be sunk! I love my girl more than I could possibly express, and I thank God for blessing me with her every single day!

March 18

- Job frustration? Remember: Work for others as though you are working for the Lord. Do everything for His glory.
- Sometimes the only way to teach responsibility is to let the child fail and bear the fullness of the consequences . . . grieves my heart . . . :(

March 19

- Post on Keith and Kathy's wedding announcement: I am so happy for you both! The ceremony was beautiful. ☺ God Bless you always!
- "Little by little, God grows us up into who we are meant to be in Him, until we have increased enough to step into the future He has prepared for us."

March 20

- "The miracle of God's guidance in our lives is not simply to bless us . . . But when God is at work opening and closing doors, our lives shine with His greatness for others to see." Greg Matte
- Note of encouragement to a hurting friend: "When you seem happy, everyone assumes that all is going well, but when you are depressed, everyone gets concerned and tries to help any way they can. The bottom line is that a lot of people love you, and in our own feeble misguided ways, we

just want to make sure that you are okay. Only God has the master plan. All we can do is to try to do as He guides us to the best of our abilities . . . all the while knowing full well that we are all very human and will make many mistakes every day."

March 21

- No matter where you are in life right now, you are no less important to God than anyone else. He wants to know YOU and draw you close to Him.
- I am blessed to know I'm going in the right direction, even though it is not always comfortable. God is good! ☺
- "If any of you lacks wisdom, he should ask God who gives generously to all without finding fault . . . but when he asks, he must believe . . . the wisdom that comes from heaven is first of all pure, then peace-loving, considerate, submissive, full of mercy and good fruit, impartial, and sincere . . ." James 1:5-6, 3:17

March 22

- While others soar, God may have you crawl in order to show you something that can't be found in the clouds.

March 23

- A HUGE burden will be lifted from your shoulders when you realize that God is in control and let Him be. No need to worry or stew, just do as He directs and all will turn out as it should. God is good!

March 24

- "Faith is blind—except upward. It is blind to impossibilities and deaf to doubt. It listens only to God." Samuel Dickey Gordon

March 27

- Do not be afraid to walk into an unknown future with a known God. HE won't leave you hangin'.

March 28

- The Spoken Word—Woman at the Well (YouTube clip)
- "Come unto me, all ye that labor and are heavy laden, and I will give you rest." JESUS in Matthew 11:28

March 29

- Encouragement from a friend's post: I will Follow you, Lord, when in doubt, when storms rise, when all else fails. I'm a believer you gave it all for me. I lift my hand to you in fear of losing this AWESOME love. Today has been made for me, and I will make the best of it!—Needed that today, thank you.

March 30

- God brings other people into our lives to help us, not to bear the whole weight of our load. Do not crush those around you with your burden. Take it All to the Father. He (God) is the only One who is able to bear the weight of our load.
- "But I tell you who hear me: love your enemies, do good to those who hate you, bless those who curse you, pray for those who mistreat you." Luke 6:27-28

March 31

- LOVE it when I get encouragement from unexpected places! Brightens my day. ☺
- Father God wants to draw you close to Him, lean into Him, and let Him grow you.
- Always value God's truth over the opinions of others.

APRIL 2011

April 1

- Amazing to see God working . . . It's not easy but Blessings abound! God is good!

April 2

- It's Amazing what a good run will do for stress . . . Got my three miles today and it feels good! ☺
- Have you ever experienced that moment when you look up and the clouds all seem to lift and everything suddenly becomes crystal clear?

April 3

- "I want not only to share my faith with you but to be encouraged by yours: Each of us will be a blessing to the other." Romans 1:12
- "Don't worry about anything; instead, pray about everything; tell God your needs, and don't forget to thank Him for His answers. If you do this, you will experience God's peace, which is far more wonderful than the human mind can understand. His peace will keep your thoughts and your hearts quiet and at rest as you trust in Christ." Psalm 40:1-3

April 4

- Encouragement from a friend: "Know therefore that the LORD your God is God; he is the faithful God, keeping his covenant of love to a thousand generations of those who love him and keep his commands." Deuteronomy 7:9
He is the friend who never fails you, never disappoints, and never stops loving you! He will do what He said He would do!
My comment: Thank you, needed that today.

- Song: "Please Don't Let Me Go" by Group 1 Crew (see Song Appendix for lyrics)
- His (Christ's) discipline is prompted by care, not cruelty.
- "We also rejoice in our sufferings, because we know that suffering produces perseverance, perseverance character, and character, hope." Romans 5:3-4
- Song: "Captured" by Toby Mac (see Song Appendix for lyrics)

April 5

- Relationship: Every emotion you have will play into your relationship with God. Talk to Him about it! He's a Big Boy, HE can take it, and HE Loves you!
- God does not bless us with things that we are not yet equipped to handle.

April 6

- The journey is not always fun or painless, but it is always what we need to become who we are meant to be.

April 8

- When you stop worrying and give everything to God, you'll be Amazed at how much extra energy you have!
- God is not merely concerned with results, but also with character; and few things produce character, like learning to wait.

April 11

- Perspective: It's not about you. It's about HIM. Stay focused.
- Song: "Stronger" by Mandisa (see Song Appendix for lyrics)
- Song: "Does Anybody Hear Her" by Casting Crowns (see Song Appendix for lyrics) {During this time, someone very close to me was going through some terrible relationship problems. My heart was breaking for their situation, and

I was trying to offer any sort of help I could. The words in this song very powerfully described her situation, so I had to share the song. I have also felt exactly the same way and don't think anyone should ever have to feel shut out, judged, or helpless.}

- The mess is there to show me where I'm hanging my hope. It is intended to drive us back to the only sure Hope we can have—Jesus.

April 13

- Inspiring day! New iPod . . . great tunes with me all the time . . . does wonders for a girl to have the right tunes in her ear all evening! ☺

April 14

- "Background (I Can Play the Background)," a stellar song by LeCrae—check it out! ☺
- Song: "Background" by LeCrae (see Song Appendix for lyrics)
- The Lord is my strength and my shield. In Him alone my heart trusts! I am privileged to be drawn closer to You each day.

April 15

- We must die completely to our old lives and let God remold us into who we are to be in Him so all will know that He and only He (God) has done it.
- Encouragement from a friend's status: "Father, forgive them, for they do not know what they are doing . . ." Luke 23:34 NIV
  He's our example, no matter how much it pains.
  My comment: We are blessed to go through pain and trials on His behalf.
- "Our identity is found in the God we trust, any other identity will self-destruct." LeCrae

April 17
- Christianity is not a get-wealthy-and-happy strategy. It's a love relationship with our Heavenly Father.
- When God shows me His miraculous plan, it overwhelms me, awes me, amazes and excites me all at the same time! God, draw me closer to you so that I can step into the future You have prepared for me.

April 18
- No longer bound by sin but am able to stand before the Father unashamed.
- When you actively walk in faith, God will use you to bless those around you more than you ever thought possible. What an Amazing feeling!

April 19
- Don't question God's motives. There is a reason why things are the way they are, and you don't always get to know why.

April 20
- SO proud of my girl . . . learning how to accept responsibility, deal with consequences, and grow from the experience. She is becoming a mighty fine young lady! ☺

April 22
- Question posed by a friend, answered by me: What does Easter mean to you?
  My answer: It means that Jesus arose on that Glorious morning, clenched the victory for us all and will walk us through this life, and allow us to live for His glory if we just surrender to Him.
  He Loves us and wants to see us all in Heaven with Him forever! God is good!
- Jesus sacrificed it ALL for us. What can we do to help each other this weekend? Even the smallest act of kindness, even

just a smile, can make a world of difference to someone in need. Let's be kind and give of ourselves. It's the Least we can do in light of the Sacrifice that was made for us through Jesus Christ.

- Gotta love it! Jaquilyn's high school youth group is watching *Passion of the Christ*' tonight. I can't think of a better way to wrap up a magnificent Good Friday for my girl! Thank you, Pastor Zach. God Bless all you do for our kids!

April 23

- "A new command I give you: Love one another. As I have loved you, so you must love one another. By this all men will know that you are my disciples, if you love one another." John 13:34-35
- "Peace I leave with you; my peace I give you. I do not give to you as the world gives. Do not let your hearts be troubled and do not be afraid." John 14:27

April 24

- Thank you, Easter Bunny, whoever you are! I just found a luscious dark chocolate bunny and assorted other chocolates at my door. ☺
- "Oh, that You would bless me indeed, and enlarge my territory; that Your hand would be with me, and that You would keep me from evil, that I may not cause pain!" 1 Chronicles 4:9-10
- It is not possible to humanly materialize God's blessings. They are Divine and from Him alone. It is for us to ask for His blessings daily; wait expectantly, patiently, and humbly; and embrace the abundant blessings He lavishes on us. May His will be my desire!

April 25

- Hard day at work? Work for others as if Christ is your customer. Difficult boss? Treat him as if Christ was in the room because He is.

- Just because a person is in a leadership role does not mean they are beyond reproach. There was only one person ever to walk the earth who was perfect. He died, rose again, and is seated next to the Father in Heaven. Never put anyone on a pedestal. No one deserves that pressure because we have ALL fallen short. Thank God for His grace!

April 26

- Finishing is better than starting. Patience is better than pride.
- "God is a God of order: He does everything by appointment. He has set a predetermined appointment to bring to pass His promise in our lives. Through the many tempestuous winds that blow against our lives, God has already prepared a way of escape. Our comfort is in knowing that, in spite of temporary circumstances, we have an appointment with destiny." T. D. Jakes
- Forgiveness is not all that is required.
  We all get hurt, and we all need to forgive, but that's not the end of the story. Do not let the fear of getting hurt again rule your emotions and decisions. There is no need to fear getting hurt again. It is just a fact. You Will get hurt again. We live in a fallen world. There is no avoiding it. Let go of the fear, give it to God, and trust that He has you in the palm of His hand and will walk with you—or sometimes carry you—through ALL of the difficulties of life. Trust in HIM and walk in His ways, and He will bless your entire life!

April 29

- If you open your eyes and heart and look around, you will find that God has brought people into your life that have already been through what you're going through or are going through something you have already overcome. Reach out to someone, extend your hand, and help them through their struggle. They may not feel they can do it alone, and they don't have to because God gave them you! ☺

A New Phase—Sharing His Lessons with Others

A while back, God laid it on my heart to start a Facebook page for single parents (I titled this page Single Parents Rock! When We Lean on The ROCK) since I've been a single mom for over sixteen years. So in obedience, I did just that. I didn't know what I would say or how it would turn out. I was scared that it would be an utter failure, but I'd learned enough to know that when God tells us to do something, there is a reason for it, and He will bless it regardless of our abilities, or lack thereof. The following are some things He has had revealed to me to share through this forum as well as things that God was revealing to me in my own personal walk with Him. Some of it I shared on my Single Parents' page, some of it on my personal page, and some of it in my personal journal. Please join me on my walk with Jesus over the past year. It has been so intense and so wonderful. Well, I just need to share it with the world. I hope it blesses you as much as God has blessed me. He has taught me so many lessons and graciously let me share them with others in the process.

NOTE: When I first started my Single Parents' page, I was scared to death that I wouldn't be able to do it right, that I wouldn't have anything useful or helpful to say to anyone. What I've learned through this process, though, is that if we are just obedient to our Heavenly Father, HE will bless our efforts. I stumbled and fumbled for a while, but He always blessed my efforts and blessed me and my walk through learning how to rely on Him and allow Him to speak through me. Truthfully, none of us have anything useful to say unless we let Him use our stories for His glory. He desires to bless others through us. We just have to learn how to get out of His way and allow ourselves to be used. I did come under attack shortly after starting this page as well. You see, the devil does **not** like it when we are obedient to God's will for our lives because God has a mighty powerful plan that will defeat the devil. As I walked out in this new form of ministry that was quite intimidating to me, I came under attack by a staunch atheist publicly on my page. I took the conversation offline and offered my personal friendship to this person. I have not heard from them much since, but they are still around. I know they are watching, and I know God is dealing with their heart issues. God encouraged me during this time so that I did not get discouraged or down on myself about what I could have or should have said. He used the experience to help me realize how founded in His word I need to be in order to be an effective ministry tool for Him. This experience did not harm me, but helped me grow and realize how much closer to Jesus I needed to be. It helped me realize how much more I needed to study the Bible and have a daily walk with the Lord. Through this experience that the enemy planned for my harm, the Lord used to grow my faith and confidence in Him. I have since learned that this is how God wants to use all of our trials. He wants to turn them around and use them for our growth and benefit, but we have to turn them over to Him first. We have to be willing to let Him in and ready and willing to hear what He has to say and do as He directs.

MAY 2011

May 1

- Doubt is an essential element of faith. Without doubt, faith would be easy, and we would not rely on God as is necessary for true Faith.
- Jesus never sinned against anyone, living a pure and just life, yet HE forgave us our many sins. Who are we if we do not forgive others' sins against us? Do we think we are better than HE who saved us? God, help us all to forgive each other as you forgave us!

May 2

- Sometimes God takes us through things so we will be tested and humbled, so that we will not forget that He is God. Without Him, we are nothing.

May 4

- Do you hear that rumble? God is moving . . . Can't wait to see what happens next! ☺ It's gonna be GOOD!

May 5

- First, not after we get our wish list, but seek first the kingdom of God and His righteousness, and all these things will be added to you.
- If God is tugging at your heart to step out of your comfort zone, get active and be His hands and feet; do not hesitate. HE wants to bless you as you bless others as He directs! Step into HIS will.

May 7

- Give all your pain to God. Let Him heal, restore, and bless you beyond your wildest dreams! Praise God. You are faithful!

May 8

- To all the single mothers: You are not forgotten on this day. God's eye misses nothing; He sees all of the sacrifices you are making in raising those He has entrusted to you. Our Father loves you beyond measure; you are priceless in His eyes! God bless and keep you all!

- Interesting: The word Forgive is mentioned in twenty-five books of the Bible; Forgiveness is in eight books of the Bible; Forgives is in three books of the Bible; Forgiving is in six books of the Bible. I get the feeling that this is very important to God. Is there anyone you need to forgive? Maybe it's time . . .

- Lord, I'm thanking you for your grace and mercy. The compassion and favor you have shown me are immeasurable. Lord, I'm asking for you to give me the wisdom and an unshakable faith to make the next move you have designed for my life.

May 9

- Something to ponder: Losing control of your temper, even just once, and lashing out against another may be a short-term stress release for you, but it may inflict permanent scars on those in your path. God, help us all treat each other as we want to be treated.

- We can try to do things under our own power all day to no avail, but when we listen to Jesus, in His timing, the harvest will be beyond our wildest dreams! (see Luke 5:4-7)

May 10

- "But Jesus often withdrew to lonely places and prayed." Luke 5:16

May 13

- We cannot change our past, but God gave us the option to change our future.

- When God truly lays something on your heart, many temptations that demanded your attention fade and lose their appeal.

May 14

- Proof: When I am focused on my desires, I am restless, doubtful, anxious, and stressed out. When I am focused on God's desires, I have joy, peace, a sense of purpose, and am oddly calm about my entire situation, even when it looks totally hopeless and impossible. Whaddaya know? We're all made to serve and praise God, not to serve and praise ourselves. Joy and purpose come only from God.
- Sometimes denying your wants helps identify what you need.
- Sometimes Faith requires us to hand our situation completely over to God and keep our hands off, knowing that HE will work everything out for the best for those who love Him. HE Always gives good gifts to His children.

May 16

- Sometimes your experiences are what make you the only one qualified to help someone else. That is the blessing inside the pain.

May 17

- The only time I have ever felt truly fulfilled and at peace is when I am in God's presence. Our Heavenly Father is so good; He is always there when we call on Him.

May 18

- security and fulfillment cannot be found in worldly things—money, possessions, people, etc.
- Single parents need as much love and support as possible! Let's encourage each other every day.

- Single parents need all the love and encouragement we can get, and that is what this page is all about. If you know anyone who may be interested or need encouragement, please share this link. God Bless! ☺

- "He also brought me up out of a horrible pit, out of the miry clay, and set my feet upon a rock, and established my steps." Psalm 40:2

- "My command is this: Love each other as I have loved you" John 15:12

  As single parents, we need to love, encourage, and help each other as much as we are able.

- Books I've found helpful:

  The Search for Significance by Robert S. McGee (Christian encouragement)

  The Single Truth by Lori Smith (Single Christian encouragement)

  Lord, Heal My Hurts by Kay Arthur (Christian healing)

  Finding God's Will by Greg Matte (finding Christian direction)

  Authentic Faith by Gary Thomas (Christian faith encouragement)

  Fix Freeze Feast by Kati Neville and Lindsay Tkacsik (Recipe book - bulk recipes)

  Sacred Marriage by Gary Thomas (Christian - What if marriage is to make us more holy than happy? I figure if singles want to get married or remarried at any point in our lives, then we should make an effort to figure out how to do it right.)

- Forgiveness Is Not All That Is Required

  by Single Parents Rock! When we lean on The Rock on Wednesday, May 18, 2011, at 9:21 p.m.

  We all get hurt and we all need to forgive, but that's not the end of the story. Do not let the fear of getting hurt again rule your emotions and decisions. There is no need to fear getting hurt again, it is just a fact, you Will get hurt again. We live in a fallen world, there is no avoiding it. Let go of the fear, give it to God, and trust that He has you in the palm of His hand and will walk with you—or sometimes carry you—through ALL of the difficulties of life. Trust in HIM and walk in His ways and He will bless your entire life!

May 19

- We can do the right things all day long, but if our hearts are not in the right place, it is all for naught. Heart Check . . . Let's get right
- "Now hope does not disappoint, because the love of God has been poured out in our hearts by the Holy Spirit who was given to us." Romans 5:5
- There is always hope in a new day. God loves you and wants to walk with you through all of today's trials. God Bless and be with you!
- "Those who know your name will trust in you, for you, Lord, have never forsaken those who seek you." Psalm 9:10
- The best advice I ever received about raising my daughter was "Tell her you love her every day," and I've done just that since. The day just isn't complete until I can hug my girl and let her know how much I love her!
- Who Am I and Why Is This Page Important to Me???
  by Single Parents Rock! When we lean on The Rock on Thursday, May 19, 2011, at 6:12 p.m.
  I think it only fair that you know a little bit about me, so you'll know where I'm coming from.
  So . . . here is a little bit about me:
  I grew up in a very small town in western Kansas, was raised in a lower middle class household. I went to church with my family when I was young, but our family stopped going to church when I was in middle school. So, there was no youth group or church influence in my life in high school or into young adulthood. I was taught to abide by the Golden Rule though, and I learned that lesson well. I didn't realize that when there is absolutely no diversity, it is easy to abide by that rule. I would later be very

disillusioned to learn that some people who were very close to me did not believe that every person deserved to be treated by the same standard (regardless of race, age, sex, etc . . . but most especially race).

Long story short, I left that small western Kansas town to join the U.S. Navy two weeks after I graduated high school. Needless to say, my world expanded quickly and I absolutely Loved the Navy! I traveled to many places and experienced many things that most Americans just don't get to experience. I was also exposed to many other cultures; most of my good friends were of different races than my own. I met and dated my daughter's father for three years, then found out that I was pregnant. My whole world turned upside down! I was now a 22 year old single, pregnant, service-member . . . I had to move out of the barracks and get a apartment in town . . . get ready to have a baby, maintain my job, deal with the stress of experiencing vicious racism not only from my own family, but from many around me who did not agree with a single white female having a baby by an African-American man (actually he is West Indian, but grew up in New York, but black is black to many people I found out . . . crazy how people can categorize everyone on the planet according to skin tone). The black women in the barracks hated me because they said I had taken one of 'their' men, the white women hated me because they saw me as a 'traitor'; my family wasn't even speaking to me. I went to a large church off the military base, but when they figured out who my baby's father was, they treated me poorly too. I learned quickly not to trust Anyone!

I got out of the Navy and went back to Kansas to raise my daughter (much to my chagrin, but I had nowhere else to go). I started to mend bridges with my family and proceeded to raise my daughter and go to school (first tech school, then community college, then a four year school for my bachelors, then back again for my master's degree). I have made my own way, paid for all of our living expenses and school on my own, and always held a full time job. I know what it is to work your fingers to the bone with no time to yourself, know what it is to feel the lonely nights close in around you when you feel like you can't even breathe . . . know what it is like to feel so alone that you just want to collapse and cry your eyes out . . . BUT, the good news is . . . through all of this I found God and HE wants you to find Him too. I started this page to encourage other single parents that ALL things are possible through Jesus Christ our Savior. Christ has healed those deep wounds that were inflicted by ignorant opinions, hard feelings, gut wrenching pain . . . I can honestly say that I have no hard feelings toward anyone in my family or those others who persecuted me during that time in my life. God loves them too and wants to draw them close to Him. I feel bad for them now and pray for them always, for they are far from the Father and that is the most hopeless feeling in the world.

My hope and prayer is that I may be some small encouragement in a world of pain to someone in a similar situation. Being a single parent in a hurting and fallen world is the hardest thing that I have ever had to go through. God is risen though and waiting for us to come to Him. Only HE can heal our deepest pain. Let's leave it all at our Heavenly Father's feet together.

God Bless you all always!

- Ten Ways to Tell Your Children . . . I Love You (I got this from a magnet someone gave me when my daughter was a tiny baby. I do not know what the original source of this material is, but it is an Excellent advice.)

  by Single Parents Rock! When we lean on The Rock on Thursday, May 19, 2011, at 8:48 p.m.

  1. Make your home a place of safety, acceptance and love.

  2. Build feelings of self-worth by showing your children how they are special.

3. Offer children opportunities to learn and succeed.
4. Make sure your children eat healthy foods, exercise regularly and get enough sleep.
5. Spend time with your children. Talk, laugh, play and enjoy each other.
6. Protect your children. Make their safety your top priority.
7. Acknowledge, praise and reward your children's successes. Don't criticize when they try but fail.
8. Set limits to make children feel secure and to teach them responsibility.
9. Make a hug, a squeeze, a loving smile an everyday occurrence.
10. Say the words, "I love you," at least once a day.

May 20, 2011

- Time crunch versus blessing: I've found if I take ten to fifteen minutes out of my day to spend with the Lord—reading his word, doing a short devotional, praying, or just basking in His presence asking for strength—He blesses our time, and I have more energy to do all the things that life demands. God Bless you and your family. Have a great Friday! ☺

May 21

- Think about it: We are told to Be Like Christ, be conformed to His likeness. When God looks at us, He sees Christ. Shouldn't we try every day to see others through Christ's eyes instead of through all the twisted filters, "standards," expectations, and norms of society?
- Simple and honest . . . couldn't ask for a better combination. ☺

May 22

- Prayer Request: There is someone very dear to my heart who is in dire need of prayer. I cannot say her name, but she needs a lot of prayer for healing, so she will be able to feel God's love. Please pray for her! Thank you so much. God Bless.

- Let us all be the body of Christ and help restore those in need.
- Have you hugged your kids today? Let them know how much they mean to you.
- Blessings often come through trials. Our God will never abandon us; He will see us through all of life's storms.
- Helping Hands . . .
  by Single Parents Rock! When we lean on The Rock on Sunday, May 22, 2011, at 7:49 p.m.
  As single parents we often find ourselves in need of things and resources that we do not have. Do not be afraid or too proud to ask for help when you are in need. God has entrusted the care of your family to you, they are counting on you to provide for them. Do not turn away a helping hand when it is extended, if you do you are not only denying yourself the blessing of receiving the needed help, you are also denying the giver the blessing of giving to someone in need. We all need help at some point in our lives. God's Word tells us to give to those in need so that they may give to us when we are in need. Helping hands are needed and half of that equation means that we need to graciously accept help when it is offered. Let the body of Christ restore you so that you may increase and give to another who has need when you are able. This is the way that God intended us to live.
- "Our desire is not that others might be relieved while you are hard pressed, but that there might be equality. At the present time your plenty will supply what they need, so that in turn their plenty will supply what you need. Then there will be equality, as it is written: He who gathered much did not have too much, and he who gathered little did not have too little." 2 Corinthians 8:13-15

May 23

- Sometimes it is very difficult to discipline our children, but just as Father God disciplines us, we must discipline our own children so they will learn and grow.
- Save Money and Be Healthier Too! Bonus! ☺
  by Single Parents Rock! When we lean on The Rock on Monday, May 23, 2011, at 8:02 p.m.
  One Great way to save money on a tight budget is to set aside a little time on the weekend and make 2 or 3 of your favorite recipes, wrap them in individual servings (or whatever serving size is just right for your family, my preferred serving size is 2) and freeze them. Then, when you need a quick meal you don't have to eat out . . . just pull out one serving package from your freezer, warm and serve! Much healthier than fast food too! ☺

May 24

- Faith = Complete trust and belief in God with no safety net. Funny thing, faith brings with it Overwhelming peace. ☺
- Let's hold each other up in prayer and be attentive to each other's needs. There is strength in numbers, especially when we call on Father God to help us all help each other. Look around and see if you can help a brother or sister out this week. Helping others often takes the focus off ourselves and gives us joy in the storm.

May 25

- There is nothing more beautiful than a person whose whole heart is seeking after God. It is a direct reflection of God's love for our fallen world. It is the image we are all supposed to reflect to be a light to this world. God is more gracious that we could ever deserve!
- We are all children of God. What is He teaching us?
- "Train up a child in the way he should go, and when he is old he will not depart from it." Proverbs 22:6

- "Let all bitterness, wrath, anger, clamor, and evil speaking be put away from you, with all malice. And be kind to one another, tenderhearted, forgiving one another, even as God in Christ forgave you." Ephesians 4:31-32
- Children Learn What They Live (This is taken from a magnet I received from a friend when my daughter was an infant. I do not know the original source of this material.) by Single Parents Rock! When we lean on The Rock on Wednesday, May 25, 2011, at 6:08 p.m.
  If children live with criticism, they learn to condemn,
  If children live with hostility, they learn to fight,
  If children live with fear, they learn to be apprehensive,
  If children live with ridicule, they learn to be shy,
  If children live with shame, they learn to feel guilty,
  If children live with tolerance, they learn to be patient,
  If children live with encouragement, they learn confidence,
  If children live with praise, they learn to appreciate,
  If children live with approval, they learn to like themselves,
  If children live with acceptance, they learn to find love in the world.
  What are your children living?
  A question we all need to ask ourselves . . .
  God Bless you and your family always!

May 25

- "Charm is deceptive, and beauty is fleeting; but a woman who fears the Lord is to be praised." Proverbs 31:30

May 26

- The true you: Be true to who Christ created you to be. Be attentive and act only on His guidance. Well-meaning family and friends will try to "help" you find your way according to their expectations and society's norms, but only God can lead you down the right path. Christ was always countercultural. We are called to follow Christ regardless of cost or comfort.

- Sometimes we go through things to humble us, so we will realize that we truly need others and so that we will learn to look Only to God for strength and direction.
- Thought: If you have people in your life that love, appreciate, and support you through thick and thin, never take them for granted. Not everyone has that luxury.
- Real Beauty . . . What Is It?

  by Single Parents Rock! When we lean on The Rock on Thursday, May 26, 2011 at 9:47pm

  I have noticed a theme in the Scripture when looking at the concept of beauty. When the Scripture talks about physical beauty, humanly beauty, it points out that people have been pre-occupied with beauty for centuries (perfect example in the story of Esther . . . she had to undergo 12 months of beauty treatments before seeing the king! 12 months!!!) and it also consistently points out that physical beauty is fleeting, it never sticks around for the long haul. Men have been distracted by the physical beauty of women that has caused them to turn from God (and I dare say women have been tempted away from God's will by the allure of 'beautiful' men as well), people have also been distracted by the physical appeal and beauty of idols (there are so many . . .golden idols, money, cars, attractive men, attractive women, houses, status, etc . . . the list goes on . . .) that has caused them to turn from God. It is sad that we still cannot grasp that Real beauty comes from God and only from God.

  Our society tells us that we must look and act a certain way and be accepted by a certain group of people to be considered 'beautiful'. The Word tells us "Your beauty should not come from outward adornment such as braided hair and the wearing of gold jewelry and fine clothes. Instead, it should be that of your inner self, the unfading beauty of a gentle and quiet spirit, which is of great worth in God's sight. For this is the way the holy women of the past who put their hope in God used to make themselves beautiful . . ." 1 Peter 3:3-5 They used to make themselves beautiful by putting their hope in God . . . they had faith and that made them beautiful.

Yes men, you can be beautiful too . . . it's not just a term used to describe women! It is a term used to describe the beauty that is granted to those who have drawn close to God and have faith. The stronger your faith, the more you walk in Christ, the more beautiful you become. Don't conform to the shallow, menial, degrading and fleeting standards of this world or our society. Don't buy what they're selling . . . you'll come up feeling empty with nothing to show for it. Seek hard after God and trust His definition of true beauty. You are fiercely loved by our loving Father and God of the universe . . . I'll take His Word over any person's opinion in a heartbeat!

God Bless and keep you always

May 27

- I have been under the weather recently, and it has reminded me how much of a blessing friends can be. Please look around if you see a brother or sister in need. Even if they may not say anything, offer them a helping hand. You will definitely be a blessing to them!

May 28

- "We will never learn the full joy of celebration if we have not pierced the depths of true sorrow and mourning." Gary Thomas
- "You are NEVER alone: Then you will call, and the Lord will answer, you will cry for help, and he will say: Here I am." Isaiah 58:9
- God will always help us in time of need; all we need to do is ask.
  "Let us therefore come boldly to the throne of grace, that we may obtain mercy and find grace to help in time of need." Hebrews 4:16

- Less Worthy??? I think not!
by Single Parents Rock! When we lean on The Rock on
Saturday, May 28, 2011, at 10:02 a.m.
I have had the unfortunate experience in my life of
running into those people (well meaning church going
folk) who have told me in no uncertain words and terms
that since I am a single parent, I am somehow lesser on
the scale of believers. They sincerely believe that they are
better than I am because they are not in a single parent
situation (and in my case, most especially a bi-racial single
parent situation). There is still a stigma in our society about
single parents; the consequences of this viewpoint can be
devastating to the single parent who is looking for love
and support in the arms of fellow believers. We need all
the love and support we can get, raising a family is tough
enough when there are two parents to care for the kids,
but when it's down to just one there is so much pressure,
so little time and so little money . . . We truly NEED each
others' love and support. When I first encountered this
viewpoint I was so hurt and angry that I turned away from
God all-together for a long time. THEN God got a hold of
me and let me know His truth.
He let me know that ALL have sinned and fallen short,
that ALL wrongdoing is sin and that everyone deserves
to die for their own sin (regardless of what it is since ALL
wrongdoing is sin, there is no sliding scale of 'better' or
'worse' sins . . . sin is sin . . . period). The good news is
that Jesus came and paid the price for ALL of our sins. We
are saved by God's grace through faith, ALL of us! God
loves ALL of his children, He does not love one more than
another.
As believers, we need to love each other as well . . . even
when another believer (however mislead they may be)
tells us that we are lesser because of our situation in life
(which we are not, and Neither are they by the way). We
need to pray for them that God will open their eyes fully

to how His grace and love works. Jesus came to this earth and died on the cross for ALL of our sins, for every single person, no one is excluded. Please do not let another person's ignorance of God's truth be reflected in your faith, do not let another person's misconceptions taint your love for the Lord, do not let another person's views based on societies norms make you turn away from God. Christ never conformed to the standards of society during the time He was on earth and we are instructed not to be conformed to the ways of the world, but be transformed by the renewing of our minds. (see Rm 12:12) None of us are better than any other, we all have the special gifts that God gave to us and will be used in different ways. (see Rm 12:3-8) We need to embrace each other, love each other, help and support each other in every way possible. God loves each and every one of us more fully and deeply than we could ever imagine. Live and walk in your faith, do not let anyone dissuade you or pull you away from the Lord. Cling to Him for truth, life, love and support. He will NEVER disappoint you!!

God Bless and keep you always

Reference verses:

1 Kings 8:46 - . . . for there is no one who does not sin . . .

Pr 20:9 - Who can say, "I have kept my heart pure, I am clean and without sin"?

Job 14:4 -Who can bring what is pure from the impure? No one!

Ro 3:22-25 -This righteousness from God comes through faith in Jesus Christ to all who believe. There is no difference, for all have sinned and fall short of the glory of God, and are justified freely by his grace through the redemption that came by Christ Jesus. Christ presented him as a sacrifice of atonement, through faith in his blood. He did this to demonstrate his justice, because in his forbearance he had left the sins committed beforehand unpunished.

Jn 8:7 - . . . If any one of you is without sin, let him be the first to throw a stone at her . . .

Jer 31:30 - . . . Instead, everyone will die for his own sin . . .

Jn 1:29 - The next day John saw Jesus coming toward him and said, "Look, the Lamb of God, who takes away the sin of the world!

1 Jn 1:7-10 - But if we walk in the light, as he is in the light, we have fellowship with one another, and the blood of Jesus, his Son, purifies us from all sin. If we claim to be without sin, we deceive ourselves and the truth is not in us. If we confess our sins, he is faithful and just and will forgive us our sins and purify us from all unrighteousness. If we claim we have not sinned, we make him out to be a liar and his word has no place in our lives.

May 29

- Praise God! The old is gone, and the new has come. Bring It!
- Take care of each other this weekend, look out for each other, encourage each other, and HAVE SOME FUN! God bless.
- Fun Fact—Love
  by Single Parents Rock! When we lean on The Rock on Sunday, May 29, 2011, at 10:26 p.m.
  Fun Fact: I have felt unloved and rejected many times and I've heard the same from others . . . so, I looked up the word "love" and "loved" in my NIV Study Bible. Did you know that, by my count, there are 519 references to the word "love" and 89 references to the word "loved" . . . I think God wants us all to know how much we're loved, wants to show us how to really love each other and how we should really love Him (God)!!! Otherwise He wouldn't bother to mention it so many times!!! Food for thought . . . God Bless . . . and He always does! ☺

May 30

- Our body wants the pleasure of relief, our spirit wants to find that pleasure or relief in God, and a holy war ensues.
- If we truly love others as we are called to, we should not try to talk them out of mourning a loss or help them "get over" something. Mourning is a necessary part of healing. We need to be patient with each other and persist with a loving and compassionate spirit.
- "Never reduce your self-worth and value to physical and emotional pleasure. Sex, money, and relationships are not what we live for." LeCrae
  I had to share this quote. Too many times, we get caught up in the things of this world and forget that we need to be focused on God.
- "Let us draw near to God with a sincere heart in full assurance of faith, having our hearts sprinkled to cleanse us from a guilty conscience and having our bodies washed with pure water. Let us hold unswervingly to the hope we profess, for he who promised is faithful." Hebrews 10:22-23
- I hope everyone had a blessed Memorial Day! Let us actually live what we claim on the coinage of our great nation, "In God We Trust."

May 31

- We love, we go, we serve . . . die to self.
- Understanding leads to true respect. True respect leads to full love . . .
- "Don't worry about anything; instead pray about everything. Tell God your needs and don't forget to thank him for his answers. If you do this, you will experience God's peace, which is far more wonderful than the human mind can understand. His peace will keep your thoughts and your hearts quiet and at rest as you trust in Christ." Philippians 4:6-7
- YOU Are Important!

by Single Parents Rock! When we lean on The Rock on
Tuesday, May 31, 2011, at 3:28 p.m.

YOU are Important! Do not neglect your own needs.
Your family is depending on you for care, if you don't take
care of your own needs you will not be able to take care
of them. Here are a few ways you can care for yourself
without taking too much time out of your hectic schedule:
Take 10-15 minutes out of the day for 'sane time' - some
alone time just to get yourself together emotionally, a little
peace and quiet.

Try to work some walking into your day - take the stairs
instead of the elevator, walk the long way around the office
to do necessary chores, work in an evening walk with the
kids even . . . they're with you, but they may enjoy the
outdoors and give you some time to decompress . . .

Try to make meals at home that will produce left-overs,
this way you do not have to eat out during the week. Just
freeze the left overs and pull them out as you need them.
This saves money and can be much healthier than eating
out too!

My favorite time to decompress when my daughter was
young was just after she went to sleep. It was a great time
to read a little or just take a long hot bubble bath with a
candle or two . . . nice and Quiet! ☺

You have other ideas that work for you?? Please feel free to
comment and share . . . ☺

- Contentment—What Is It?
  by Single Parents Rock! When we lean on The Rock on
  Tuesday, May 31, 2011, at 9:28 p.m.

  Being Content is a tall order and not for the faint of heart!
  It takes an abundant faith to truly be content in what God
  has given us, especially when our circumstances are very
  difficult and we just don't like them. The Word shows us
  that it IS possible to be content. Paul writes the following
  to the Philippians (4:11-13) "I am not saying this because
  I am in need, for I have learned to be content whatever

the circumstances. I know what it is to be in need, and I know what it is to have plenty. I have learned the secret of being content in any and every situation, whether well fed or hungry, whether living in plenty or in want. I can do everything through him who gives me strength." And we learn that ". . . godliness with contentment is great gain." (1 Timothy 6:6)

The following excerpt shed a little more light on the subject for me, I hope you find it helpful as well: "Contentment is being okay with something (or a lot of things) you're not okay with. It's being satisfied with what you have. It's the ability to open up wide and swallow whole the lot life has given you. Contentment is beauty. People who are content radiate peace, a warm acceptance of life, and love and concern for others. Contentment is a determination of the will. It's not a higher state of consciousness in which you never again desire what you don't have. It's not waking up every day to sunshine with a smile on your face. Some days, it's realizing that you're about to turn 37 and the biological clock you thought had settled down is about to explode. It's having to go through all those feelings one more time. It's determining to deal with it one more time. It doesn't always feel good. To be content is to accept the gifts of God with thankfulness and a willingness to do His will. You don't have to feel like it. You just have to do it."
Taken from "The Single Truth" by Lori Smith

It is not an easy pill to swallow, but we are called to praise God and if we are to praise God, we need to be thankful for all He has given us in every circumstance. Sometimes it truly is a sacrifice of praise as in Hebrews 13:15-16 "Through Jesus, therefore, let us continually offer to God a sacrifice of praise - the fruit of lips that confess his name. And do not forget to do good and to share with others, for with such sacrifices God is pleased."
God Bless you always!

JUNE 2011

June 1

- Faith is not believing that God can do anything. Faith is believing that God WILL do what He promised He will do.
- If you are musically inclined, like I am, it really helps to load your iPod or mp3 player with as many uplifting inspiring Christian songs as possible. That way, when you're struggling or having a hard day, you have your positive inspiration right in your pocket! ☺ I know there are many days when I need all the help I can get!

June 2

- Encouragement from a friend: We are allowed the problems we need in our life to fix the things about ourselves that need fixing, with Jesus's help. The worst suffering occurs when you run from your suffering instead of running to Him. It's not the snake bite that's the problem; it's running from the snake that pumps venom to your heart—that's the problem.
  My response: Wow . . . Amen!
- "During those days when you feel completely abandoned and unloved . . . Please remember God's promise: The poor and needy seek water, but there is none, their tongues fail for thirst. I, the Lord, will hear them; I, the God of Israel, will not forsake them." Isaiah 41:17
- God's Word: "Because he has set his love upon Me, therefore I will deliver him; I will set him on high, because he has known My name. He shall call upon Me, and I will answer him; I will be with him in trouble; I will deliver him and honor him." Psalm 91:14-15

June 4

- Great way to spend a Saturday: Take the kids to the park and have a picnic. Go to the lake, Go to the backyard toss the ball around, and grill out. Spend some time outside and enjoy the wonderful summer weather God has given us! ☺ Have a great weekend!
- "Let all those rejoice who put their trust in You; let them ever shout for joy, because You defend them; let those also who love Your name be joyful in You. For You, Oh Lord, will bless the righteous; with favor you will surround him as with a shield." Psalm 5:11-12

June 5

- Interesting observation: Oddly enough, life often seems a little less overwhelming when the house is clean and in order. Try to take one room at a time, <u>un</u>clutter and clean. When you can walk into a tidy house, the mood just isn't as gloomy, and you'll have a safe, comfortable place to relax after a very busy day.

June 6

- Change of perspective: If you're upset with your situation, shift your focus to God. Let Him lead you and give praise. Your whole outlook on life will be transformed! Guaranteed.
- Contempt is conceived with expectations. Respect is conceived with expressions of gratitude.
- Let us never forget to give thanks to God for all the blessings in our lives. No matter how small, they're still blessings! No matter how many hardships we have to endure, count your blessings every day. It helps keep things in perspective.
- "Contentment is about resting, about removing ourselves from the vain strivings of the world and finding peace and quiet in God's will." Gary Thomas

June 7

- Thought: If you can't be content with what God has given you when you are single, you are not going to be able to be content in a relationship. You must be okay with yourself before you can be okay with anyone else.
- When a loved one dies, when a friend moves away, when something in our life changes, we can choose to thank God for the joy he gave us in the past, or we can wallow in misery over the joy we think we will be denied in the future. The choice is ours.
- "Let your roots grow down into him and draw up nourishment from him. See that you go on growing in the Lord, and become strong and vigorous in the truth you were taught. Let your lives overflow with joy and thanksgiving for all he has done." Colossians 2:7
- Everyone needs to be loved and appreciated. Please take the time to tell those closest to you how much you appreciate them; they need that affirmation and love. Allow God to fill you with love, appreciation, and thankfulness for your family and show them how much they mean to you.

June 8

- "Trust in the Lord with all your heart and lean not on your own understanding; in all your ways submit to Him, and He will make your paths straight." Proverbs 3:5-6
- "Now may the God of patience and comfort grant you to be like-minded toward one another, according to Christ Jesus, that you may with one mind and one mouth glorify the God and Father of our Lord Jesus Christ. Therefore receive one another, just as Christ also received us, to the glory of God." Romans 15:5-7
- Accountability Partners
  by Single Parents Rock! When we lean on The Rock on Wednesday, June 8, 2011, at 6:28 p.m.
  Find someone who you can be accountability partners with, someone who you trust and trusts you. Share your

goals with them (from spiritual goals to everyday tasks that you want and need to complete), then make a schedule for goal completion and check in with each other on a regular basis to track progress. Lovingly encourage and help motivate each other . . . you may be surprised how much this helps you stay on track! God Bless!

Ref verses:

1 Corinthians 12:12-31 (One Body Many Parts)

Galatians 6: 1-10 (Doing Good to All) Brothers, if someone is caught in a sin, you who are spiritual should restore him gently. But watch yourself, or you also may be tempted. Carry each other's burdens, and in this way you will fulfill the law of Christ . . . .

• Marriage by Richard Schmidt

by Cynthia Johnson on Wednesday, June 8, 2011, at 4:22 p.m.

I am not married, but a married friend of mine posted this (as a couple status posts) and I had to share it. Several of my friends (you know who you are ☺) have recently been married, newly engaged or are in very serious relationships. I read the following and just can't resist sharing! Thank you Richard S. for posting.

Marriage is much more than a contract between couples; it is a covenant before the Almighty. It is a solemn agreement between two God-fearing souls that honors heaven with vows of commitment on earth. Marriage is sacred to your Savior Jesus, because it communicates His love through the most intimate love between a husband and a wife.

True love transitions from the thought of living together—to the commitment of living together forever in marriage. It is not a man-centered conditional love, but a Christ-centered unconditional love. There is fidelity of focus on their faith in God and their faith in each other. Couples with true love see marriage as a reflection of their relationship with Jesus.

On the third day a wedding took place at Cana in Galilee. Jesus' mother was there, and Jesus and his disciples had also been invited to the wedding. John 2:1-2

- Song: "God Speaking," a Very Beautiful Music Video for Anyone in Need (see Song Appendix for lyrics)
  The message in this song by Mandisa is really meaningful for anyone who is a Christian. Listen to this and please share it with someone else who needs uplifted today.

June 9

- "The Lord himself is my inheritance, my prize. He is my food and drink, my highest joy! He guards all that is mine. He sees that I am given pleasant brooks and meadows as my share! What a wonderful inheritance!" Psalm 16:5-6

June 10

- "Faith is like love; it cannot be forced." Arthur Schopenhauer
- Had the day off today and got to spend most of it just kickin' around with my girl. ☺ I Love the days I get to spend with her! Enjoy your kids while you can. Time just seems to go so fast! Thank you, God, for giving me this precious time with my daughter!
- Concentrate on changing the world for Christ's sake instead of changing your condition (single, married, job, house, etc.) for your sake. When we do what we are called to do, God blesses us abundantly!

June 11

- Oh, God and King, please expand my opportunities and my impact in such a way that I touch more lives for Your glory. Let me do more for You!
- God loves you. God loves you. God loves you. God loves you! Rest in the fact that you are truly and fiercely loved, and love each other in a way that honors God's love for you. ☺

June 12

- "Shout for joy, O heavens; rejoice, O earth; burst into song, O mountains! For the Lord comforts his people and will have compassion on his afflicted ones." Isaiah 49:13
- Loneliness vs. Comfort . . .

by Single Parents Rock! When we lean on The Rock on Sunday, June 12, 2011, at 8:56 a.m.

I have felt very lonely at times, as a single parent, and I know first-hand how difficult that feeling is to deal with. It struck me this morning while I was in my Bible, that there are literally zero references in my NIV to the word 'alone' and only two references to the word 'lonely'; they are:

Ps 68:6: God sets the lonely in families, he leads forth the prisoners with singing; but the rebellious live in a sun-scorched land.

Lk 5:16 - But Jesus often withdrew to lonely places and prayed.

It struck me because the first verse that lonely is used is an encouragement to the lonely, it is a positive thing for lonely believers and also a warning to those who choose to rebel against God. The second verse where lonely is used is a reference to Christ going to a lonely place to get alone with Father God, where there would be no distractions to his interaction and communication with the Father. Christ is our ultimate example of how we should live our lives, so it occurs to me that we need to strive to find those lonely places from time to time to commune with God. Other than that . . . the negative concept of 'lonely', as in that everyone (including God) has abandoned us, that we are unworthy of others company, that we are unloved . . . I truly believe those concepts come from the accuser. God tells us over and over again that we are loved and that we need to be in community with other believers, lift each other up, comfort and pray for each other. God is truly our God of comfort. So, on thinking of these things I looked up comfort and here is what the word says about comfort:

Isa 49:13 - Shout for joy, O heavens; rejoice, O earth; burst into song, O mountains! For the Lord comforts his people and will have compassion on his afflicted ones.

Isa 51:12 - I, even I, am he who comforts you. Who are you that you fear mortal men, the sons of men who are but grass.

2 Co 7:5-6 - For when we came into Madeconia, this body of ours had no rest, but we were harassed at every turn - conflicts on the outside, fears within. But God, who comforts the downcast, comforted us . . .

2 Co 1:3-11 - Praise be to the God and Father of our Lord Jesus Christ, the Father of compassion and the God of all comfort, who comforts us in all our troubles, so that we can comfort those in any trouble with the comfort we ourselves have received from God. For just as the sufferings of Christ flow over into our lives, so also through Christ our comfort overflows. If we are distressed, it is for your comfort and salvation; if we are comforted, it is for your comfort, which produces in you patient endurance of the same sufferings, so also you share in our comfort. We do not want you to be uninformed, brothers, about the hardships we suffered in the province of Asia. We were under great pressure, far beyond our ability to endure, so that we despaired even of life. Indeed, in our hearts we felt the sentence of death. But this happened that we might not rely on ourselves but on God, who raises the dead. He has delivered us from such a deadly peril, and he will deliver us. On him we have set our hope that he will continue to deliver us, as you help us by your prayers. Then many will give thanks on our behalf for the gracious favor granted us in answer to the prayers of many.

In 2 Co 1:3-11 Paul is writing to the Corinthians to let them know that God has comforted him in all his troubles and that God will comfort them in all their troubles as well. That they need to comfort others by telling them how God has comforted them during their trials, so that we may all mature in our faith realizing that we will always face hardships, but that we are never abandoned by our gracious God. Paul explains that sometimes the reason for these kinds of trials, the kind that make a person's heart despair and 'feel the sentence of death', is to ensure that we rely on God and not ourselves. Paul encourages the Corinthians to pray for him and each other so that 'many will give thanks on our behalf for the gracious favor granted us in answer to the prayers of many'. We need to heed Paul's words and pray always for each other and ourselves, so that we will rely on God and not ourselves, to walk (and sometimes carry) us through the trials of this life.

God bless you always

June 14

- Scripture for Encouragement: Psalm 119:73-96
  by Single Parents Rock! When we lean on The Rock on Tuesday, June 14, 2011, at 6:04 p.m.
  Your hands made me and formed me; give me understanding to learn your commands. May those who fear you rejoice when they see me, for I have put my hope in your word. I know, O Lord, that your laws are righteous, and in faithfulness you have afflicted me. May your unfailing love be my comfort, according to your promise to your servant. Let your compassion come to me that I may live, for your law is my delight. May the arrogant be put to shame for wronging me without cause; but I will meditate on your precepts. May those who fear you turn to me, those who understand your statutes. May my heart be blameless toward your decrees, that I may not be put to shame.
  My soul faints with longing for your salvation, but I have put my hope in your word. My eyes fail, looking for your promise; I say, When will you comfort me? Though I am like a wineskin in the smoke, I do not forget your decrees. How long must your servant wait? When will you punish

my persecutors? The arrogant dig pitfalls for me, contrary to your law. All your commands are trustworthy, help me, for men persecute me without cause. They almost wiped me from the earth, but I have not forsaken your precepts. Preserve my life according to your love, and I will obey the statues of your mouth.

Your word, O Lord, is eternal; it stands firm in the heavens. Your faithfulness continues through all generations; you established the earth, and it endures. Your laws endure to this day for all things serve you. If your law had not been my delight I would have perished in my affliction. I will never forget your precepts, for by them you have preserved my life. Save me, for I am yours; I have sought out your precepts. The wicked are waiting to destroy me, but I will ponder your statutes. To all perfection I see a limit; but your commands are boundless.

- Our ROCK!

by Single Parents Rock! When we lean on The Rock on Tuesday, June 14, 2011 at 6:31pm.

Genesis 49:24-25: But his bow remained steady, his strong arms stayed limber, because of the hand of the Mighty One of Jacob, because of the Shepherd, the Rock of Israel, because of your father's God, who helps you, because of the Almighty, who blesses you with blessings of the heavens above, blessings of the deep that lies below, blessings of the breast and womb.

Deuteronomy 32:4: He is the Rock, his works are perfect, and all his ways are just. A faithful God who does no wrong, upright and just is he.

2 Samuel 22:2-3: He said: The Lord is my rock, my fortress and my deliverer; my God is my rock, in whom I take refuge, my shield and the horn of my salvation. He is my stronghold, my refuge and my savior - from violent men you save me. I call to the Lord, who is worthy of praise, and I am saved from my enemies.

Psalm 18:2-3: The Lord is my rock, my fortress and my deliverer, my God is my rock, in whom I take refuge. He is my shield and the horn of my salvation, my stronghold. I call on the Lord, who is worthy of praise, and I am saved from my enemies.

Psalm 19:14: May the words of my mouth and the meditation of my heart be pleasing in your sight, O Lord, my rock and my Redeemer.

Psalm 40:2-3: He lifted me out of the slimy pit, out of the mud and mire; he set my feet on a rock and gave me a firm place to stand. He put a new song in my mouth, a hymn of praise to our God. many will see and fear and put their trust in the Lord.

Psalm 61:2-3: From the ends of the earth I call to you. I call as my heart grows faint; lead me to the rock that is higher than I. For you have been my refuge, a strong tower against the foe.

Psalm 92:15: The Lord is upright; he is my Rock, and there is no wickedness in him.

Isaiah 26:4: Trust in the Lord forever, for the Lord, the Lord, is the Rock eternal.

Isaiah 51:1: Listen to me, you who pursue righteousness and who seek the Lord: Look to the rock from which you were cut and to the quarry from which you were hewn

Matthew 7:24: Therefore everyone who hears these words of mine and puts them into practice is like a wise man who built his house on the rock.

1 Corinthians 10:3-4: They all ate the same spiritual food and drank the same spiritual drink; for they drank from the spiritual rock that accompanied them, and that rock was Christ.

1 Peter 2:7-10: Now to you who believe, this stone is precious. But to those who do not believe, "the stone the builders rejected has become the capstone", and, "A stone that causes men to stumble and a rock that makes them fail". They stumble because they disobey the message -

which is also what they were destined for. But you are a chosen people, a royal priesthood, a holy nation, a people belonging to God, that you may declare the praises of him who called you out of darkness into his wonderful light. Once you were not a people, but now you are the people of God; once you had not received mercy, but now you have received mercy.

June 15

- Rely on the Lord to be your strength: "In all these things we are more than conquerors through him who loved us. For I am convinced that neither death nor life, neither angels nor demons, neither the present nor the future, nor any powers, neither height nor depth, nor anything else in all creation, will be able to separate us from the love of God that is in Christ Jesus our Lord." Romans 8:37-39

June 16

- "Faith brings man to God; love brings Him to man." Martin Luther
- As parents, it is our duty to discipline our children and instruct them in the ways of the Lord. Discipline is never easy because we love our children, but that is precisely why we need to discipline them, so that they will learn, grow, and be healthy both physically and spiritually.
- "The rod of correction imparts wisdom, but a child left to himself disgraces his mother." Proverbs 29:15

June 17

- Our Heavenly Father loves us enough to discipline and guide us for our eternal good. Let us embrace Him and follow His example so that we may point our own families to Him and give praise in every situation.
- "He said: 'The Lord is my rock, my fortress and my deliverer; my God is my rock, in whom I take refuge, my shield and the horn of my salvation. He is my stronghold,

my refuge and my savior—from violent men you save me. I call to the Lord, who is worthy of praise, and I am saved from my enemies.'" 2 Samuel 22:2-3

- Let Us Submit to Our Heavenly Father's Discipline by Single Parents Rock! When we lean on The Rock on Friday, June 17, 2011, at 9:32 a.m.

  Let us submit to the discipline of our Heavenly Father so that we may grow in our faith and be better equipped to lead and train our families in the ways of our Lord.

  "Our fathers disciplined us for a little while as they thought best; but God disciplines us for our good, that we may share in his holiness. No discipline seems pleasant at the time, but painful. Later on, however, it produces a harvest of righteousness and peace for those who have been trained by it. Therefore, strengthen your feeble arms and weak knees. Make level paths for your feet, so that the lame may not be disabled, but rather healed." Heb 12:10-12

- Praise God we are so dearly loved that He would take the time to discipline and guide us for our eternal good.

June 18

- When the right choice is not clear, remember the Lord says, "I will guide you along the best pathway for your life. I will advise you and watch over you." Psalm 32:8

- Lord, help us be reflections of You to our families and to the world.

  "May the words of my mouth and the meditation of my heart be pleasing in your sight, O Lord, my rock and my Redeemer." Psalm 19:14

- Father's Day is very challenging and sad for some of us who have children in our homes who have no earthly father in their lives. Please know that God will fill all the gaps for them and for you. It is not humanly possible to always be strong. Rely on God to be your strength and portion for your heart, especially when it aches more than words can describe for your children.

- "My flesh and my heart may fail, but God is the strength of my heart and my portion forever." Psalm 73:26

June 20

- Being transparent in your struggles is sometimes the most powerful encouragement to others.
- "Be temperate, trustworthy in everything . . ."
- Do NOT let anyone but God define you! God loves each and every one of us so much that he has bequeathed to us an inheritance in Glory that will never dwindle or fade! Let the world say what it will—we are children of God and are priceless in His eyes!
- "Praise be to the God and Father of our Lord Jesus Christ! In his great mercy he has given us new birth into a living hope through the resurrection of Jesus Christ from the dead, and into an inheritance that can never perish, spoil or fade—kept in heaven for you, who through faith are shielded by God's power until the coming of the salvation that is ready to be revealed in the last time. In this you greatly rejoice, though now for a little while you may have had to suffer grief in all kinds of trials. These have come so that your faith—of greater worth than gold, which perishes even though refined by fire—may be proved genuine and may result in praise, glory and honor when Jesus Christ is revealed." 1 Peter 1:3-7

June 21

- God's got your back . . . Glad HE does! I know I need Him.
  "But you will not leave in haste or go in flight; for the LORD will go before you, the God of Israel will be your rear guard." Isaiah 52:12
- C. S. Lewis re our heart: "If you want to make sure of keeping it intact, you must give your heart to no one, not even to an animal. Wrap it carefully round with hobbies and little luxuries; avoid all entanglements; lock

it up safe in the casket or coffin of your selfishness. But in that casket, safe, dark, motionless, airless—it will change. It will not be broken; it will become unbreakable, impenetrable, irredeemable."

- We will never have the quality relationships we are meant to have until we put our relationship with God FIRST!
- It is impossible to be all we are called to be and do all we are called to do unless we abide each day in Christ. When we rely on HIM for our strength, courage, wisdom, and steadfastness, He will guide us; and when we are weak, we can take shelter in His loving arms. Praise God!

June 22

- I'm so blessed to have friends who aren't afraid to check on me when something seems out of place! You know who you are. Thank you! ☺
- God always loves us no matter what! Count yourself abundantly blessed if you also have people in your life who love you even when you're a mess.
- Great?? Expectations???
  by Single Parents Rock! When we lean on The Rock on Wednesday, June 22, 2011, at 7:09 p.m.
  Be careful how you treat people and how you allow people to treat you. I've seen first-hand how easy it is to get used to people treating you poorly. After a short time you begin thinking that it is NORMAL for people to treat you poorly and actually come to expect that kind of treatment from others in your life. Pretty soon, you're a magnet for people who act this way . . . you're in a very destructive rut! The kicker is . . . you may not even realize that you are in such a Dangerous place! When a person is in this mentality they slowly plod along, regretfully accepting what life has thrown their way, thinking it is a normal and unavoidable situation. The TRUTH is that we were all MADE TO BE LOVED AND PURSUED FIERCELY by the God of the Universe!!! Our Heavenly Father made us to love Him and

to be LOVED AND BLESSED by Him! Praise God!!!
Please look around you today . . . if you see anyone in this
destructive rut PLEASE show them some love and let them
know how important they really are! It will take a LOT of
time to get through to them, but every encouraging word is
one step closer to them realizing that they Truly are loved
and WORTH IT! NEVER give up on them . . . you will
probably be thoroughly frustrated with them many times.
Please realize that they are in a VERY VERY VERY deep
hole . . . it may take Years of encouragement and prayer,
constantly encouraging them and lifting them to the
Father before they are able to escape the bondage they are
living in . . . Please don't give up . . . If you are the person
in this bondage, please don't give up!!! Even if you can't see
it right now YOU ARE WORTH IT! YOU ARE LOVED
AND WORTH LOVING!!!
God Bless and keep you always

June 24

- "Only be careful, and watch yourselves closely so that you
  do not forget the things your eyes have seen or let them slip
  from your heart as long as you live. Teach them to your
  children and to their children after them." Deuteronomy 4:9
- Psalm 46
  by Single Parents Rock! When we lean on The Rock on
  Friday, June 24, 2011, at 8:19 a.m.
  I was frustrated the other day and God directed me to
  this Psalm so I thought I would share The thought that
  occurred to me is this . . . God IS the Almighty . . . with
  all He has done and continues to do throughout history He
  can certainly handle my troubles, which pale severely in
  comparison to His Power and Majesty!
  Psalm 46:
  God is our refuge and strength
  an ever-present help in trouble.
  Therefore we will not fear, though

the earth give way and the mountains fall into the heart of
the sea,
though its waters roar and foam and the mountains quake
with their surging.
There is a river whose streams make glad the city of God,
the holy place where the Most High dwells.
God is within her, she will not fall;
God will help her at break of day;
Nations are in uproar,
kingdoms fall;
he lifts his voice,
the earth melts,
The Lord Almighty is with us;
the God of Jacob is our fortress.
Come and see the works of the Lord,
the desolations he has brought on the earth.
He makes wars cease to the ends of the earth;
he breaks the bow and shatters the spear,
he burns the shields with fire.
Be still, and know that I am God;
I will be exalted among all nations,
I will be exalted in the earth.
The Lord Almighty is with us;
the God of Jacob is our fortress.
God bless and keep you always!

- Share Your Story . . . Unashamed
by Single Parents Rock! When we lean on The Rock on
Friday, June 24, 2011, at 8:34 a.m.
Share your story with your family, don't be ashamed of the
places you have been . . . Show them the strength of the
Lord and how He has brought out of those places, guided
you back to the right path, shone His glory on you and
blessed your life! This will give them hope and they will
know that even after they have strayed and made some bad
decisions (as we ALL do in our lives) that God still loves

them and still wants to bless their lives abundantly for His good purpose!!!

Dt 4:9—Only be careful, and watch yourselves closely so that you do not forget the things your eyes have seen or let them slip from your heart as long as you live. Teach them to your children and to their children after them.

- Why do most men assume that ALL women want the big house in the best neighborhood with the best loaded SUV that money can buy? Is it really that rare to want a nice cozy house, a vehicle that is reliable, and time with the people you love?

June 25
- Forgive those who have wronged you, forget the past, and press on to your future in Christ Jesus; He works everything for the good of those who love Him. Stay strong in the Word and rely on Him to be your strength.
- "Brethren, I do not count myself to have apprehended; but one thing I do, forgetting those things which are behind and reaching forward to those things which are ahead, I press toward the goal for the prize of the upward call of God in Christ Jesus." Philippians 3:13-14

June 26
- We are deeply loved, completely forgiven, fully pleasing, totally accepted, and complete in Christ—complete in Christ, not missing Anything, holy and perfect because of the blood that Christ shed for us to pay for our sins and satisfy the righteous wrath of God. How Blessed we are!
- "Once you were alienated from God and were enemies in your minds because of your evil behavior. But now he has reconciled you by Christ's physical body through death to present you holy in his sight, without blemish and free from accusation." Colossians 1:21-22
- Let God Fill Your "Holes" and Rest in Him

by Single Parents Rock! When we lean on The Rock on
Sunday, June 26, 2011, at 9:56 p.m.
Please allow God to fill all of the 'holes' in your life . . . all
the pain that is tucked down so deep inside you have to
work to show anyone how bad it REALLY hurts . . . all of
the un-forgiveness that has been festering and causing you
pain in your heart and relationships . . . all of the angst
that comes with worrying where the next paycheck, meal
or pair of much needed set of school clothes is coming
from . . . give it ALL to God and REST in His provision.
He Loves you and will take care of you . . . you are His
child and He will Never abandon you!

June 28

- "Rejoice in the Lord: Let all those rejoice who put their
trust in You; let them ever shout for joy, because You defend
them; let those also who love your name be joyful in You.
For You, O Lord, will bless the righteous; with favor you
will surround him as with a shield." Psalm 5:11-12

- I have a teenage daughter, and if anyone else out there
is dealing with teenage girls, well, you know they're all
drama all the time! LOL. I wouldn't trade her for the world
though. She will be out of the house in just a few short
years, and I can't seem to get enough time with her. Enjoy
your kids while you have them. Time goes by way too fast!

June 29

- Waiting faithfully: Sometimes it is much more difficult to
obey God when He calls us to wait on Him to bring things
into our lives in His time. Wait peacefully with faithful
anticipation of our promised blessings instead of waiting
begrudgingly like little kids waiting for the all-important
cupcake that promptly gets snarfed down as soon as it hits
the plate. God's timing is perfect. Let us wait faithfully
upon Him.

June 30

- "You can't control today's outcome but you can control your effort. Push through it." LeCrae

  My comment: I don't know about you, but I needed this one today, so I thought I'd share. God Bless you in all you do!

July 2011

July 1

- Don't block your own blessing by refusing to walk the path God has laid before you. Just take Jesus's hand, let Him lead you, and know that He has good plans for you, plans to prosper you and not harm you, plans to give you hope and a future!
- Lord, please help me stay focused on You. I will empty out my life before I put You on a shelf.
- Draw close to God. He wants to heal you and make you whole. He wants to walk with you, and even carry you if necessary, through every difficult time in your life. He uses the difficult times to shape our character and our lives to look more and more like Christ Jesus. Praise God, the Eternal Love of our lives!
- "When outward strength is broken, faith rests on the promises. In the midst of sorrow, faith draws the string out of every trouble and takes out the bitterness from every affliction." Robert Cecil

July 2

- "The Lord is far from the wicked but he hears the prayer of the righteous." Proverbs 15:29
- Party People or Straight Course . . .
  by Single Parents Rock! When we lean on The Rock on Saturday, July 2, 2011, at 12:20 p.m.
  When deciding what kind of people to spend your time, space and life with . . . remember . . . "Folly delights a man who lacks judgment, but a man of understanding keeps a straight course." Proverbs 15:21
  People who are focused on God, seeking His council, don't revel in lust, greed or selfish behavior; they constantly seek God's direction and obey even when it goes directly against

their fleshly desires. It is very difficult for any of us to deny ourselves and seek God's kingdom wholeheartedly and we cannot do it without His divine guidance and strength. It is WORTH it in the long run though (eternal rewards beyond our imagination instead of temporary physical or monetary earthly rewards!!) . . . the last things any of us need are more drama and more distractions from God. He is the only One who can make us whole and guide us to fulfillment in Him. There is NO fulfillment in earthly things, people or places. God please help us all to stay strong and on Your straight course. God bless you in all you do and don't do according to His good will! ☺

July 3

- Walk out in your faith every day. Let your life reflect Jesus in every attitude you have and in everything you say and do.
- If God is working relentlessly on your weak spots, don't be angry. Give praise! For the greatest blessings come out of the most difficult lessons. Thank You, Jesus, for so patiently and lovingly molding me into the woman You created me to be!
- Song: "Someone Watching Over Your" by Yolanda Adams (see Song Appendix for lyrics)
- If, in your distress, you turn to another for help and they direct you to our good Lord and Savior, they are a wise friend indeed because no person on the planet can make it through this world and go on to live in Heaven with our Beloved Savior without the divine guidance and discipline of Father God.
- No matter what anyone in the past has told you or what anyone is telling you right now, you ARE WORTH IT! Never let anyone steal your self-esteem. God loves you and sent His Son to die on the cross for you. No person can diminish your true worth!

- Hearing Isn't Enough . . . We Must Put the Word into
  Practice in Our Lives
  by Single Parents Rock! When we lean on The Rock on
  Sunday, July 3, 2011, at 9:57 a.m.
  Do not merely listen to the word, and so deceive
  yourselves; do what it says: anyone who listens to the word
  but does not do what it says is like a man who looks at his
  face in a mirror and, after looking at himself, goes away
  and immediately forgets what he looks like. But the man
  who looks intently into the perfect law that gives freedom,
  and continues to do this, not forgetting what he has heard,
  but doing it - he will be blessed in what he does. If anyone
  considers himself religious and yet does not keep a tight
  rein on his tongue, he deceives himself and his religion is
  worthless. Religion that God our Father accepts as pure
  and faultless is this: to look after orphans and widows in
  their distress and to keep oneself from being polluted by
  the world. James 1:22-27
  Father God . . . please give us the strength and wisdom to
  not only hear Your word, but to put it into practice in our
  lives every single day!
  God bless you always . . .
- God Will Lift Us Up in Due Time . . . ☺ And RESTORE
  Us!!!
  by Single Parents Rock! When we lean on The Rock on
  Sunday, July 3, 2011, at 3:04 p.m.
  Humble yourselves, therefore, under God's mighty hand,
  that he may lift you up in due time. Cast all your anxiety
  on him because he cares for you. Be self-controlled and
  alert. your enemy the devil prowls around like a roaring
  lion looking for someone to devour. Resist him, standing
  firm in the faith, because you know that your brothers
  throughout the world are undergoing the same kind of
  sufferings, and the God of all grace, who called you to
  his eternal glory in Christ, after you have suffered a little
  while, will himself restore you and make you strong,

firm and steadfast. To him be the power forever and ever.
Amen. 1 Peter 5:6-11Praise God!

- Put your biggest issue squarely in the hands of the Lord
  and walk away from it, as scary as it seems, to relinquish
  control. Giving it to God is better than constantly living in
  the pain the issue causes every day!

July 4

- Song: "Shackles" (Praise You) by Mary Mary (see Song
  Appendix for lyrics)
- "God has said, 'Never will I leave you; never will I forsake
  you.' So we say with confidence, 'The Lord is my helper;
  I will not be afraid. What can man do to me?'" Hebrews
  13:5-6
- No More Negativity . . . Practice Positive Reinforcement!
  by Single Parents Rock! When we lean on The Rock on
  Monday, July 4, 2011, at 1:00 p.m.
  If you have been fed a bunch of negativity for a long time
  (like I have) practice believing God's truths for your life.
  Recite God's promises and truths about who you are in
  Him and what He has in store for your future. Write
  out the most encouraging verses on 3x5 cards and put
  them around the house where you can find them . . .
  (the bathroom mirror, the refrigerator, behind the visor
  in the car, the kitchen sink window . . .) anywhere you
  will see them and read them each and every day. It only
  takes a minute to read a verse off of a 3x5 card or scrap of
  paper . . . and you'll be Amazed at the impact that God's
  promises spoken into your life have if you meditate on
  them every day! The more you practice, recite and remind
  yourself of your true worth in Christ, the more His
  truth will become a part of who you are and the negative
  message of the world will gradually fade away . . . Stay
  close to God and HE will make you whole! We are whole
  and complete only when we are in His will. We are all built
  with a natural space for God to fill and He is the only One

who can fill it. There are other spaces in our lives for our loved ones, friends and family . . . but only God can fill the God spot. Let HIM have His space in your life and you'll be surprised at how much joy you will find in your current situation . . . even if you don't like where you are in life, God will give you true joy while you're on the journey. Praise God who does what we, in our limited capacities to understand anything, think is impossible!

God Bless you always . . .

July 5

- No matter how impossible your situation appears, never doubt what God has shown and promised you. God does not lie to His children. Your future is secure in Him.
- Don't let yourself be a slave to the destructive past mistakes of others. God has set you free from what they did to you. Embrace God's love and healing!
- If you have ever thought of yourself as "damaged goods," remember God specializes in Restoring "damaged goods" and making them shine for His glory!
- Can you say . . . I just got Checked Up? Wow . . . "When I am consumed by my problems-stressed out about my life, my family, and my job-I actually convey the belief that I think the circumstances are more important than God's command to always rejoice. In other words, that I have a "right" to disobey God because of the magnitude of my responsibilities." Francis Chan, *Crazy Love*
- Suffering is a privilege, a means to draw closer to our Heavenly Father like never before, a chance to model God's grace, an opportunity to become more like our Lord Jesus Christ. Thank You, Lord, for this chance to draw even closer to You.
- Are you following Jesus close enough to hear and obey His call? To actually walk in what He has for you? If not, I would challenge you to draw closer to our Heavenly Father.

You will not be complete and healed until you are fully walking in what He has for you.

- Something to think about: "When I am consumed by my problems—stressed out about my life, my family, and my job—I actually convey the belief that I think the circumstances are more important than God's command to always rejoice. In other words, that I have a 'right' to disobey God because of the magnitude of my responsibilities." Francis Chan, *Crazy Love*

- If we coddle our children in an attempt to compensate for a less than desired situation, we do them a great disservice! No matter our situation, whether we like it or not, we are obligated to teach our children love, respect, discipline, and self-control. Otherwise, they will not be equipped to be responsible adults.

- AMAZING LOVE PROMISE!!!
  by Single Parents Rock! When we lean on The Rock on Tuesday, July 5, 2011, at 9:17 p.m.
  "I will betroth you to Me forever; I will betroth you in righteousness and justice, in love and compassion. I will betroth you in faithfulness, and you will acknowledge the Lord." Hosea 2:19
  How AMAZING is that?!?! God wants to betroth us to HIM forever!!! You can't ask for a better promise than that! No matter what anyone thinks of you, no matter how many times you have been rejected, put down or used by other people . . . God wants to betroth you to HIM forever!!! Praise God!
  What is love?? What some in the world call 'love' is not real love at all!
  "Beloved, let us love one another, for love is of God; and everyone who loves is born of God and knows God. He who does not love does not know God, for ***God is love***. In this the love of God was manifested toward us, that God sent His only begotten Son into the world, that we might live through Him. In this is love, not that we loved

God, but that He loved us and sent His Son to be the propitiation (Propitiation means that the wrath of someone who has been unjustly wronged has been satisfied. It is an act that soothes hostility and satisfies the need for vengeance. Jesus paid the price for our sins on the cross, therefore; satisfying the righteous wrath of God so that we may be saved by faith through grace.) for our sins. Beloved, if God so loved us, we also ought to love one another, no one has seen God at any time. If we love one another, God abides in us, and His love has been perfected in us." 1 John 4:7-12

July 6

- Rely on God's strength to get you through your struggles every day. Not only will He get you through your trials, no matter how intense, He will bless and restore you in the process.

July 7

- Your suffering is temporary, a necessary step to allow God to refine your character and grow your faith. Be blessed in your suffering for God is with you!
- Sometimes we must realize how much God loves us and let Him heal us before we are truly able to love another the way we were meant to love.
- Security doesn't come from people or money. Security comes only from God.
- "This is a sane, wholesome, practical, working faith; that it is man's business to do the will of God; second, that God Himself takes on the care of that man; and third, that therefore that man ought never to be afraid of anything." George MacDonald
  PRAISE GOD as we walk in His will and are NOT afraid any longer! God bless you always . . .
- Your past does not define you. God has defined you as fully loved and fully pleasing to Him, covered by the blood

of his only son, Jesus Christ, so that you may receive the Father's grace and have eternal life! Don't let anyone tell you that you're worth any less. God never lies!

- "The Lord has appeared of old to me, saying: 'Yes, I have loved you with an everlasting love; therefore with loving-kindness I have drawn you.'" Jeremiah 31:3

July 8

- Never let anyone use shame to diminish your worth. Own up to your mistakes, hold your head up high, cling to God, and let Him walk you through it with your self-worth intact!
- "Rejoice in the Lord always. I will say it again: Rejoice! Let your gentleness be evident to all, the Lord is near. Do not be anxious about anything, but in everything, by prayer and petition, with thanksgiving, present your requests to God. And the peace of God, which transcends all understanding, will guard your hearts and your minds in Christ Jesus." Philippians 4:4-7

July 9

- When you are lonely, remember Lust is a powerful weapon in Satan's arsenal because it impairs our ability to love. REAL love is not only about the physical. It requires patience, understanding, and sacrifice. There is no greater example of love than Christ's sacrificial love for us. Anyone who just wants the physical from you does not really love you.
- Encouragement from a friend: "⁴ Love is patient, love is kind. It does not envy, it does not boast, it is not proud. ⁵It does not dishonor others, it is not self-seeking, it is not easily angered, it keeps no record of wrongs. ⁶Love does not delight in evil but rejoices with the truth. ⁷It always protects, always trusts, always hopes, always perseveres. ⁸Love never fails . . ." 1 Corinthians 13:4-8

My response: Wow . . . God is so good! I truly needed this one this morning. Thank you for posting. I'm right there with you. I'm pondering this verse this morning too, along with my situation and where God is taking me as well. I love how God brings his children together to bless each other just simply by being open and honest about where we are in our walk.

- Don't let loneliness turn you away from Godliness.
- If it seems that God is asking you to walk alone for a season, listen more carefully. He may be asking you to walk solely with HIM for that blessed season so that He can grow you in ways that you can't even imagine! Don't get caught up in the loneliness, lean hard into our Heavenly Father, and let Him guide, teach, and grow you into the person you are meant to be.
- Looking for Love?? Show Love . . .
  by Single Parents Rock! When we lean on The Rock on Saturday, July 9, 2011, at 9:38 a.m.
  If we are truly looking for love, we need to give love in everything we do and say: Love is patient, love is kind. It does not envy, it does not boast, it is not proud. It does not dishonor others, it is not self-seeking, it is not easily angered, it keeps no record of wrongs. Love does not delight in evil but rejoices with the truth. It always protects, always trusts, always hopes, always perseveres. Love never fails. 1 Corinthians 13
  Ask yourself 'Am I showing all of the real qualities of love to everyone in every situation in my life?'
  Even if you are not 'looking' for love . . . we are all called to be more like Christ and if God IS Love . . . well . . . 'nuff said!
  Heavenly Father, please help all of us show real love to everyone in every situation in our lives. Help us to be more and more like You each and every day.

July 10

- "My brothers and sisters, whenever you face trials of any kind, consider it nothing but joy, because you know that the testing of your faith produces endurance; and let endurance have its full effect, so that you may be mature and complete, lacking in nothing." James 1:2-4
- God Is Love . . . Love Is Patient . . .
by Single Parents Rock! When we lean on The Rock on Sunday, July 10, 2011, at 8:58 p.m.
When God has you in a 'holding' pattern, He may be giving you the gift of time so you can heal and be restored so you will be able to handle the blessings that He longs to give you. Remember . . .
LOVE IS PATIENT:
Exodus 23:27-30I will send my terror ahead of you and throw into confusion every nation you encounter. I will make all your enemies turn their backs and run. I will send the hornet ahead of you to drive the Hivites, Canaanites and Hittites out of your way. But I will not drive them out in a single year, because the land would become desolate and the wild animals too numerous for you. Little by little I will drive them out before you, until you have increased enough to take possession of the land.
God takes care of his children, but he does not give them more than they are prepared to handle at one time. He patiently gives us our portion, little by little, increasing it as we grow and are capable of handling the bountiful blessings He has in store for us. It is our duty to grow and increase and to petition Him with a pure heart and right motives for our blessings. In this fashion we are to walk in His will and do His work for His kingdom. If we do this with a pure heart and right motives, when we petition Him with the true desires of our heart, he will be faithful to bless us more bountifully than we can possibly imagine!
- God's Eyes vs. Man's Eyes . . .
by Cynthia Johnson on Sunday, July 10, 2011, at 6:38 p.m.

1Sam 16:7 The Lord does not look at the things man looks at. Man looks at the outward appearance, but the Lord looks at the heart."

Wouldn't it be Wonderful if people looked at the world through God's eyes??? When we look at each other we see all of the barriers that this world and society tell us 'matter', when they don't matter at all to God. In fact, God made us all different and I must believe that He values those differences and made us all EXACTLY like we are for His perfect purpose! Instead of seeing things like race, sex, height, weight, disabilities, social status, economic status, age, etc . . . we should be loving and helping EVERYONE as we have been commanded.

(1 John 3:23-24 And this is his command: to believe in the name of his Son, Jesus Christ and to love one another as he commanded us. Those who obey his commands live in him and he in them. And this is how we know that he lives in us: We know it by the Spirit he gave us.)

God, please give us all new eyes and a refreshed heart to look at each other as YOU look at us instead of through our own limited and encumbered vision. Give us all hearts to help everyone you put in our paths with true servant's hearts with no limitations. Thank you so much for all of your blessings . . . in Your name . . . Amen.

July 11

- "Peace I leave with you, My peace I give to you; not as the world gives do I give to you; let not your heart be troubled, neither let it be afraid." John 14:27

- PEACE: "And let the peace of God rule in your hearts, to which also you were called in one body; and be thankful." Colossians 3:15

  "The Lord will give strength to His people; the Lord will bless His people with peace." Psalm 29:11

"Peace I leave with you, My peace I give to you; not as the world gives do I give to you; let not your heart be troubled, neither let it be afraid." John 14:27

- When you have peace in the midst of the storm, the world does not understand why you're not stressed. Don't let this dissuade you or make you doubt anything that God has told you. God is with you and will give you peace in the midst of ANY storm. All you need to do is ask and believe. God bless you always!

July 12

- God is so good! Getting answers from places that are undeniably and completely from HIM. On-point and on time! ☺

- No matter what kind of heartache and trials you are dealing with, if you put God first, let Him handle your life in His strength, His time, and in HIS way, HE (God) will take care of you. He will heal, restore, and bless you beyond your imagination, but you MUST give control over to Him.
  God bless you always!

July 13

- "Take delight in the Lord, and he will give you your heart's desires. Commit everything you do to the Lord. Trust him, and he will help you." Psalm 33:18-20

- A troubled history can be made into a beautiful thing by God. It pays generous spiritual dividends when we do things God's way. Even when we're sinned against, we can grow through the experience by the grace of God. HE will shape our character and spirit into something so incredibly beautiful that it will be a testimony to everyone around us! Praise God!
  Lord, please use each and every one of us for Your glory!

July 14

- Do what you are called to do regardless if you are where you want to be or not. The lessons you are learning and blessings you are receiving are mandatory steps toward the future God has for you. Rejoice always!
- YouTube clip: "I will wait for you" by Official P4CM Poet JANETTE . . . IKZ
- "Don't worry about anything; instead, pray about everything. Tell God what you need, and thank him for all he has done. Then you will experience God's peace, which exceeds anything we can understand. His peace will guard your hearts and minds as you live in Christ Jesus." Philippians 4:6-7
- "My comfort in my suffering is this: Your promise preserves my life." Psalm 119:50
  God is ALWAYS there for us. No matter how big our troubles seem, GOD IS BIGGER! ☺

July 15

- Stop fighting it. Open your heart, embrace your struggles, and let God use them to shape you into who He made you to be. Your beauty is your Godliness. If someone else can't see that, they are not the one God has for you.
- Loving, Discerning Teacher . . .
  by Single Parents Rock! When we lean on The Rock on Friday, July 15, 2011, at 7:45 a.m.
  I am starting to teach my daughter how to drive lately and the experience has reminded me how patient, loving and discerning our Heavenly Father is with us. My daughter and I were talking the other day . . . she was letting me know that she really does want to learn to drive, but that the thought scares her . . . there are so many things that could happen that have dire consequences and she doesn't want to get hurt or hurt anyone else. I found myself re-assuring her that I would never allow her to take the vehicle into any situation where I knew she was not capable

of handling it. She is still not so sure, but I know she will do very well when push comes to shove. Our Heavenly Father does the same thing for us . . . HE does not bless us with things that we are not yet equipped to handle and He does not allow us to go through any situation that HE cannot help us get through. Granted, we may not be able to do it completely on our own power, but we're not supposed to do anything completely on our own power. We are supposed to rely on God's strength, wisdom and power to get us through our struggles. Our loving, patient and discerning Heavenly Father knows what is best for us in every phase of our lives. We do not have the capability to see things with His vision and foresight, but quite honestly . . . that's why we need Faith . . . lean hard on your faith every single minute of every single day and I promise you that God will lead you down the right path. There are going to be times when you don't think you can bear what you are going through . . . times when you think it's all just too much to handle . . . just call on our Heavenly Father and He will comfort you and give you peace and strength to make it through. It is not going to be an easy road, but HE will always be with you to heal, restore, encourage and grow you into the person He created you to be, if you let Him. God bless you always!

July 16

- Our culture is SO self-centered it's hard not to buy into it, But we've got it backwards. It should be God FIRST, die to self.
- NEVER settle for less than God's best! You are a priceless gem in God's eyes. Rely on Him to lead you to the right relationship and be obedient when He tells you to move on. If you keep holding on to something that is hurting you, there is no room for God to bring something truly good into your life.
- Nobody can be strong all the time. We all need love.

July 17

- "Do not worry about tomorrow, for tomorrow will worry about its own things. Sufficient for the day is its own trouble." Matthew 6:34
  "I will life up my eyes to the hills . . . From whence comes my help? My help comes from the LORD, Who made heaven and earth." Psalm 121:1-2
  Praise God Who is always with us!
- Got one of those tough reminders today . . . must not be upset with God's agenda and timing, HE directs us on how we need to manage our time, and we Must be obedient. HE will sustain us and give us strength and peace for the journey.
- Ever notice that training for something can be excruciating (studying for finals, getting a master's degree, running a race, excelling at a sport, etc.) but completing the task has great rewards? Sometimes when life is excruciating, God is training us so we will be prepared for our future.

July 19

- I fall short because I am human. I can go on because God is gracious and has forgiven me for all my short comings. Praise God for His patience and grace!
- Waiting is God putting you in a place of unhindered, undistracted, and inescapable time with Him. Give him all of your worries and concerns and just be with him.
  "Humble yourselves, therefore, under the mighty hand of God so that at the proper time he may exalt you, casting all your anxieties on him, because he cares for you." 1 Peter 5:6-7
- Love moments of clarity . . . there is peace in clarity. Thank You, Jesus. ☺
- The purpose of waiting is Jesus, the point of waiting is the relationship, and the work of waiting is worship.
  "Wait for the Lord; be strong, and let your heart take courage; wait for the Lord!" Psalm 27:14

- When we keep God as the focal point of our lives, He truly takes care of us. We need not worry, stew, or fret. God is always with us, and His plans are always better than our own.

July 20

- God can turn the deepest pain in your life into your biggest blessing and the most powerful part of your testimony! Don't let the pain define you. Let God use it to Refine you.

July 21

- Love who you are. God does! ☺

July 22

- When you love, ALWAYS love God first. Seek God first. HE will complete you, give you direction, and fill you with His Spirit so that you may bless those that you love the way HE intended you to bless them.
- God is so good. God is so very, very good! Find some time to spend alone with HIM. Let HIM regenerate you so that you may press on in His will. God bless you always!

July 23

- Be who God created you to be. No matter what anyone else says or does, do not let anything distract you from the Lord. HE has a plan for your life and will bring it to pass regardless of the opposition.
- "Take up your cross daily and follow Me . . ." Hummm . . . means you don't live this life for you, you live for HIM. Stop complaining when things don't go your way. They're not supposed to. They're supposed to go His way.
- Many times you cannot predict or control the circumstances in which you find yourself, but you can control how you handle them.

- I'm feeling so blessed to have such an amazing and beautiful daughter!
- Be upstanding and honorable in all you do so that you may reflect Christ's likeness to this fallen world. Christ is the only One who can heal this world and all the pain in it. If we contribute to the anger, pain, and suffering, we are not being part of the solution or following Christ's will for our lives. HE never promised it would be easy, but HE did promise that it will be worth it! God bless you always!

July 24

- When God lays something on your heart, do it.
- "If my people, which are called by my name, shall humble themselves, and pray, and seek my face, and turn from their wicked ways; then will I hear from heaven, and will forgive their sin, and will heal their land." 2 Chronicles 7:14
- Don't forget to set aside some time just for yourself and our Heavenly Father. Downtime is a must. Without it, we cannot rest and regenerate. Remember to set some time aside just for yourself and the Father so that you may rest in His arms.
- "Fold the arms of your faith and wait in quietness until the light goes up in your darkness. Fold the arms of your faith, I say, but not of your action. Think of something you ought to do, and go do it. Heed not your feelings. Do your work." George MacDonald

July 25

- Sometimes you just have to walk in faith. When the night seems the darkest and things do not seem to be going the way you want them to go, lean on our Heavenly Father. HE will see you through.

July 26

- When we realize how much God loves us, we begin to realize our true worth. Then it is easier to let God heal our hearts and move forward.
- Encouragement from a friend: When you have cried out to God in desperate times, you have wondered if your prayers are even heard. But God is never late. He turns up at the eleventh hour. He answers our prayers in unexpected ways, stretching our faith to the limit. It's in these times we trust Him as we are taken way out of our comfort zone. BUT God is a complete show off! He likes to do things in a big way. He wants to show off in your world!
- Encouragement from a friend: "But the LORD said unto me, Say not, I am a child: for thou shalt go to all that I shall send thee, and whatsoever I command thee thou shalt speak. Be not afraid of their faces: for I am with thee to deliver thee, saith the LORD." Jeremiah 1:7-8
- Growing in faith is never easy. It usually comes through many very tough struggles. Take time out to be refreshed. Take some "sane time" for yourself where you can just relax and clear your heart and head for a little while. Then get alone with God so He can give you the guidance, encouragement, and strength you need to continue the journey.
- Our weaknesses don't matter. It's God's power that completes the mission that God calls us to.

July 27

- Habits: I need and want water, but my mind keeps telling me that I want soda. Good grief! Funny how bad habits keep rearing their ugly head and overstay their welcome.
- One step at a time, one breath at a time, let Jesus lead you minute by minute.
- Song: "Song of Restoration" by LeShawn Daniel (NOTE: I could not find the lyrics to this song on the Internet. Please

look it up and listen to it at your leisure. It is a wonderful song!)

- "³⁴Then Peter replied, "I see very clearly that God shows no favoritism. ³⁵In every nation he accepts those who fear him and do what is right. ³⁶This is the message of Good News for the people of Israel—that there is peace with God through Jesus Christ, who is Lord of all." Acts 10:34-37
- "Faith begins where reason sinks exhausted." Albert Pike
- If you are still living for your blessings, you are living for yourself. We are called to live for our Heavenly Father. Our blessings are nice perks, NOT the goal.

July 28

- When life gets overwhelming, remember others are overwhelmed too. Treat everyone with patience, kindness, understanding, and tender-hearted mercy. Treat others how you would like to be treated.
- God created women to be emotional, and I'd say He did a Spectacular job, maybe too good! Good thing, He calls us all to be patient and kind with each other. We'd all be in trouble otherwise!
- "Finally, all of you, live in harmony with one another, be sympathetic, love as brothers, be compassionate and humble. Do not repay evil with evil or insult with insult, but with blessing, because to this you were called so that you may inherit a blessing." 1 Peter 3:8-9
- It really is amazing to see God working a healing process in you when you can look in the mirror and back over the recent past and see how much you have grown. God is truly amazing and will do miraculous things with your life if you just give HIM control. SOOO Blessed! ☺
- Fears Don't Stand a Chance When God Is in the House ☺ by Single Parents Rock! When we lean on The Rock on Thursday, July 28, 2011, at 9:57 p.m.

When you turn around and look your fears directly in the eye, they can look like a insurmountable mountain which cannot be moved, conquered, ducked around, tunneled under, flown over or avoided . . . the TRUTH is that alone, that mountain cannot be overcome. However, all we have to do to conquer all of our fears is let our Heavenly Father take our hand and walk with us through the pain, fear, anger, worry, loss . . . HE can and will conquer our fears for us if we'll just give Him total control of our lives and hearts . . . If we just open our hearts to His healing power and love and submit our lives to His perfect will, He will restore and bless us beyond our wildest dreams! HIS love conquers all!

July 29

- Encouragement from a friend: Sometimes God allows thing to happen so that He can take us into the future He has planned for us. Next time you are feeling in the depths of despair, don't look out at your circumstances, instead look up.
  "Behold, I make all things new . . ." Revelations 21:5 NKJV
  My response: So timely! Love this one! ☺
- Listen carefully to the Father and follow His lead. He will lead you if you let Him. God is so good! ☺ When you hear His call and feel Him nudging you in the right direction, be obedient, and you will be blessed!

July 31

- Encouragement from a friend: Ladies, get your mind off a man and put it on God and His Kingdom and everything else will be added, including the RIGHT man. Amen, Somebody!
  My response: Amen!
- Don't let the stress of this world get to you. God has a bigger plan for your life, and He is bursting to show you

His will. Look up to our Heavenly Father and ask Him today. Father, please show me Your way and Your will for my life. I surrender all to You and ask for your guidance, mercy, and strength. In Your precious name, I pray . . . Amen.

- Safe in HIS Arms
  by Single Parents Rock! When we lean on The Rock on Sunday, July 31, 2011, at 6:47 p.m.
  I can't begin to tell you how many times I've gone to bed thoroughly in distress and petitioned the Father longingly in prayer to just PLEASE come down and hold me tight in HIS arms so I would have the strength to just make it through the night . . . knowing that I didn't have the strength to do it on my own. Every single time I've petitioned my Heavenly Father in genuine heart-felt prayer to come and hold me HE has never failed to do just that! Our Heavenly Father is so loving, kind, gentle and merciful!!! HE will hold his children close to comfort them and give them strength for a new day every single time they ask to feel His presence. HE has held me when I've just wanted to feel close to Him . . . God NEVER FAILS us! If you are longing for the Father, needing strength to face the trials and tribulations of this life . . . just call on His name and He will answer, He will pull you close to love, protect and strengthen you . . . all you have to do is ask and you shall receive . . .
  All praise be to Jesus Christ our Savior, Lord, King and loving Heavenly Father!

AUGUST 2011

August 1

- Encouragement from a friend: "Whoever sows to please their flesh, from the flesh will reap destruction; whoever sows to please the Spirit, from the Spirit will reap eternal life. Let us not become weary in doing good, for at the proper time we will reap a harvest if we do not give up." Galatians 6:8-9
  My response: Needed this one this morning, thank you for posting.
- Song: "Stronger" by Mandisa (From the Upcoming Album *What If We Were Real*) (see Song Appendix for lyrics)
- I'm thankful for our loving Heavenly Father every single day. ☺
- Trials Are Not Meant to torture, But to Refine . . .
  by Single Parents Rock! When we lean on The Rock on Monday, August 1, 2011, at 8:11 p.m.
  Do not begrudge your current trials . . . allow yourself to learn the lessons that are right in front of you, for it is these very lessons that will allow you to step into the future that God has for you. Your trials are not here to torture you, but to help you learn, to refine you, to bring you closer to the Father . . . allow your heart to be teachable and accept His refinement so you can courageously and honorably step into His perfect will for your life.
  God bless you always!

August 2

- Fact: everyone will be rejected by other people at some time in their lives. This hurts, but God will heal the hurt if you let Him. Fact: God will NEVER reject or forsake you.

- People aren't fillers, don't use them as a band-aid for the pain. Let God walk you through it and truly heal your heart.

August 3

- Set your goals and GO FOR IT! Don't let anyone tell you that you Cannot attain the goals that are in your heart. I can do ALL things through Christ who strengthens me! God Bless you always

August 5

- Song: "Cover Me" by 21:03 (see Song Appendix for lyrics)
- Song: "Holding on to You" by 21:03 (see Song Appendix for lyrics)
- Song: "Chozen" by 21:03 (see Song Appendix for lyrics)
- Song: "You" by 21:03 (see Song Appendix for lyrics)
- Song: "Love Song" by LeCrae (see Song Appendix for lyrics)
- Only heart change brings life change.
- If you are looking for Love, all you have to do is look UP! God's love is the only completely fulfilling, lasting and eternal love. People can only love as people love. God's love is divine and never-ending. He will teach us how to love each other. If we don't know how to embrace His love, we can never love each other the way He intended for us to love each other.
  God love and bless you always!
- Lord, help us to pray for and encourage each other always . . .
- Ladies, don't rely on what a man makes ($$), just work your Faith. God is the ultimate provider; HE will take care of you.
- God is love.

August 6

- Encouragement from a friend: When God renews us He brings about change—new life, new strength, new growth, new fruitfulness. God's life springs up within us like the sprouting grain in springtime, making the winter season of the heart productive once again.

His Renewing lifts us up to new heights, carries us over all barriers, and causes us to behold things we've never seen before.

"But they that wait upon the LORD shall renew their strength; they shall mount up with wings as eagles; they shall run, and not be weary; and they shall walk, and not faint." Isaiah 40:31

My response: ☺

- I wish everyone realized just how powerful God's love truly is. Human love always falls short while God's love never fails. When we see our own worth through God's eyes, instead of relying on others opinions of us, we aren't so devastated when we don't hear the human "I love you" when we'd like to.

- Only God has the authority to define you. Let His will direct your steps and shape your life into His beautiful reflection no matter how nontraditional and countercultural it may appear to others.

- When we settle for less than God's best in relationships, we're telling God that we're not good enough for the real thing. God created us in His own image and sent His Son to die for our sins. HE knows our worth. Do we?

- Step Out of the Drama . . .
  by Single Parents Rock! When we lean on The Rock on Saturday, August 6, 2011, at 7:54 p.m.
  Although the world and many people in it would drag us into every sort of drama out there, we must step out of the drama and abide by God's commands. God gives us Peace and Grace . . . His children need not be walking daily in drama and being drug down by the world.
  Titus 2:11-14 For the grace of God that brings salvation has appeared to all men, it teaches us to say "No" to ungodliness and worldly passions, and to live self-

controlled, upright and godly lives in this present age, while we wait for the blessed hope - the glorious appearing of our great God and Savior, Jesus Christ, who gave himself for us to redeem us from all wickedness and to purify for himself a people that are his very own, eager to do what is good.

As children of God, we must strive to do what is good and not allow others to make us doubt our faith or cause us to quarrel amongst ourselves

Titus 3:1-11 Remind the people to be subject to rulers and authorities, to be obedient, to be ready to do whatever is good, to slander no one, to be peaceable and considerate, and to show true humility toward all men. At one time we too were foolish, disobedient, deceived and enslaved by all kinds of passions and pleasures. We lived in malice and envy, being hated and hating one another. But when the kindness and love of God our Savior appeared, he saved us, not because of righteous things we had done, but because of his mercy. He saved us through the washing of rebirth and renewal by the Holy Spirit, whom he poured out on us generously through Jesus Christ our Savior, so that, having been justified by his grace, we might become heirs having the hope of eternal life. This is a trustworthy saying. And I want you to stress these things, so that those who have trusted in God may be careful to devote themselves to doing what is good. These things are excellent and profitable for everyone. But avoid foolish controversies and genealogies and arguments and quarrels about the law, because these are unprofitable and useless. Warn a divisive person once, and then warn him a second time. After that, have nothing to do with him. You may be sure that such a man is warped and sinful, he is self-condemned.

Don't let the world catch you in its snare . . . ALWAYS look to God for inspiration and guidance.

God bless you always!

August 7
- Song: "Get Low" by LeCrae (see Song Appendix for lyrics)
- Song: "Take Me as I Am" by LeCrae (see Song Appendix for lyrics)
- "Forgiveness . . . is an act of self-defense, a tourniquet that stops the fatal bleeding of resentment." Gary Thomas
- Don't wait until you're down and out to call on the name of the Lord. Call on Him day and night and allow Him to guide you through this life. He wants to bless you, to love you, and to give you strength. Ask and you shall receive. Seek and you shall find.
  God bless you always . . .

August 8
- God is my Father, my Rock, my Salvation, my Light. He is always gracious, loving, kind, and just. He loves me more than I can comprehend. He shows me how to love others. I will always fall short of His mark but will never stop trying to live how He shows me and to follow the path He lays before me.
- Sometimes we may think to heck with all this being strong stuff. All I want is a mate to share my life with! But God really does know best. Our lives are not our own. We belong to our Heavenly Father, and His eternal rewards are exponentially better than any temporary earthly pleasure or fleeting happiness . . . HE gives us true joy and eternal life with Him in Heaven.
- Faith is believing in the Father's promises without any evidence, other than HIS word, that they will come to pass. If we start putting time tables and conditions on His promises and then start to doubt when our conditions are not met, it's not true faith. Give it ALL to God and leave it in His hands. He will never leave nor forsake you.
- Love One Another . . . What Does This Really Mean?? by Single Parents Rock! When we lean on The Rock on Monday, August 8, 2011, at 8:19 p.m.

We are commanded many times in the Bible to love one another. All commands of God are to be taken very seriously, but it strikes me how many times this one particular command is repeated and reinforced throughout the Word. We all know that all people are 'hard of hearing' sometimes, especially when we're being told to do something that is not easy or that we just do not want to expend the effort to do. God makes no bones about this one, we are called and commanded to LOVE ONE ANOTHER. But . . . what does this mean??? The following scripture sheds a little light on the subject.

1 John 4:7-21 Dear friends, let us love one another, for love comes from God (from God, not anyone or anywhere else). Everyone who loves has been born of God and knows God. Whoever does not love does not know God because God is love. This is how God showed his love among us: He sent his one and only Son into the world that we might live through him. This is love: not that we loved God, but that he loved us and sent his Son as an atoning sacrifice for our sins (so we should love others even when they do not love us, we should treat them with love and respect, so that we may be the reflected image of our Savior Jesus Christ, even when they spit in our faces and mock our beliefs. Jesus died for the whole world when we were all sinners and we crucified Him on the cross, but Jesus still loved us anyway, He didn't say . . . Ok God, I'll die for the nice people who are just ignorant, but I won't die for those who participated in my crucifixion . . . no . . . He died for all). Dear friends, since God so loved us, we also ought to love one another. No one has ever seen God: but if we love one another, God lives in us and his love is made complete in us. We know that we live in him and he in us, because he has given us of his Spirit. And we have seen and testify that the Father has sent his Son to be the Savior of the world. If anyone acknowledges that Jesus is the Son of God, God lives in him and he in God. And so we know and rely on

the love God has for us. God is love. Whoever lives in love lives in God, and God in him. In this way, love is made complete among us so that we will have confidence on the day of judgment, because in this world we are like him. There is no fear in love (NO fear in love, if we have fear in our hearts, we need to pray that the love drive out the fear because fear is not from God). But perfect love drives out fear, because fear has to do with punishment. The one who fears is not made perfect in love. We love because he first loved us (He first loved us when we were very unlovable by any reasonable standard . . . we cannot wait until we feel like loving someone to actually love them and treat them like we love them), if anyone says, "I love God," yet hates his brother, he is a liar (we cannot truly love until we have forgiven those who have wronged us). For anyone who does not love his brother, whom he has seen, cannot love God, whom he has not seen. And he has given us this command: Whoever loves God must also love his brother.

1 Corinthians 13:4-8a Love is patient, love is kind. It does not envy, it does not boast, it is not proud. It is not rude, it is not self-seeking, it is not easily angered, it keeps no record of wrongs. Love does not delight in evil but rejoices with the truth. It always protects, always trusts, always hopes, always perseveres. Love never fails. If we are impatient, unkind, envious, boastful, proud, rude, self-seeking, easily angered, if we keep a record of the wrongs that others have done to us, if we delight in malicious ways, seeking revenge and gossiping, if we feel a sense of satisfaction when we take revenge on others because 'they finally got theirs', if we harm others, mistrust others, doubt and are stir crazy, expecting everything on our own schedule . . . if we have issues with any of these, we need to seek to be filled with God's love. Seek to be more like Him so that we may receive His blessings, live our lives for His glory instead of our own and abide in a deeply personal relationship with our Savior and King Jesus Christ. None

of us are perfect, we have all fallen short, but with the daily guidance, strength and grace of God we can live lives that honor our Heavenly Father. Jesus yearns for us to draw close to Him, to have a deeply personal relationship with our Heavenly Father . . . Lord, please help us to draw closer to You each and every day . . .

God Bless and keep you always!

August 9

- Authentic faith is letting go of Everything and truly BELIEVING all of God's promises for your life Will come to pass, not that they're merely possible.
- Something to think about: Maybe it's so much harder to trust God for the day-to-day difficulties and challenges because it actually requires us to relinquish control and actively believe NOW. Trusting for salvation seems so vague, but trusting God now, in every passing minute, requires immediate action on our part.
- Do not be afraid to believe God's promises for your life, even if they're very specific and appear to be completely impossible. God cannot and does not lie.
- People hurt other people, sometimes intentionally and sometimes accidentally, which breeds distrust. But getting hurt, even repeatedly, by people is no reason to distrust our Heavenly Father.
- "The golden rule for understanding in spiritual matters is not intellect, but obedience." Oswald Chambers

August 10

- It's okay if it takes longer than you'd like to work through things. God's timing is always perfect. ☺
- I will walk in God's glory, not my own.
- Encouragement from a friend: LOVE HEALS. We are all wounded in all various ways, and loving people as they really are is powerful. Love is the healing balm that God uses to help restore the lives of others. We can

become disillusioned with people very easily by putting expectations upon them. Yet we need to let people to be free to be themselves and not hide behind masks. As we walk in love, we will learn how to see the best in others. We will find that our own peace and power are the results of walking in love.

My response: So True . . . Peace . . . ☺ Thank you, Jesus . . .

August 11

- "But blessed is the man who trusts in the Lord, whose confidence is in him. He will be like a tree planted by the water that sends out its roots by the stream. It does not fear when heat comes; its leaves are always green. It has no worries in a year of drought and never fails to bear fruit." Jeremiah 17:7-8

- Don't adore anyone or anything more than you adore God.

- Enjoy God's Majesty and Splendor and Share His Love with All
  by Single Parents Rock! When we lean on The Rock on Thursday, August 11, 2011, at 5:49 a.m.
  A friend showed me this poem last night and I just had to share it with all of you. My prayer is that we would all shine like our Lord and Savior Jesus Christ in this fallen world and bring light and hope to all around us . . . that we would all take the time to enjoy and appreciate God's splendor and majesty and share it with all we know.
  Poem:
  I've heard it said the world is a dismal place
  But I know better
  For I have seen the dawn, and walked in the splendor of the morning sun. Blinked at the brilliance of the dew, and beheld the gold and crimson of an autumn landscape.
  I've heard it said the world is sad
  I can't agree

For I have heard the cheerful songs of a feathered
masters . . . heard the low laughter of the leaves
and the everlasting chuckle of a mountain brook.
I've heard it said the world's a musty sordid thing
It can't be true
For I have seen the rain . . . watched it bathe
the earth, the very air . . . and I've seen the
sky, newly scrubbed and spotless blue from
end to end . . . and I've watched the winter's
snow drape tree and bush, to look like natures
freshly laundered linen hung to dry.
I've even heard the world is evil
But they are wrong
For I have known its people . . . watched them
die to save a freedom, bleed to save a life . . .
spend of themselves to stem disaster, of
their wealth to ease distress . . . and I have
watched them live, love and labor . . . watched
them hope, dream and pray, side by side.
I've heard them say these things
But I would disagree
Because, for every shadow, I have seen a
hundred rays of light . . . for every plaintive
note, I've heard a symphony of joy . . . for
every penny weight of bad, I have found a
ton of good . . . good in nature, in people,
in the world
and I am thankful I belong.
Author Unknown
God Bless us all and help us to be the rays of light, the
shining city on the hill that our good Lord and Savior
has called us to be in this fallen world. Let us enjoy
His splendor and majesty and share His Love with
everyone . . .

August 12

- Will you allow your struggles to draw you closer to Jesus and extend grace to others or to repel you away from our Heavenly Father and view those around you with a critical eye and unforgiving heart?
- "Significance is found in giving your life away, not in selfishly trying to find personal happiness." Gary and Betsy Ricucci
  Good, typical blues, with a biblical line or two in it. The biblical Law of the Harvest is True!
- "Devote yourselves to prayer, being watchful and thankful." Colossians 4:2
- "Let the peace of Christ rule in your hearts, since as members of one body you were called to peace. And be thankful. Let the word of Christ dwell in you richly as you teach and admonish one another with all wisdom, and as you sing psalms, hymns and spiritual songs with gratitude in your hearts to God. And whatever you do, whether in word or deed, do it all in the name of the Lord Jesus, giving thanks to God the Father through him." Colossians 3:15-17
- God has a purpose for EVERYONE. There are no exceptions. ☺
- Real Love . . .
  by Single Parents Rock! When we lean on The Rock on Friday, August 12, 2011, at 8:06 a.m.
  I am convinced that most people truly do not understand what real love is . . . Our heavenly Father really, truly loves us . . . Not only did He send His only Son to die for our sins . . .
  John 3:16-17: For God so loved the world that he gave his one and only Son, that whoever believes in him shall not perish but have eternal life. For God did not send his Son into the world to condemn the world, but to save the world through him. He was also so concerned about how His disciples would feel after he was crucified that He gave

them the following words of encouragement to prepare them and to let them know that He was not leaving them permanently . . .

John 14:1-4: Do not let your hearts be troubled. Trust in God, trust also in me. In my Father's house are many rooms: if it were not so, I would have told you. I am going there to prepare a place for you. I will come back and take you to be with me that you also may be where I am. You know the way to the place where I am going.

Our heavenly Father also loved the entire world so much that before He was crucified, He prayed for Himself, He prayed for His disciples, and He prayed for ALL believers so that we may all become one, united with Jesus the Son and God the Father. He prayed for us even before we were created because He loves us so much!!! How amazing is that!?!

Our Lord wants to comfort us through all of our troubles, He wants to be there for us through all of our hardships, He wants to spend eternity with us in heaven . . . He sent His only Son to die on the cross for our sins, to conquer death and pay our debt for all of our sin past, present and future . . .

It amazes me that we, as fallen people, try so hard to rely on other people to show us love . . . when we have the most magnificent example of true, unfailing, UN-conditional love ever shown in our Heavenly Father . . . My prayer is that we would all look up every single day and rely totally and completely on our Heavenly Father for our every need. May God bless you always!

- God Delivers Us Out of Our Mess . . . But We Must Actively Follow Him
  by Single Parents Rock! When we lean on The Rock on Friday, August 12, 2011, at 5:02 p.m.
  There is no better source of strength, wisdom, courage and joy than our Heavenly Father. It is never easy to actively seek His will and make all of the sacrifices necessary to

stay in His will, but . . . I did things my way long enough to know that His way is much less stressful and everything ALWAYS turns out much better when Christ is the center of it. When I was doing everything my way I was Always stressed, sapped of strength and didn't even know what real joy was . . . too much anxiety and worry to be the best mom I can be to my girl . . . Praise God He delivers us out of the depths of our mess!!!

August 13
- Love the book of James. ☺
- The Armor of God
  by Single Parents Rock! When we lean on The Rock on Saturday, August 13, 2011, at 8:57 a.m.
  Finally, be strong in the Lord and in his mighty power. Put on the full armor of God so that you can take your stand against the devil's schemes. For our struggle is not against flesh and blood, but against the rulers, against the authorities, against the powers of this dark world and against the spiritual forces of evil in the heavenly realms. Therefore, put on the full armor of God, so that when the day of evil comes, you may be able to stand your ground, and after you have done everything, to stand. Stand firm then, with the belt of truth buckled around your waist, with the breastplate of righteousness in place, and with your feet fitted with the readiness that comes from the gospel of peace. In addition to all this, take up the shield of faith, with which you can extinguish all the flaming arrows of the evil one. Take the helmet of salvation and the sword of the Spirit, which is the word of God. And *pray in the Spirit on all occasions* with all kinds of prayers and requests. With this in mind, be alert and *always keep on praying for all the saints.* Ephesians 6:10-18
  God bless you always!

August 14

- We are called to be servants: "To become a servant is to become radically strong spiritually. It means you are free from the petty demands and grievances that ruin so many lives and turn so many hearts into bitter cauldrons of disappointment, self-absorption, and self-pity. There is true joy when true service is offered up with a true heart." Gary Thomas

  Something to think about: How can I be a servant today?

- "Through Christ you have come to trust in God. And because God raised Christ from the dead and gave him great glory, your faith and hope can be placed confidently in God." 1 Peter 1:21

- The Armor of God . . . Why Do We Need to Wear the Armor of God??

  by Single Parents Rock! When we lean on The Rock on Sunday, August 14, 2011, at 10:19 a.m.

  Finally, be strong in the Lord and in his mighty power. Put on the full armor of God so that you can take your stand against the devil's schemes. Ephesians 6:10-11

  It is necessary for us to wear the armor of God, because without it we cannot be strong in the Lord, we have no real strength outside of the Lord. His mighty power is far greater than any power we think we wield on our own. If we are to truly walk in His will, be a witness for Him and reflect His love into this fallen world we MUST rely on HIS power. Without Him we can do nothing and with Him we are more than conquers!

  Romans 8:31-39 What, then, shall we say in response to these things? If God is for us, who can be against us? [32]He who did not spare his own Son, but gave him up for us all—how will he not also, along with him, graciously give us all things? [33]Who will bring any charge against those whom God has chosen? It is God who justifies. [34]Who then is the one who condemns? No one. Christ Jesus who died—more than that, who was raised to life—is at the right hand of God and is also interceding for us. [35]Who shall separate us from the love of Christ? Shall trouble or hardship or persecution or famine or nakedness or danger or sword? [36]As it is written: "For your sake we face death all day long; we are considered as sheep to be slaughtered." [37]No, in all these things we are more than conquerors through him who loved us. [38]For I am convinced that neither death nor life, neither angels nor demons, neither the present nor the future, nor any powers, [39]neither height nor depth, nor anything else in all creation, will be able to separate us from the love of God that is in Christ Jesus our Lord.

2 Samuel 22:33-37 It is God who arms me with strength and makes my way perfect. He makes my feet like the feet of a deer, he enables me to stand on the heights. He trains my hands for battle; my arms can bend a bow of bronze. You give me your shield of victory; you stoop down to make me great. You broaden the path beneath me, so that my ankles do not turn.

Apart from God we can do nothing, but WITH HIM we can do ALL things through the One who gives us strength . . . Our Lord and Savior Jesus Christ! Therefore, we MUST put on the entire armor of God so that we may stand firm in our faith and walk the path to which HE is calling us.

God Bless you always!

August 15
- Song: "Beautiful Things" by Gungor (see Song Appendix for lyrics)
- "Little acts of sacrifice will not always be rewarded or even noticed . . . that's what can make them all the more difficult over the passage of time. But if we guard our hearts from bitterness and resentment, we will receive affirmation where it counts and where it means the most—from our Heavenly Father." Gary Thomas

- God makes everything beautiful.
- "He who is of a proud heart stirs up strife, but he who trusts in the Lord will be prospered. He who trusts in his own heart is a fool, but whoever walks wisely will be delivered." Proverbs 28:25-26
- "We have such trust through Christ toward God. Not that we are sufficient of ourselves to think of anything as being from ourselves, but our sufficiency is from God." 2 Corinthians 3:4-5
- Overwhelmed??

  by Single Parents Rock! When we lean on The Rock on Monday, August 15, 2011, at 5:17 p.m.

  Overwhelmed: When your burdens seem too heavy to carry, remember there are those out there who are much less fortunate than you . . . those with no house, no car, no appropriate clothing to wear, no job to go to, no food to set on the table for their children, some have spouses who beat them every night . . . Maybe, when we're feeling overwhelmed with our own burdens, we should look out into the world and see how we can help others with through their trials . . . when we take the focus off of ourselves and do something to bless others, God is pleased and we in turn are blessed more than we knew possible. God bless you always!

August 16
- He'll never give you more than you can handle with His help. Without Him, it's always too much to handle.
- If God has laid something on your heart, GO FOR IT! "For the Spirit God gave us does not make us timid, but gives us power, love and self-discipline." 2 Timothy 1:7
- Ladies, never settle for less than God's best for you.
- "Be still before the Lord and wait patiently for him; do not fret when men succeed in their ways, when they carry out their wicked schemes. Refrain from anger and turn from wrath; do not fret—it leads only to evil. For evil men will

be cut off; but those who hope in the Lord will inherit the land." Psalm 37:7-9

- "My God is my rock, in whom I take refuge, my shield and the horn of my salvation. He is my stronghold, my refuge and my savior—from violent people you save me." 2 Samuel 22:3

August 18

- "Let the morning bring me word of your unfailing love, for I have put my trust in you. Show me the way I should go, for to you I entrust my life." Psalm 143:8

August 17

- All of my trials are temporary, how liberating! I get the pleasure and privilege of stepping into God's work. HE will take care of the opposition; I just have to be obedient. Much JOY and Peace come with walking with Jesus! ☺
- No matter who stands with you or who stands against you, if God has given you something to say, say it. HE will never leave or forsake you.

August 18

- Listen, really listen, and HE will show you which way to go.
- Song: "The Light in Me" by Brandon Heath (see Song Appendix for lyrics)
- Is walking in abundant blessings, affirmation, and peace today . . . God is so good!
- "Let the morning bring me word of your unfailing love, for I have put my trust in you. Show me the way I should go, for to you I entrust my life." Psalm 143:8

August 19

- Don't underestimate God's plan for YOU. He doesn't just lead others on the dynamic, faith-filled, "grand tasks" in life. He has BIG plans for you too.

- YOUR will, Not mine, Lord.
- My heart must want His will for my life so intensely that I purposely deny my will and graciously and thankfully walk in what He has for me with a happy heart.
- Song: "Yes" by John Waller (see Song Appendix for lyrics)
- Song: "Commission My Soul" by Citipointe (see Song Appendix for lyrics)
- "Remind the people to be subject to rulers and authorities, to be obedient, to be ready to do whatever is good, to slander no one, to be peaceable and considerate, and to show true humility toward all men." Titus 3:1-2
- Don't lose faith because the immediate future doesn't look good to you. We don't have God's road map for our future; we don't have the same perspective He does. He promises us hope and a future, to prosper us, love us always, and never forsake us. If we're in the maze of life, sometimes we must turn our back on the things that we want the most in order for God to bless us in the ways we are intended to be blessed in the long run. Keep the faith!

August 20
- Encouragement from a friend: We all serve someone. Better to serve Christ than sin.
  My response: That could possibly be THE understatement of the century!
- Encouragement from a friend: In my search for me, I discovered Truth. In the search for the Truth, I discovered Love. In the search for Love, I discovered GOD, and in GOD, I found EVERYTHING.
- "But the wisdom that comes from heaven is first of all pure; then peace-loving, considerate, submissive, full of mercy and good fruit, impartial and sincere." James 3:17
  Lord, please give me wisdom.
- "The love of money is a root of all kinds of evil, for which some have strayed from the faith in their greediness, and pierced themselves through with many sorrows. But you,

O man of God, flee these things and pursue righteousness, godliness, faith, love, patience, gentleness." 1 Timothy 6:10-11

- Grace Isn't Just for Me . . .
  by Single Parents Rock! When we lean on The Rock on Saturday, August 20, 2011, at 10:54 a.m.
  God is eternally faithful to His children. He keeps all of his promises and is exceedingly patient with us as we lean on Him to get through our struggles. Therefore, we should remember to extend grace to those around us, for they are wrestling with their struggles, hurdles and challenges too. We need to be patient, loving, kind and extend the grace of God to everyone we meet. We don't have a monopoly on God's grace and should not be critical of others as they struggle. We need to encourage, support and love each other in every situation.
  God bless you always!

August 21

- Sometimes helping others heal is a matter of getting out of the way and turning the whole situation over to our Heavenly Father. HE is the only One who can truly put us back together.
- I have decided to participate in a program, with my church, to read the Bible in ninety days. I have committed to do this with my daughter, and she has graciously agreed to read with me. (NOTE: I had not been reading the Bible with any directed purpose until I started this reading program. I was on the Bible on a regular basis but never purposely and intentionally in any particular section. I was searching, but until this point, I had been very scattered with my approach to learning the Word. Upon putting all of this together, I never realized, before this point, just how much scripture is in this book and was utterly flabbergasted! God is so very good! He had given me exactly what I needed, even though my approach had been

poor and scattered at best. You don't have to be a Bible scholar to search for and find God. HE will come find you and give you exactly what you need. You just need to be doing your best to meet with Him, and He'll make good on His promise to meet you exactly where you are. May God continue to bless and keep you and yours always.)

- Encouragement from a friend: I am embracing everything God has for me. What God has for me, it is for me. My response: Couldn't be more on-point for me . . . thanks for sharing.

- Surrender your weaknesses completely to our Heavenly Father; let Him be strong for you while He gives you the strength and wisdom to conquer them.

- Surround yourself with loving, caring, encouraging believers. No one can make it through this life alone; we need all the encouragement we can get. When you surround yourself with people who constantly encourage and uplift you, those you share your Christian walk with, they will encourage you and you them by sharing the Lord's blessings in your lives. Share your blessings with those around you as well. You never know who needs to hear a good word. God bless you always!

- B90X
  by Cynthia Johnson on Sunday, August 21, 2011, at 5:07 p.m.
  I have decided to participate in a program, with my church, to read the Bible in 90 days. I have committed to do this with my daughter and she has graciously agreed to read with me. It should be a Wonderful growing experience for us both, I'm so very excited to be able to walk through the entire Bible with my girl in this way!!! I have no doubt that God will bless us abundantly during the coming days of delving head first and immersing ourselves in His word!
  So . . . I couldn't pass up the opportunity to invite you to do the same. If you would like to participate, the schedule is as follows (see B90X Reading Schedule in the back of the book)

August 22

- I'm walking into my purpose.
- One of the most difficult things for me to do is to BE STILL, yet I am commanded to Be Still and know that God is God and HE alone will take care of me. Lord, please give me grace and strength to be obediently still and know that You are God.

  He says, "Be still, and know that I am God; I will be exalted among the nations, I will be exalted in the earth." Psalm 46:10

  The LORD Almighty is with us; the God of Jacob is our fortress.
- Best path: My will and God's will are never quite the same thing. The difference is that God can see the whole picture, where I only see one little piece from one perspective. HIS will is always better, even though it is often difficult and can appear to be a dead end. God always makes a way where there seems to be no way. God is faithful; He always comes through for His children!
- "Have I not commanded you? Be strong and courageous. Do not be afraid; do not be discouraged, for the LORD your God will be with you wherever you go." Joshua 1:9
- Do not let your fears drive you! You DO have a choice how you react to every situation in your life. Don't let yourself panic when a past wound is opened. Truly give the past trauma to Jesus and let Him heal you. When Jesus heals, He replaces fear and anxiety with peace and joy. Don't let anxiety and fear rule your life! Take your life back by giving it completely to our Heavenly Father.
- Know Christ's Love . . .

  by Single Parents Rock! When we lean on The Rock on Monday, August 22, 2011, at 11:55 a.m.

  [16]I pray that out of his glorious riches he may strengthen you with power through his Spirit in your inner being, [17]so that Christ may dwell in your hearts through faith. And I pray that you, being rooted and established in love, [18]may

have power, together with all the Lord's holy people, to grasp how wide and long and high and deep is the love of Christ, ¹⁹and to know this love that surpasses knowledge— that you may be filled to the measure of all the fullness of God.

²⁰Now to him who is able to do immeasurably more than all we ask or imagine, according to his power that is at work within us, ²¹to him be glory in the church and in Christ Jesus throughout all generations, forever and ever! Amen.

Ephesians 3:16-21

August 23

- The place where you're the least comfortable may be where God needs you most, to shine His light into the darkness. Trust that HE has you in the right place. Set aside your own emotions and obey. God will bless you through it.
- If God gives you a heart for something, pay attention to it, walk in it. It is a blessing waiting to happen!

August 24

- When it feels like you must face the world and all your trials alone, remember Jesus is always with you. No matter how alone you feel, Jesus will never leave or forsake you. He loves you!
- ssYou are a new creation in Christ. Let your old life fall away. I know it's scary, but it only brought you hardship and pain. Jesus promises to prosper you and not to harm you! Let past pain and habits go and walk anew with Jesus.
- Find praise in each day, even and especially when you do not like where you're at. Giving praise actually lifts your spirit and lets you reflect the glory of God even when you're struggling.

God, please help me to give thanks to You each and every day, regardless of my circumstances.

August 25

- Today is a new day. Thank You, Lord, for granting me grace as I learn to be more like You. I'm not always a graceful student.
- God . . . Amazing Faithful Protector of His People . . . by Single Parents Rock! When we lean on The Rock on Thursday, August 25, 2011, at 7:26 p.m.
  The Lord God will protect you every single day just as he protected the Israelites when he led them out of Egypt. He led them by day in the form of a pillar of cloud and by night in the form of a pillar of fire. He led them to camp by the sea. When the Egyptians pursued them with a fierce army, the angel of God who had been traveling in front of Israel's army, withdrew and went behind them. The pillar of cloud also moved from in front and stood behind them, coming between the armies of Egypt and Israel. (God put Himself between the His children and their enemies so that His children could not be harmed).Then God made a way out, where there was previously no way (He drew the sea back and let His children cross to the other side on dry ground) then he closed the way and the Egyptians who meant to harm the children of God perished. God fiercely and endlessly loves His children. When you are in distress, call out to our heavenly Father . . . He will hear your cries and help you in your time of trouble. (See Exodus chapter 14)
  God bless you always!

August 26

- The more thankful you are for what God has graciously given you, the happier you will be. Quit looking at what you don't have and give thanks for all your blessings.

August 27

- No One Is as "Good" as They Appear . . . Share Your story, It May Save Someone's Life . . .

by Single Parents Rock! When we lean on The Rock on
Saturday, August 27, 2011, at 9:16 a.m.

Sometimes helping another is as simple as sharing your
story, skeletons in the closet and all, and letting them know
how God has brought you out of the dark places you have
been and into His light. Letting them know that no one
else is as 'good' as they seem on the outside, that everyone
- including you - have deep, dark, shameful secrets . . . But
that God forgives and loves us ALL unconditionally and
He wants to love them unconditionally too . . . all they
have to do is open the door and let Him in.

God bless you always!

- Let Go and Let GOD . . . HE Will Transform You Like
  You Never Believed Possible!

  by Single Parents Rock! When we lean on The Rock on
  Saturday, August 27, 2011, at 11:30 a.m.

  Let go of whatever it is that you're clinging to so tightly.
  When we give EVERYTHING to God and let Him use
  us and guide us, Amazing things happen!!! He will guide
  you down paths that you never dreamed possible, He will
  walk you through things and bless you in ways that will
  absolutely blow your mind!

  I can speak on this because God has taken me from a
  completely broken, battered and hopeless situation into
  a very empowered, growing, thriving and completely
  dependent on HIM situation. The more I lean on Him,
  the more He heals me, provides for me, and leads me
  deeper and deeper into His plan and shows me more of
  Himself and of His love than I ever thought I would see or
  experience. I have never felt so fulfilled and excited to move
  forward in His work! Keeping in mind that I NEVER
  wanted to be single and struggle with it daily, but God has
  fulfilled my every need and desire and now the greatest
  desire of my heart is to serve Him in any way He calls me
  simply because it is HE who is calling me. I was convinced
  in the past that I would never be able to attain a decent

financial or emotional condition without a spouse. Now I am completely convinced that unless I attain the spiritual maturity that Christ longs to draw me into, I will never be able to have a healthy, blessed and fulfilling marriage the way that God intended.

When I gave everything to my heavenly Father, HE changed the desires of my heart and is drawing me closer to Him every single day. It is a daily struggle to sacrifice self, but He never said The Way would be easy. He simply calls us to follow Him, to pick up our cross (which is a very difficult task) DAILY and follow Him, to allow Him to lead us through our struggles, to rely on Him alone for the strength and peace that we need in order to bless others the way we're called to bless them . . . to stay completely focused on Him and He will grant us the true desires of our hearts . . . in HIS time.

God bless you always!

• My personal journal entry: 8/27/2011 4:56 PM
I am starting this journal because the other day at work it occurred to me that maybe I should write some things down, God has grown me so immensely in the past couple years and I feel like I'm on the edge of something great and wonderful . . . I said something about writing something down to my mom, she thinks it is a good idea, then I said something to a couple of my Bible study ladies, they thought it was a good idea, then a dear friend of mine called this morning and out of the blue mentioned that he thought I should write down my journey so that it will be an encouragement to me later when I get frustrated. He mentioned that he writes things down so that when he is having a difficult time, he can go back in his writings and see how God has been working in his life and it is a huge encouragement to him. He had no idea that I had been thinking along these lines. He is a dear friend whom I met through his ministry page on Facebook of all places! We have struck up a friendship and God has spoken to

me greatly through him and what he has gone through. I value our friendship a great deal and am so thankful that our heavenly Father uses such unconventional means of connecting His children and giving encouragement in such a way that only HE can!

I appear to be at a crossroads in my life . . . a pinnacle, if you will, and I have no doubt that God has great plans for me. I do not yet know what He has in mind, but I know that I am being called to step into some kind of ministry. God has given me a huge heart for single mothers and people in disadvantaged social situations. I do not know exactly where this is going to take me, but I know that it will be somewhere spectacular! I never dreamed that God would have such spectacular plans for me. He has brought me through so many things in my life and in many ways I feel like I'm just now (at the age of 37 years old) coming into my real purpose. I have made so many bad decisions and tried to do things under my own power for so long . . . it's amazing that I am so stubborn and that it has taken me this long to be able to totally surrender my entire life and future to my heavenly Father! I am so very thankful for all that He is showing me and where He is taking me . . . I get very impatient though and need to check my emotions at the door often. God has been so gracious to me! In the past two years I've gotten a tour of all of the significant men in my life and I feel like God has shown me my future husband. I had totally given up on any good man and also on my future for myself. I had decided that I would just settle for whatever my life currently contained and muddle through . . . at that very moment God dropped someone very special into my life and showed me, through him (although the guy showed me everything that was wrong with him and all of his flaws) God showed me a BEAUTIFUL heart that beat for Him! Funny . . . a man who is completely flawed, just like everyone else on the planet, was used to show me such a wonderful heart

for God. God let me know, in no uncertain words and
terms that THIS man is my man, this man who lives and
breathes to serve God, this man who has just as many
flaws as any other person on the planet, this is the man I
will be with. HE also showed me though, that I have a lot
of work to do and a lot of spiritual growth to do before
this union is possible. I have to grow and maintain a very
intimate relationship with my heavenly Father, to let my
Jesus fill all my spaces and gaps and let HIM heal me and
grow me into the Godly woman I need to be in order to be
a blessing to my future husband. (NOTE: I realized much
later, after this journal entry, that God was showing me
qualities of my future husband, not necessarily the person
in whom I would find them. HE was giving me a picture of
the heart of the man I will marry, and what a picture it is!
I will never forget what he showed me in this person, and
it will certainly be unmistakable when I see these qualities
in the man I will marry. I know now that God gave me
this picture for this very reason, so that when I do meet my
husband at the right time, I will most certainly recognize
him! God is always good to us, just sometimes not in the
way we would like right at that moment. Trust Him. He
truly does know what is best for you. He is not cruel, but
unendingly loving, loving to the point of willing to let us
go through a lot of heartache so that our hearts will be
turned to Him first. You see, if our hearts are not turned to
Him first, no relationship we have here on this earth will
go well. Without Jesus at the center of our hearts and lives,
we cannot possibly bring glory to Him and lead others to
be saved by His love and grace.)
God has shown me that I need to do some things right
here in my town (much to my chagrin, as I've never wanted
to stay here . . . lol . . . HE does have a sense of humor
and teaches me so many things through tough love and
putting me in situations from which there is no escape . . .
it is up to me if I'm going to change my attitude and gain

God's blessing or if I'm going to pout and make myself miserable). He has let me know that I need to step up in my leadership of a local Christian singles ministry—I've been involved, but not actively for a long time—I have been told that I need to be Actively involved and I am walking in that now . . . it is awkward, but I can feel His leading and I know He is growing me in necessary ways. HE has also led me to apply to be a mentor at a local women's ministry (a refuge for single women and their children who are in troubled situations). I am very excited about this and have an interview scheduled with a lady from the women's ministry this coming Thursday. I must turn in an application, have church and personal references (which I do have . . . all 3 pastors at my church said they would be more than happy to give me a reference and a close friend of mine and Bible study lady, has offered to be a personal reference since she knows my story). Anyway, I have an interview Thursday, when I'll tour the ministry's local location and turn in the application then they need to do a background check on me, then I find out if I can be a mentor. I really feel God is calling me to do this so I think all will go well. I know God has a blessing in this for me. Well . . . I need to go to a leadership meeting soon, so must go for now. I will do my best to keep up this journal so that I may be obedient in what I feel God leading me to accomplish . . . part of which apparently includes this journal (NOTE: Little did I know HE would later let me know that my personal journal entries were intended to be published publicly in book form). I hope and pray I can step into God's plan and do it justice . . . I'll need so many prayers . . . I never want to lose touch with my heavenly Father again . . . this world is way too difficult and painful to go through without having HIS arms wrapped around me. What a wonderful, magnificent and generous Healer HE is!!! I so don't deserve His mercy, yet He freely gives it anyway . . . Thank You Jesus . . .

August 28

- "Wait for the LORD: Be strong and let your heart take courage; yes, wait for the LORD." Psalm 27:14
- God has defined who you are; men do not have that right, so don't give it to them. Listen to God and walk in HIS plan for your life, and you will be blessed!
- No One Can Do It Alone . . .
  by Single Parents Rock! When we lean on The Rock on Sunday, August 28, 2011, at 8:59 a.m.
  No one can do everything we've been called to do alone, it's just simply not the way God designed it. I doubt anyone would argue with me if I said that Moses was an extraordinary man who was extremely courageous and obedient to God. He was a man to be sure and had his faults, but to go to Pharaoh and do all of the things God told him to do, to say all the things that God told him to say knowing full well that Pharaoh (who had full power and authority to KILL him) would not take it well at all . . . That takes pure courage and obedience to God, it takes a very strong faith in God to face death and trust that He will deliver you.
  As strong as Moses was in his own right, he could not ensure that the Israelites did not perish in the desert by himself. When they met the Amalekites and had to go to battle, it was Moses' job to lift his hands up to the throne of the Lord. As long as his hands were lifted the Israelites prevailed in the battle, as soon as he dropped his hands, they began to lose. God did not wish for His children to perish in the desert, but Moses could not ensure their safety by himself . . . So, he took with him Aaron and Hur to perform the task with him, when his strength was fading and he could no longer hold his hands up to the throne of the Lord, Aaron and Hur held his hands up for him. You see . . . not even a pillar of obedience; courage and strong faith like Moses could do it all alone! We need to take a lesson from Moses and realize that we CANNOT do it

all alone. We are not called to be an island unto ourselves and save the world all by ourselves. We are called to be the BODY of Christ, all of whom have different skills, abilities and talents and ALL of whom are NEEDED to do the work that God has called us to do.

Don't feel bad if this is a lesson that is slow to come though, even after the battle with the Amelekites, Moses got another lesson in delegation. You see . . . he had set himself up as judge for all of the people's problems and disputes. His very wise father in law came to him and asked him what in the world he was doing. He said the following . . . "What you are doing is not good. You and these people who come to you will only wear yourselves out. The work is too heavy for you; you cannot handle it alone. Listen now to me and I will give you some advice, and may God be with you. You must be the people's representative before God and bring their disputes to him. Teach them the decrees and laws, and show them the way to live and the duties they are to perform. But select capable men from all the people - men who fear God, trustworthy men who hate dishonest gain - and appoint them as officials over thousands, hundreds, fifties and tens. Have them serve as judges for the people at all times, but have them bring every difficult case to you; the simple cases they can decide themselves. That will make your load lighter, because they will share it with you. If you do this and God so commands, you will be able to stand the strain, and all these people will go home satisfied." Exodus 18:17-23

Moses, again, had to re-think the way he was doing things . . . he had to take wise council from a trustworthy source, he had to rely on another part of the Body of Christ in order for things to go as God had designed.

We need to do the same . . . If we learn to lean on each others' strengths and help each other in our weaknesses, we will all be much more successful and less frustrated along the journey.

God bless you always!

August 30

- Encouragement from a friend: Waiting is just a gift of time in disguise, a time to pray wrapped up in a ribbon of patience, because the Lord is never late.
- Did you ever notice when you're working toward a goal, people are encouraging right up until you surpass their current status then they start discouraging you from reaching your goal? Wish people would just be supportive regardless if others' goals are different from their own.
- Don't "front" when it comes to your faith. Be REAL with people. They can see through your front anyway.
- My house is WAAAAAAAAAAYYYYYYYYYY too quiet! Daughter is at work, cat is sleeping . . . Had a hectic day, busy and noisy . . . Now it's so quiet it's loud . . . Forgot that you can actually Hear silence sometimes . . .
- Be careful with what you let drop out of your mouth when you're frustrated. People tend to remember your worst moments the most.
- Do your best to be a witness for God in ALL you do and say.
- No one can be strong all the time. When you're feeling worn down, do yourself a favor and take a break. Find a trusted friend and vent. Find a quiet place to rest/meditate/ pray. Spend some one-on-one time with the Big Man (our Heavenly Father). When your tank is empty, it is impossible to accomplish everything your life requires. Let God fill your tank then proceed.

August 31

- "Strength will rise as we wait upon the Lord . . . ☺"
- Light bulb moment: Why do we expect people who are not walking with Jesus to be faithful in relationships?

Faithfulness is a fruit of the Spirit (Galatians 5:22). If people do not know Jesus and are not listening to and abiding by the guidance of the Holy Spirit, they cannot bear the Fruit of the Spirit! Never settle for less than God's best. HE knows you deserve it. Do you?

God bless and guide you always!

- "But the fruit of the Spirit is love, joy, peace, patience, kindness, goodness, faithfulness, gentleness, self-control; against such things there is no law. Now those who belong to Christ Jesus have crucified the flesh with its passions and desires." Galatians 5:22-24

- Wow . . . The Creator of the Universe Really Does Love ME! ☺

by Single Parents Rock! When we lean on The Rock on Wednesday, August 31, 2011, at 10:26 p.m.

Isaiah 43:1, 4-5a

¹But now, thus says the LORD, your Creator, O Jacob,
And He who formed you, O Israel,
"Do not fear, for I have redeemed you;
I have called you by name; you are Mine!
4"Since you are precious in My sight,
Since you are honored and I love you,
I will give *other* men in your place and *other* peoples in exchange for your life.
5"Do not fear, for I am with you . . .

This verse is so amazing to me! The LORD is speaking to us . . . He first announces who He is so there is no doubt who is speaking, then he proceeds to let His children know that He sees them (us) as precious in His sight, He sees us as honored and He loves us. The Lord God, Father of all the universe SEES US AS PRECIOUS AND HONORED and truly LOVES us! That is HUGE!!!! I don't know about you, but I have never had a relationship with a man who truly loved and honored me; so to hear the God of all Creation express His love for me in such vast and unending terms just blows my mind! God is so good and wants the best for us always . . . no matter what anyone else tells you please believe in our Father's unending, unfailing love; it is expressed throughout the bible in many, many ways . . . HE really wants us to know His love and realize how much we are really truly worth to Him. HIS is the one and only love story that Always has a happy ending and HE is the only One who will NEVER leave or forsake you, no matter what.

Just had to share that thought . . .

God bless you always!

September 2011

September 1
- I am along for the ride. I don't pretend to know or understand Your will. Where You lead me, I will follow . . . faith on high, pride on low . . . nothin' like blind faith to draw a girl closer to the Father!
- Song: "I Will Rise" (Live) by Chris Tomlin (see Song Appendix for lyrics)

September 2
- When it looks hopeless and you feel helpless, when it seems to be taking so long that you begin to wonder if it will ever happen, just keep taking one step at a time and know that God has it handled. He is faithful and just and Always keeps His promises!
- Encouragement from a friend: My Princess . . .
  Love is not a game
  Listen to me, My princess. Love is not a game it is a gift. I know there are those who don't sincerely care for your heart, but I say that your heart is priceless. Reflect on your relationships, My royal one. Who are you allowing into your private world? Do they draw you closer to Me, or do they weaken your faith in Me and draw you away? I gave you life so you could be free. I don't want you to play "relationship games" to get the approval of people. If you choose to play these games, you will miss out on all I have for you. I am your Father, and I know what's right for My daughter. Hold on to Me and let go of those who harm you. Then you'll be free from their power, and you'll be wise enough to see what a real, lasting relationship is meant to be.
  Love,
  Your King who bought you

"You are not your own; you were bought at a price. Therefore honor God with your body." 1 Corinthians6:19-20 NIV

My response: Wish more realized this . . .

- The more time I spend with my Jesus, the better I get to know Him, the more peace He gives me! So Cool!

- God keeps His word, He does not lie, and He does not neglect to love and protect His children.

  "God is not a man, that he should lie, nor a son of man that he should change his mind. Does he speak and then not act? Does he promise and not fulfill?" Numbers 23:19

- Are We Really Obedient???

  by Single Parents Rock! When we lean on The Rock on Friday, September 2, 2011, at 9:25 p.m.

  It struck me while I was reading in Numbers (Numbers 9:15-23) that we, the children of God, are called to absolute obedience to our Lord. The Israelites were commanded to travel as follows:

  Numbers 9:15-23 - "On the day of the tabernacle, the Tent of the Testimony, was set up, the cloud covered it. From evening till morning the cloud above the tabernacle looked like fire. That is how it continued to be; the cloud covered it, and at night it looked like fire. Whenever the cloud lifted from above the Tent, the Israelites set out; wherever the cloud settled, the Israelites encamped. At the Lord's command the Israelites set out, and at his command they encamped. As long as the cloud stayed over the tabernacle, they remained in camp. When the cloud remained above the tabernacle a long time, the Israelites obeyed the Lord's order and did not set out. Sometimes the cloud was over the tabernacle only a few days; at the Lord's command they would encamp, and then at his command they would set out. Sometimes the cloud stayed only from evening till morning, and when it lifted in the morning, they set out. Whether by day or by night, whenever the cloud lifted, they set out. Whether the cloud stayed over the tabernacle for two days or a month or a year, the Israelites would remain in camp and not set out; but when it lifted, they would set out. At the Lord's command they encamped, and at the Lord's command they set out. They obeyed the Lord's order, in accordance with his command through Moses."

We are called to follow God, when He says, how He says in the manner in which He says . . . How many times must the Israelites have been thoroughly frustrated with God's timing? They never knew how long they were going to be anywhere, they never knew if they were going to have to set out in the middle of the night or at daylight . . . if the cloud lifted and you happened to be in the middle of a bath or a good book, or a sporting event which meant a lot to you . . . wherever you were you had to stop what you were doing and set out as the Lord commanded. How many times do we get frustrated with the Lord's timing and start grumbling and complaining? How many times do we forget all of the miraculous things that the Lord has done in our lives and how many trials and snares He has delivered us from? How He saved our eternal lives by sacrificing His only Son as an atonement for our sins (past, present AND future!). How many times should we fall to our knees and plead with our heavenly Father to please forgive us once again and refresh our hearts so that we may listen to His Spirit which is within us . . . so that we may follow the Father and do all that He has called us to do as He calls us to do it.

Dear heavenly Father . . . please refresh our hearts, minds, souls and spirits so that we are more compelled to seek wholeheartedly after YOU, to seek out Your will for our lives and to follow Your direction promptly, with full faith that You will complete the work you have started in each of us . . . and may we do this without grumbling . . . In Your precious name we pray . . . Amen

God bless and keep you always!

September 3

- God has been revealing Himself in powerful ways to me through this experience. I have found that it truly helps me to read the excerpt about each book of the Bible in *The Essential Bible Companion Guide* before reading each book. All the details were very frustrating until I had a better perspective on its purpose. Then it was actually beautiful and I felt God's blessing as I obediently read through it.
- Beautiful day to spend with my girl . . . Got to sleep in, soooo nice. ☺ Now I get to enjoy the day with no agenda, no schedule, no expectations . . . just a nice, relaxing, fun day with my girl. ☺ Sweet!

September 4

- Jesus is my all in all. No matter what is going on in my life, I know that He has His plan well in hand and will see me through.
- Always give grace to those around you. You have no idea what kind of pain is hidden in their hearts.
- God's vision amazes me! He sees so many people who need renewal, restoration, and recovery then He places opportunities (and assignments) in front of all of us to experience (and help others experience) His healing, restoration, renewal, and recovery, right in our own neighborhoods, towns, and churches. God is SO Good!
- When it hurts so bad you feel like your chest is going to cave in and your whole world is going to collapse, take it all to the feet of the Father. He wants to hold you, comfort you, and see you through this storm. He does not come in uninvited though. We need to invite Him into our lives and embrace His guidance, love, and protection (even when His protection feels like an isolation booth). God loves and protects His children for their own good. God bless and keep you always!
- "He who claims never to have doubted does not know what faith is, for faith is forged through doubt." Paul Tournier

- No pain, No gain: God grows us out of pain and brokenness. Embrace the pain, recognize it, FEEL it. Do not run away from it! Know that God wants to heal you of your pain, but sometimes that means walking through it. It is heart-wrenching, but allow God to heal and change your heart. If you allow God to work through your pain, HE will bless you more than you may believe possible, and you WILL be a much stronger person on the other side. God bless and keep you always!

September 5

- If we allow anyone or anything to become our main focus, God will rearrange our priorities. Tough love can be Exceedingly painful! We must have faith that God really does love us and will work all things for good for those who love Him.
- Song: "The Living Proof" (2011) by Mary J. Blige (see Song Appendix for lyrics)
- Song: "Crawl" by Superchick (see Song Appendix for lyrics)
- Encouragement from a friend: My Chosen Daughter, You are royalty even when you don't feel like a princess. How you feel about yourself will never change the truth of who you are in Me. You are My treasure, and I have chosen you. If you ever begin to doubt your significance, just look to the cross and remember I gave my life to prove your worth. I see your heart, and I know you fight to find truth. So start by recognizing who I am, the King of Kings and Lord of Lords and your Daddy in heaven. Saturate yourself in My truth and you will discover how loved and treasured you are.
- You Will get knocked down. When you do, stop, catch your breath, assess what issue you need to address then rely on God's strength and wisdom to do what needs to be done. God Always keeps His promises and specializes in the "impossible." Don't lose faith!

- If you look around and find yourself in the middle of someone else's mess, allow God to extract you no matter how painful it is right now. If you stay, the pain will only increase. Allow God to rip off the band-aid of an unhealthy situation/relationship and let Him heal you.
- When you are hurt, shut your mouth and hit your knees.

September 6

- Fear is a dangerous enemy! Fear cannot dwell where love and peace reside. Thank you, Jesus!
- Society's standards do not define me. God's love defines me!
- I love my friends, so much understanding and encouragement when I need it! You guys rock!
- As long as Jesus is my no. 1, the enemy will never overtake me! ☺
- Funny thing . . . heart change brings peace . . . and relief . . . and joy . . . wow . . . too cool! ☺
- My personal journal entry: 9/6/2011 8:59 PM The most amazing thing happened to me today!!! Well, I'll catch you up from my last entry. I met with the lady from the local women's ministry; actually she has resigned but still has a heart for the program. Anyway, she was impressed with my testimony and forwarded it to the head lady, along with my volunteer application. Long story short, they no longer have a mentor program, but are looking for financial budget advisors as well as someone to lead a bible study on God's love. Kind of ironic that they're looking for someone to lead a bible study on God's love since my bible study has been on God's love and we've felt the need to address this very same issue in the single's group and I've personally had some healing to do in this area. God brought up a situation that uncovered some VERY BIG pain from my past. I've been dealing with issues of fear, pain and feelings of being left and degraded self-esteem. God has shown me who I am in HIM and has allowed me to uncover this HUGE

pain so that I would realize it is still an issue and surrender it completely to Him. So . . . after a major breakdown (a very long call to my best friend along with a sleepless night, much angst, fear, dread and physical symptoms of much stress, and losing it in the shower for a huge cry . . .) God has brought me to a place of peace about it all. I now firmly know that no matter what my physical situation in this world, no matter how dreary things look or feel; that God is with me and HE keeps ALL of His promises. He WILL keep His promises He has made to me about my future! He will provide me with a Godly husband and take care of my daughter for her whole life. No matter how long it takes until HE provides me with my husband, I know that I will be ok. God will always take care of me, not because of my own strength, but because of His Spirit that lives in me. I am so very relieved; I know that I do not have to do it on my own. I know that HE will always be my strength, my fortress, the lover of my soul. God will ALWAYS go to battle for me and keep me safe in His arms, no matter the storm around me. I have never felt so very secure in my entire life! I know that I do not need a husband to feel secure. FINALLY, I KNOW that I do not need a husband to feel secure!!!!!! How amazing is that for a woman who has firmly believed this LIE that the enemy has driven into my head for the last I don't know how many years??!!!?? So Amazing . . . in a couple days of complete misery and one evening of complete relief that God can make such a TREMENDOUS transformation. True, it was years in the making and the revelation was in this short period of time, but it is so very amazing to me. Nothing less than a miracle! No one can tell me that miracles no longer happen!

Of course, with the good comes the challenging. I just lost my temper with my daughter because she lost her temper about her homework. She stayed up very late last night doing homework because she hadn't gotten it done on the weekend and she fell asleep when we were doing our bible reading. Now she is overwhelmed and feels that she won't be able to get her homework done. So, she was throwing her stuff around the living room and was basically giving up instead of just taking it one step at a time and trying to get it done. Kinda funny though . . . I've done that as a grown up with my spiritual walk. I've seen things that look like they're impossible and instead of just taking one step at a time, I've looked at the whole daunting task and freaked out! Funny, how God has me teach these lessons to my child as I'm going through similar things on a different level. After she gets done with her homework I need to talk to her about this . . . when we're both calm again.

I am very thankful for wonderful friends. During the worst part of my day, when I was full of angst to the point where my hands were shaking . . . a dear friend was texting me to check on me and walked me through the trial. I thank God that He has brought such wonderful, Godly people into my life to help me in the midst of my trial. I even got to speak to (another dear friend) tonight over FB instant chat, which is amazing because first I haven't talked to him in a while and second because my modem is bad and I was 'borrowing' some time on an unsecured network . . . which was gone when I checked again later. Coincidence?? I think not! God so knows what I need and provides in Amazing ways! HE is so good to me!

I am looking forward to see what God has in store for me tomorrow. It's been such a roller coaster this past week, but God is bringing a massive amount of healing and peace into my life and heart and I'm so filled with hope right now. I'm just almost giddy! I can't wait to feel great instead of so gloomy . . . I've felt dread for so many years and am so completely relieved to know that I don't have to feel that anymore. I need to stay in God's word to reinforce His promises and goodness until they're so engrained that nothing can ever possibly make me doubt again though and I plan to do just that. The closer I walk with Jesus the more peace I have, the more I feel his presence—almost physically at times—and the more I know that no matter how difficult a trial I face that HE will always see me through. I know that there will be pain and tears in the years to come, but I also know that Jesus will be right there holding my hand through it all . . . and then I'll get to go see my maker in heaven when I pass from this fallen world! How much better could it possibly get?!? This life and all its trials are temporary and God is with me and will see me through it all as well. Praise God!!! Wow . . . well, I'd better get for now. I will do my best to keep this journal going. I know not all days are going to be as positive at this one, but Praise God HE has delivered me from my bondage and I no longer have to live in the oppressive lies of the enemy! I am free indeed!!!!!! My past will never rule my present or future again!

September 7
- Your tests are your testimony. Persevere and God will bless you abundantly!
- Our lives are to be a "living sacrifice" to our Lord and Savior. If you're just giving up and revising what is easy, what you're not attached to, that is not true sacrifice. True sacrifice comes when there is true love and the willingness to give ALL we truly love to our Heavenly Father, even when it is painful. He is faithful to see us through and will bless us exceedingly for our obedience and faithfulness to Him.
- When you start to get scared that the wonderful future God promised will never get here, remember: "Seek first the kingdom of God, and all these things will be added unto you." Matthew 6:33
  Make sure your priorities are in line with God's, and things will go much better.

- My personal journal entry: 9/7/2011 9:33 AM Well, I'm sitting at the house waiting on the cable repair man, bored to death. I did the dishes, straightened up my bedroom, put together the two boxes for the church rummage sale and took them out to the truck. Now, it's just sit and wait . . . I'm really not good at just sitting and waiting! Speaking of waiting, I know it is still going to be very difficult to wait on God's timing for my future. I don't like being alone and even though I have peace and know that God always has and always will take care of me, I am acutely aware that He never does things the way I want or expect. Just because He has shown me some of what He has for my future does not mean that it is going to happen any time soon or that it is going to happen the way I want it to happen. I know that and just hope not to get disheartened as I encounter the inevitable bumps in the road. I am going to try to stay focused on what I need to do day to day and try to stay thankful for all that He is constantly doing in my life. I never want to lose the faith that He has given me and want to grow it even more. I know it is difficult to grow faith and trials are mandatory along the way . . . I do not like or want any more trials, but if that is what it takes in order for me to be even closer to Jesus, then I will walk through it. I have never felt so loved and wanted in my entire life as when I can feel Jesus' heavenly arms wrapped around me, holding me tight. HE always lets me know that He is never going to leave me or forsake me . . . I am holding onto that truth for all I'm worth and believing it with everything I have. I've been left, forsaken, forgotten, used and abused by every other man that has ever been in my life and have a very difficult time trusting anyone. Jesus is showing me how trustworthy HE is and always will be. By the time He brings my future husband to me He will have taught me how to trust again and I will be able to have a healthy relationship with the husband that He has for me. I don't want any other man

129

anyway . . . . I've been with too many guys who were NOT the right guy and do not want to feel any of that pain ever again! I will wait! I will truly wait for the man Jesus has for me, he is the only man I'm interested in and that is not going to change. I know I will get tired of waiting, shoot . . . I'm tired of waiting right now, but I do know that I have some more work to do to be the right wife for him as well and I definitely want to be a blessing to my man and not a burden. So . . . I will do the work I need to do, and try my best to do it with a happy heart.

Not to mention, I have my hands full with my daughter. She is a very good kid, but a teenager nonetheless! We definitely have our times, like last night. But, I do have to say . . . the night ended on a very good note and we had a talk about what needed to happen instead of the temper tantrum. She said she understood that getting mad didn't help anything and that if she would have calmed down and stepped through what she needed to do that it would have been better. I truly hope that she will be able to calm down a little bit first next time and just concentrate on one step at a time. I guess she does take after her mamma though . . . and I need to work on the same thing! Lol . . . well the cable man is here . . . gotta go for now . . .

September 8
- Honesty should be expected in ALL relationships (family, friends, significant others, etc.)
- When you get hurt, accept your portion of the blame, lay it all at the feet of the Father, and ask HIM to heal all involved. Retaliating in kind or acting out will only cause everyone more pain.
- Let GO and Let GOD!
  by Single Parents Rock! When we lean on The Rock on Thursday, September 8, 2011, at 6:10 a.m.
  Faith is about spiritual maturity and trust in our Heavenly Father. You must have faith that no matter what the

circumstances that HE will work everything for good for those who love Him. He will bless your future, but remember: You cannot always rely on others (even godly people) to make the right decisions (you must be spiritually mature enough in your own right to make Godly decisions and lay EVERYTHING at the feet of the Father, otherwise you will never be able to be equally-yoked to another believer in a healthy relationship). Everyone gets hurt and acts out of pain and selfish motives (you never know what pain someone is dealing with or has had to walk through in their past, emotional pain can make anyone act in ways that are unpleasing to the Father, so do NOT judge!). YOU must be the one to make the right decisions, even when it means stepping back from a good person because they are in a bad place. Love them, pray for them and encourage them, but from a distance . . . *take responsibility for your part in the mess*, step back and let God handle the situation. *HE is the only One qualified to do so!!!* God bless and keep you always!

September 9

- Strong people NEED a soft place to fall too! Just don't make the mistake of thinking a person can fulfill this task. Jesus is the only reliable "soft place" to land for true comfort and restoration.
- Trust that whatever you are walking through is a necessary experience to allow you the opportunity to learn what you need to learn to grow into who HE made you to be. Learn it and Live it! ☺
- Song: "Everything Good" by Ashes Remain (see Song Appendix for lyrics)

September 10

- I am exceedingly grateful for the wonderful godly ladies at the woman's miniretreat. The speaker was excellent and an amazing woman of God! Thank you, Jesus, for touching my heart. I so needed Your touch today!

- Knee-Jerk Reaction—Don't do it! Do not allow yourself to act badly when you get treated badly. Rise above it by hitting your knees and asking our Heavenly Father to tie your tongue and heal the pain. Vengeance is Mine saith the Lord.

- "[17]Do not repay anyone evil for evil. Be careful to do what is right in the eyes of everyone. [18]If it is possible, as far as it depends on you, live at peace with everyone. [19]Do not take revenge, my dear friends, but leave room for God's wrath, for it is written: It is mine to avenge; I will repay,[a] says the Lord . . . [21]Do not be overcome by evil, but overcome evil with good." Romans 12:17-19, 21

- When God calls you to do something, even if you're walking in what seems like unbearable pain, just keep putting one foot in front of the other. The things the Father is asking you to do will bring you healing. Through obedience, faith, and perseverance, you WILL come out of this on the other side a stronger and better person, and God will use your trials and persistence through them to minister to others. Praise God our Savior loves us like no other! Praising Him in the pain.

September 11

- Teenagers: It's not easy raising a teenager. They still throw fits from time to time. They're VERY emotional. They push the limits and break all the rules. They think they can get away with anything. But we never stop loving our teenagers. They require a firm hand (which is not fun for them or us) and a LOT of love! We must be God's teenagers. HE loves us enough to give us tough love so we can learn and grow.

- My daughter: "Mom, you know how football players have John 3:16 on their face?"
  Me: "Yes"

My daughter: "Wouldn't it make more sense if they put
Matthew 19:26?"
Matthew 19:26: "With God all things are possible."
I LOVE MY GIRL!

- Song: "Times" by Tenth Avenue North (see Song Appendix
  for lyrics)
- Standing on this truth: "And Jesus answered saying to
  them, Have faith in God. Truly I say to you, whoever says
  to this mountain, 'Be taken up and cast into the sea,' and
  does not doubt in his heart, but believes that what he says
  is going to happen, it will be granted him. Therefore I say
  to you, all things for which you pray and ask, believe that
  you have received them, and they will be granted you."
  Mark 11:22-24
- Grace Is Required
  by Single Parents Rock! When we lean on The Rock on
  Sunday, September 11, 2011, at 12:50 p.m.
  Grace: It is exceedingly difficult to extend grace to those
  who have harmed us. When someone inflicts emotional
  damage, we need to extend to them the grace of God.
  Many times we need to get out of the situation for our
  own health and safety, but we must also forgive and leave
  'justice' up to the Lord. Our own brand of justice would
  never do anyway . . . Why forgive and give grace you
  ask??? Because Christ died so you could be forgiven of your
  sins . . . they are no different . . . we are all fatally flawed,
  the best we can do is try to imitate Christ every day . . .
  and HE forgave us all!
  God bless and keep you always!
- God's Refining Fire . . . Let Him Do His Work in You . . .
  by Single Parents Rock! When we lean on The Rock on
  Sunday, September 11, 2011 at 8:46pm
  When you give your life over completely to the Lord, He
  is faithful and just and will refine you into what you are
  meant to be. The definition of refine is:
  re·fine

/rɪ ˈ faɪn/ Show Spelled [ri-fahyn] Show IPA verb, -fined,
-fin·ing.
-verb (used with object)
1.to bring to a fine or a pure state; free from impurities: to
refine metal, sugar, or petroleum.
2.to purify from what is coarse, vulgar, or debasing; make
elegant or cultured.
3.to bring to a finer state or form by purifying.
4.to make more fine, subtle, or precise: to refine one's
writing style.
-verb (used without object)
5.to become pure.
6.to become more fine, elegant, or polished.
7.to make fine distinctions in thought or language.
—Verb phrase
8.refine on / upon, to improve by inserting finer
distinctions, superior elements, etc.: to refine on one's
previous work.

Just to get a good picture of what refining looks like, this is
the process for refining silver:

Silver ore and scrap silver have to go through a refining
process in order for the pure silver to be separated from
the dross. Cupellation is when it is heated to 1,200 degrees
Celsius in a special furnace. First though, the silver scrap or
ore is placed in a solution of 30 percent to 35 percent nitric
acid. It takes an ounce and a half of nitric acid to dissolve
one ounce of silver. The solution produces a white powder,
silver chloride. When sodium carbonate is mixed with
the silver chloride and placed in a cupellation furnace, the
heat causes a chemical reaction and makes table salt and
silver. The process works without the addition of sodium
carbonate as well but then the heat releases poisonous
chlorine gas as it produces the pure silver.

Now, picture yourself as the silver ore and scrap silver that
has to go through this process. First you must endure the

acid, then parts of you are turned into white powder, then you're mixed with another solution and placed in a 1,200 degree furnace which causes an intense chemical reaction which makes table salt and silver totally and completely changing your physical properties. OR you could just be tossed into the furnace without the other solution and you would emit poisonous gas in the process and all of your physical properties are still totally and completely changed. When God refines us, IT HURTS!!!!!! It is NOT a pleasant process! Parts of us are being stripped away, melted away, made into powder and burning off as poisonous gas. Our sin that is tucked deep in our hearts, our deepest hurts and fears . . . these do not come out of us easily or voluntarily. Even if we want to walk away from them, they are so ingrained into our very person from years and years of inhabiting our bodies, minds, souls and spirits that we are not able to get rid of them ourselves. Let the Lord refine you. Let HIM purge you of everything that is impure and unpleasing in His sight. Let HIM make you pure, into the form He created you to be, the person He will do many good works through. Let Him refine you into that precious jewel in His kingdom who will bring joy to Him and do His work always!

It is a painful process . . . but . . . as I sit here today, typing this note to you, I am being refined. It hurts, I am very much in pain to the point of physical pain . . . but I know as sure as I am breathing that God is using me and He will use all of this for His glory. There is no better reward than being used for the King's service.

May God bless and keep you always!

September 12
- "As the Lord's servant, you must not quarrel. You must be kind toward all, a good and patient teacher, who is gentle as you correct your opponents, for it may be that God will

135

give them the opportunity to repent and come to know the truth." 2 Timothy 2:24-25
- Song: "Commission My Soul" by Citipointe (see Song Appendix for lyrics)
- YouTube clip: "I will wait for you" by Official P4CM Poet JANETTE . . . IKZ (see script content on July 14)
- Calling: We aren't always called to do what we Want to do. We are called to do what God has equipped us to do and has set before us (said with many tears and much heartache.).
- Take everything to the Father in prayer. When you petition Him with a sincere heart, waiting anxiously and expecting His answer, He will be faithful and answer. You may not always like His answers, but they are the answers that will lead you into His promised future for you. Thank you, Father God, for being so faithful and loving with your rebellious children!
- Wrong Actions = Wrong Motives, No Matter Who You Are!
  by Single Parents Rock! When we lean on The Rock on Monday, September 12, 2011, at 5:55 a.m.
  Do not get angry with God when supposedly 'upright' people treat you poorly. No one is above sin and everyone has the capacity to do the most devious deeds. If you see anyone acting inappropriately, never assume that they still have right motives. Immediately step away from the situation, examine your own actions, give it to the Lord in prayer and accept what He tells you . . . no matter how painful . . . . if He tells you to walk away and you persist in the situation, you will get hurt worse in the long run.
  God bless and keep you always!

September 13
- Surrendering your own will can be the most difficult part of following God's will for your life.

- Like pieces of a puzzle, God puts us together with what He has called us to do. I am thoroughly and completely Amazed! God is so good! All the pain and growth are worth it. I feel like I'm on a roller coaster ride and just about to the top of the really steep climb at the beginning . . . Time to GOOOoooooooo . . . ☺
- Thank you, Jesus, for all of the blessings you have given us today! We don't deserve your mercy and grace, but you are faithful and will never leave us! Thank you, Father God . . .

September 14

- Walk your talk to the core and beyond. Don't just speak it. BE it!
- Song: "Still Here" (Live) Sunday Morning Edition by 21:03 (see Song Appendix for lyrics)
- I am complete, I am whole, I am fully loved in Him . . . couldn't ask for a better thought to end the day with . . . ☺
- Ladies, don't rely on men to bail you out of singleness. Rely on your faith. God is waiting for you to turn to Him. HE will provide all your needs. Our Heavenly Father will always hold you in the palm of His hand. He never promised it would be easy, and sometimes it seems unbearable, but I can tell you from experience that if you lean on Him, HE WILL bring you through, and you will be stronger and better for it! Trust Him.

September 15

- "Trust in the Lord with all your heart and lean not on your own understanding; in all your ways submit to him, and he will make your paths straight." Proverbs 3:5-6
- Never tell anyone they are unlovable or dispensable either by your words or actions. You'd be surprised how deeply this can be ingrained in their heart and soul. Everyone is precious in God's eyes!
- Life change happens when heart change makes you want to change the way you make decisions. When your heart is

right, your actions will follow. They don't have a choice at
that point.
- Take care of each other. If you see a friend in need, help
them out. The smallest gesture can mean so very much to
someone who is going through a hard time. Take the time
to show someone some genuine love today.
God bless and keep you always!

September 16
- Walk: I've heard so many people say, "I wish I had (insert
someone's name here)'s walk with Jesus." This is such a silly
statement. Everyone can have a close walk with Jesus. The
kicker is that you must do the work to get there. Never
wish you had someone else's blessing. You have no idea
what they had to walk through to get there.
- Encouragement from a friend: "He will wipe every tear
from their eyes. There will be no more death or mourning
or crying or pain, for the order of things has passed away."
Revelations 21:4NLT ♥
Carry me away on the wings of a dove,
To the faraway heavenly place up above
No sorrow, no suffering, nor memory of pain
Just my Father, His glory, His book with my name . . . ♥
Amen. ♥
- A woman would be much better off if she could distinguish
the difference between a man that flatters her and a man
that compliments her, a man that spends money on her and
a man that invests in her, a man that views her as property
and a man that views her properly, a man that lusts after
her and a man that loves her, a man that believes he is
God's gift to women and a man that REMEMBERS a
woman was God's gift to man. Know your self-worth! God
doesn't make junk. He makes jewels!
- Love yourself enough to walk away from destructive people
and situations when they show themselves. You deserve a

healthy, godly, loving relationship. Don't settle for less than God's best for you!

September 17

- The Christian Walk
  by Single Parents Rock! When we lean on The Rock on Saturday, September 17, 2011, at 12:19 p.m.
  Ephesians 4

[17]So this I say, and affirm together with the Lord, that you walk no longer just as the Gentiles also walk, in the futility of their mind, [18]being darkened in their understanding, excluded from the life of God because of the ignorance that is in them, because of the hardness of their heart; [19]and they, having become callous, have given themselves over to sensuality for the practice of every kind of impurity with greediness. [20]But you did not learn Christ in this way, [21]if indeed you have heard Him and have been taught in Him, just as truth is in Jesus, [22]that, in reference to your former manner of life, you lay aside the old self, which is being corrupted in accordance with the lusts of deceit, [23]and that you be renewed in the spirit of your mind, [24]and put on the new self, which in *the likeness of* God has been created in righteousness and holiness of the truth.

[25]Therefore, laying aside falsehood, SPEAK TRUTH EACH ONE *of you* WITH HIS NEIGHBOR, for we are members of one another. [26]BE ANGRY, AND *yet* DO NOT SIN; do not let the sun go down on your anger, [27]and do not give the devil an opportunity. [28]He who steals must steal no longer; but rather he must labor, performing with his own hands what is good, so that he will have *something* to share with one who has need. [29]Let no unwholesome word proceed from your mouth, but only such *a word* as is good for edification according to the need *of the moment*, so that it will give grace to those who hear. [30]Do not grieve the Holy Spirit of God, by whom you were sealed for the day of redemption. [31]Let all bitterness

and wrath and anger and clamor and slander be put away
from you, along with all malice. [32]Be kind to one another,
tender-hearted, forgiving each other, just as God in Christ
also has forgiven you.

Heavenly Father, let us all strive to walk wholely with You,
to put aside our old selves and to walk in Your likeness,
being kind, gentle and understanding with each other . . .
putting all sinful things aside and embracing and showing
Your love to each other. In Jesus precious name . . . amen

September 18
- Song: "You Make Beautiful Things Out of the Dust" by
  Gungor (see Song Appendix for lyrics)
- God is not in our story; we are in God's story. We are
  not the Author nor do we have the authority to write our
  own script. We are the pawns of our Father to be used for
  His SERVICE. This means action. It is our responsibility
  to listen to His guidance and DO as He tells us to do,
  regardless of our own will and desires.
- Get to Know Jesus Every Single Day . . .
  by Single Parents Rock! When we lean on The Rock on
  Sunday, September 18, 2011, at 8:27 a.m.
  As followers of Jesus we are supposed to show Christ's love
  to the world and do our best to reflect His image always.
  One of the most helpful things I've found to help me do
  this is to discipline myself to be in the Word every single
  day . . . the closer I get to Jesus, the more I understand His
  character and love and the easier it is for me to understand
  how I need to be a reflection for Him in this lost world.
  Without a constant reminder of who my Jesus is, it is all
  too easy to fall back into old ways and slip away from my
  Redeemer.
  God bless and keep you always!
- Praise God Who Works Everything for Good!
  by Single Parents Rock! When we lean on The Rock on
  Sunday, September 18, 2011, at 8:35 a.m.

Praise God!!! Thank You for allowing me to go through
my trials, for You are fashioning me more into Your image
every day . . . giving me strength and courage, building my
faith into an unwavering faith . . . giving me the wisdom
and knowledge that You will truly never leave me no matter
how bad my circumstances appear . . . letting me realize
that You are my Rock and my Redeemer and you will work
everything for good for those who truly love You and put
You and Your work above all else! Thank you father God . . .
I am not worthy, yet You love and keep me anyway . . .

September 19

- Just got reminded: "You are beautiful, you are sacred, you
  are HIS." Thank You, Jesus . . .
- A lot of people see God in the OT (Old Testament) as a
  harsh and judgmental God, and out of context, I can see
  where they get that. What keeps coming to my attention is
  just how much grace, mercy, and patience God extended to
  the people of the OT (Old Testament), especially in Kings
  when all of the kings keep messing up, over and over and
  over again, generation after generation. God keeps loving
  them. Yes, He does have to punish them for their wrongs,
  but HE always keeps His promises to them and loves them
  anyway. That is truly Amazing to me! How many times do
  we give up on each other after just one wrong? And God
  keeps giving us more chances to get it right and come back
  to Him. Now THAT is true Love!
- Humbled: In order for God to heal you, He must expose
  all of the damaged parts. I am truly and completely
  humbled and thankful that He does not walk away from
  us when He sees all that is in us.
- "Fear imprisons, faith liberates; fear paralyzes, faith
  empowers; fear disheartens, faith encourages; fear sickens,
  faith heals; fear makes useless, faith makes serviceable—
  and, most of all, fear puts hopelessness at the heart of life,
  while faith rejoices in its God." Harry Emerson Fosdick

- WHY Can't You Believe You're Loved???
by Single Parents Rock! When we lean on The Rock on
Monday, September 19, 2011, at 3:32 p.m.
REAL love is much more than physical, in fact, the
physical is SUPPOSED to be a perk, NOT the substance
of love. Real love is spiritual, emotional, intellectual . . .
real love is self sacrificing - not self indulging . . . real
love shows patience, kindness, grace, mercy and keeps
no record of wrongs . . . real love does not guilt you into
doing something you should not do . . . real love has little
to nothing to do with sex. Physical affection is supposed
to be a way to show love to someone, but too many people
use it as a tool to manipulate instead of a gift to be freely
offered (only in the right context) with a servant heart.
Real love serves the one it loves, it does not demand
services to be rendered and then walk away until services
are needed again. Real love is shown to us over and over
again in the Bible . . . God shows us the meaning of real
love when He sent Christ to die for us on the cross. HE
values each and every one of us so much that He sent His
only son to die for our sins so that each one of us could be
saved! Everyone is priceless in His eyes. If we could only
truly believe and understand how much Christ loves us,
I truly believe that many more people would treat others
as they should because they would respect themselves and
know how much they are worth. When people respect
themselves and love themselves (in a healthy way, not
egotistical), they are much more capable of loving others
properly and treating them as they should be treated. If
a person has never experienced true love (on any level), it
is nearly impossible for them to understand that they are
loved because they don't know how to be loved or how to
truly love others. Show someone some real love today . . .
be genuine with everyone in your life . . . you never know
what wounds you may help heal in another who may have
never experienced any kind of real love in their lives. Be a

true friend, confidant, boyfriend, girlfriend, spouse, sister, brother, mother, father, etc . . . truly love one another

September 20

- Give God the key to your heart. Anyone who is truly worthy will win it when they seek HIM to find you.
- Food for thought: Sometimes people hold on so tight because they're used to others bailing. It is hard to expect something good when all you've seen is bad.
- Encouragement from a friend: This is for all the strong ladies who have been through a lot in life and survived! Say this out loud, "I am strong because I know weakness. I am compassionate because I have experienced suffering. I am alive because I am a fighter. I am wise because I have been foolish. I can laugh because I have known sadness. I can love because I have known loss." Repost if you are a strong woman who has weathered the storm but still loves to dance in the rain.
- Encouragement from a friend: End of Day Blessing: May you rest in the knowledge that God is in control. May you release your burdens and pick up His promises. May you remind yourself daily that you are the object of His affection. And tonight, may you relax for a moment and count the blessings in your day. Sleep well.
  My response: ☺
- You are not your own. Be a living sacrifice. Live it. Embrace HIS will for your life joyfully. Walk it out. Sacrifice your own will, do as HE directs, and let Him give you joy.
- "He answered their prayers because they trusted in him." 1 Chronicles 5:20b

September 21

- Stubborn is a package deal with Strong. Sorry, but the two cannot be separated. It's just the way it is. It's not always a good thing, but our greatest strengths are also our worst

Achilles's heel. Letting go and letting God does not come easy for strong people. We try to do it ourselves to our own detriment. Give us time, though. We're all a work in progress. ☺

- Food for thought: It takes more energy to be in a bad place than to let God walk you through a tough period of growth to get to a good place. In a bad place, where you're still trying to be in control, you have to worry about all the logistics and actually try to "drive" on an uncontrollable journey. (Epic fail!) In a good place, where God is driving, there will be pain along the way, but it is temporary. HE will heal you, and then you get to walk into a glorious future!

- Truth is life is messy. Talk to God about it (whatever IT is). HE will never fail you.

- Who am I to take things into my own hands? I am sorry . . . It's Yours, Father . . . It's ALL yours.

- We are all so very, very messed up. Please try to be patient with one another. When someone says or does something or specifically does not say or do something that hurts, offends, or annoys you, please remember that you have probably done the same to someone else, maybe even the person who just offended you, very recently. Have some grace, bite your tongue, and walk away. Sometimes walking away without saying anything is the kindest and most responsible thing we can do.

- True friends stand by each other in good times and bad. True friends listen to you when you're down and party with you when you're happy. Real friends check on you for no reason because they were just thinking about you. Be a real friend to someone today. You could be the only bright spot in someone's day. ☺

September 22
- "What if trials of this life are Your mercies in disguise . . ."
  Laura Story

- If the only thing that changes about the decisions you make are the people involved, you will continue to get the same results. To get different results, you must change your motives and your methods.
- When you are no longer devastated by your trials but can abide in the hope God provides in the midst of the storm, your faith is growing stronger.
- Many people know the right decisions to make, but it takes a very disciplined and self-controlled person to actually make the right decisions.
- Living to Please Others . . . This Struck Me When I Read It, So I Had to Share . . . God Bless
  by Single Parents Rock! When we lean on The Rock on Thursday, September 22, 2011, at 4:59 p.m.
  Romans 15
  Living to Please Others
  ¹We who are strong must be considerate of those who are sensitive about things like this. We must not just please ourselves. ²We should help others do what is right and build them up in the Lord. ³For even Christ didn't live to please himself. As the Scriptures say, "The insults of those who insult you, O God, have fallen on me." ⁴Such things were written in the Scriptures long ago to teach us. And the Scriptures give us hope and encouragement as we wait patiently for God's promises to be fulfilled.
  ⁵May God, who gives this patience and encouragement, help you live in complete harmony with each other, as is fitting for followers of Christ Jesus. ⁶Then all of you can join together with one voice, giving praise and glory to God, the Father of our Lord Jesus Christ.
  ⁷Therefore, accept each other just as Christ has accepted you so that God will be given glory. ⁸Remember that Christ came as a servant to the Jews to show that God is true to the promises he made to their ancestors. ⁹He also came so that the Gentiles might give glory to God for his

mercies to them. That is what the psalmist meant when he
wrote:
"For this, I will praise you among the Gentiles;
I will sing praises to your name."
[10]And in another place it is written,
"Rejoice with his people,
you Gentiles."
[11]And yet again,
"Praise the Lord, all you Gentiles.
Praise him, all you people of the earth."
[12]And in another place Isaiah said,
"The heir to David's throne will come,
and he will rule over the Gentiles.
They will place their hope on him."
[13]I pray that God, the source of hope, will fill you
completely with joy and peace because you trust in him.
Then you will overflow with confident hope through the
power of the Holy Spirit.
God bless you always!
• Wait for the Lord . . .
by Cynthia Johnson on Thursday, September 22, 2011, at
8:21 p.m.
Psalm 27
A Psalm of Fearless Trust in God.
A Psalm of David.
1The LORD is my light and my salvation;
Whom shall I fear?
The LORD is the [a]defense of my life;
Whom shall I dread?
[2]When evildoers came upon me to devour my flesh,
My adversaries and my enemies, they stumbled and fell.
[3]Though a host encamp against me,
My heart will not fear;
Though war arise against me,
In *spite of* this I [b]shall be confident.
[4]One thing I have asked from the LORD, that I shall seek:

That I may dwell in the house of the LORD all the days of my life,
To behold the [c]beauty of the LORD
And to [d]meditate in His temple.

[5]For in the day of trouble He will conceal me in His [e] tabernacle;
In the secret place of His tent He will hide me;
He will lift me up on a rock.

[6]And now my head will be lifted up above my enemies around me,
And I will offer in His tent sacrifices [f]with shouts of joy;
I will sing, yes, I will sing praises to the LORD.

[7]Hear, O LORD, when I cry with my voice,
And be gracious to me and answer me.

[8]*When You said*, "Seek My face," my heart said to You,
"Your face, O LORD, I shall seek."

[9]Do not hide Your face from me,
Do not turn Your servant away in anger;
You have been my help;
Do not abandon me nor forsake me,
O God of my salvation!

[10][g]For my father and my mother have forsaken me,
But the LORD will take me up.

[11]Teach me Your way, O LORD,
And lead me in a level path
Because of [h]my foes.

[12]Do not deliver me over to the [i]desire of my adversaries,
For false witnesses have risen against me,
And such as breathe out violence.

[13][j]*I would have despaired* unless I had believed that I would see the goodness of the LORD
In the land of the living.

[14]Wait for the LORD;
Be strong and let your heart take courage;
Yes, wait for the LORD.

Psalm 33
Praise to the Creator and Preserver.
[1]Sing for joy in the LORD, O you righteous ones;
Praise is becoming to the upright.
[2]Give thanks to the LORD with the lyre;
Sing praises to Him with a harp of ten strings.
[3]Sing to Him a new song;
Play skillfully with a shout of joy.
[4]For the word of the LORD is upright,
And all His work is *done* in faithfulness.
[5]He loves righteousness and justice;
The earth is full of the lovingkindness of the LORD.
[6]By the word of the LORD the heavens were made,
And by the breath of His mouth all their host.
[7]He gathers the waters of the sea together [a]as a heap;
He lays up the deeps in storehouses.
[8]Let all the earth fear the LORD;
Let all the inhabitants of the world stand in awe of Him.
[9]For He spoke, and it was done;
He commanded, and it [b]stood fast.
[10]The LORD nullifies the counsel of the nations;
He frustrates the plans of the peoples.
[11]The counsel of the LORD stands forever,
The plans of His heart from generation to generation.
[12]Blessed is the nation whose God is the LORD,
The people whom He has chosen for His own inheritance.
[13]The LORD looks from heaven;
He sees all the sons of men;
[14]From His dwelling place He looks out
On all the inhabitants of the earth,
[15]He who fashions [c]the hearts of them all,
He who understands all their works.
[16]The king is not saved by a mighty army;
A warrior is not delivered by great strength.
[17]A horse is a false hope for victory;
Nor does it deliver anyone by its great strength.

[18]Behold, the eye of the LORD is on those who fear Him,
On those who [d]hope for His lovingkindness,
[19]To deliver their soul from death
And to keep them alive in famine.
[20]Our soul waits for the LORD;
He is our help and our shield.
[21]For our heart rejoices in Him,
Because we trust in His holy name.
[22]Let Your lovingkindness, O LORD, be upon us,
According as we have [e]hoped in You.

Psalm 37
Security of Those Who Trust in the LORD, and Insecurity
of the Wicked.
A Psalm of David.
[1]Do not fret because of evildoers,
Be not envious toward wrongdoers.
[2]For they will wither quickly like the grass
And fade like the green herb.
[3]Trust in the LORD and do good;
Dwell in the land and [a]cultivate faithfulness.
[4]Delight yourself in the LORD;
And He will give you the desires of your heart.
[5]Commit your way to the LORD,
Trust also in Him, and He will do it.
[6]He will bring forth your righteousness as the light
And your judgment as the noonday.
[7][b]Rest in the LORD and wait [c]patiently for Him;
Do not fret because of him who prospers in his way,
Because of the man who carries out wicked schemes.
[8]Cease from anger and forsake wrath;
Do not fret; *it leads* only to evildoing.
[9]For evildoers will be cut off,
But those who wait for the LORD, they will inherit the
land.
[10]Yet a little while and the wicked man will be no more;

And you will look carefully for his place and he will not be
there.
[11]But the humble will inherit the land
And will delight themselves in abundant prosperity.
[12]The wicked plots against the righteous
And gnashes at him with his teeth.
[13]The Lord laughs at him,
For He sees his day is coming.
[14]The wicked have drawn the sword and bent their bow
To cast down the afflicted and the needy,
To slay those who are upright in conduct.
[15]Their sword will enter their own heart,
And their bows will be broken.
[16]Better is the little of the righteous
Than the abundance of many wicked.
[17]For the arms of the wicked will be broken,
But the LORD sustains the righteous.
[18]The LORD knows the days of the [d]blameless,
And their inheritance will be forever.
[19]They will not be ashamed in the time of evil,
And in the days of famine they will have abundance.
[20]But the wicked will perish;
And the enemies of the LORD will be like the [e]glory of
the pastures,
They vanish—like smoke they vanish away.
[21]The wicked borrows and does not pay back,
But the righteous is gracious and gives.
[22]For those blessed by Him will inherit the land,
But those cursed by Him will be cut off.
[23]The steps of a man are established by the LORD,
And He delights in his way.
[24]When he falls, he will not be hurled headlong,
Because the LORD is the One [f]who holds his hand.
[25]I have been young and now I am old,
Yet I have not seen the righteous forsaken
Or his [g]descendants begging bread.

²⁶All day long he is gracious and lends,
And his [h]descendants are a blessing.
²⁷Depart from evil and do good,
[i]So you will abide forever.
²⁸For the LORD loves [j]justice
And does not forsake His godly ones;
They are preserved forever,
But the [k]descendants of the wicked will be cut off.
²⁹The righteous will inherit the land
And dwell in it forever.
³⁰The mouth of the righteous utters wisdom,
And his tongue speaks justice.
³¹The law of his God is in his heart;
His steps do not slip.
³²The wicked spies upon the righteous
And seeks to kill him.
³³The LORD will not leave him in his hand
Or let him be condemned when he is judged.
³⁴Wait for the LORD and keep His way,
And He will exalt you to inherit the land;
When the wicked are cut off, you will see it.
³⁵I have seen a wicked, violent man
Spreading himself like a luxuriant [l]tree in its native soil.
³⁶Then [m]he passed away, and lo, he was no more;
I sought for him, but he could not be found.
³⁷Mark the [n]blameless man, and behold the upright;
For the man of peace will have a [o]posterity.
³⁸But transgressors will be altogether destroyed;
The [p]posterity of the wicked will be cut off.
³⁹But the salvation of the righteous is from the LORD;
He is their strength in time of trouble.
⁴⁰The LORD helps them and delivers them;
He delivers them from the wicked and saves them,
Because they take refuge in Him.

September 23

- It is okay to cry. The times I've felt the closest to my dear Jesus is when He has held me while I was crying an ocean of tears because I was so completely broken and hopeless. HE is always there. It's okay to cry. He will always give you His shoulder to cry on, and then He'll help you dry your tears and take the next step on your journey to Him. ☺ Thank you, Lord Jesus.
- It is absolutely amazing how much reading the Bible will boost your faith! So many examples of God's faithfulness in the face of human unfaithfulness, and He still hasn't given up on us! God is so abundantly good to us!
- If there is anything in your past that you haven't worked through properly and given to God, BEWARE. Fairly minor events in the present can trigger Major reactions due to past baggage! Work it out, give it to God, and let Him give you peace. Your future is waiting.
- Encouragement from a friend: You'd never invite a thief into your house. So why would you allow thoughts that steal your JOY to make themselves at home in your mind? "Do not conform any longer to the pattern of this world, but be transformed by the renewing of your mind. Then you will be able to test and approve what God's will is-his good, pleasing and perfect will." Romans 12:2

September 24

- Hope everyone has a wonderful day! Beautiful weather outside here . . . time to enjoy the weekend! ☺
- Love it when God teaches me something through my daughter. I found myself telling my girl that being mad at her homework was not going to make it go away. Funny thing, being mad at our situations in life do not make them go away either. We just have to do what we're supposed to do to walk through life, holding God's hand and heeding His guidance, whether we like it or not, and

sometimes we're not going to like it. Huh . . . amazing how God teaches me while I teach my daughter . . .

- "He sought God during the days of Zechariah, who instructed him in the fear of God. As long as he sought the Lord, God gave him success . . . But after Uzziah became powerful, his pride led to his downfall. He was unfaithful to the Lord his God . . ." 2 Chronicles 26:5, 16a

- Encouragement from a friend: Women "Stop" looking for men. Your mate will find you.
  My comment: Any woman looking for A man will find one. Anyone looking for the right man will be found by him.

September 25

- Share who you are, what you've done, and how God has helped you, pulled you out of the pit, and blessed your life in spite of yourself. Others NEED encouragement. Some are convinced that they are too messed up for God to help. They need to know that you are not perfect, we're all fatally flawed, and the only hope for ANY of us is the great God Almighty! Fearlessly share your story with someone today.

- Share a smile with someone today. Let them know you care.

- "I believe in the sun even when it is not shining; I believe in love even when I do not feel it; I believe in God even when He is silent." Author Unknown

- The things we're called to do are often times the things that appear to be the most difficult. Always rely on the Lord's strength and guidance to complete the tasks He has assigned. No one can do any of these things under their own power. Always seek the Lord.

- Encouragement from a friend: Stop Crying over what God have already solved.
  My comment: You have no idea how timely this Word is . . . Thank you for passing it along. God bless you abundantly!

- God is so good! Just when it is most difficult, HE gives us wonderful, amazing examples of others who are not scared or ashamed to share how He has worked in their lives. Thank you, Father God, for the timely encouragement to keep about Your work!
- I have the best daughter EVER! We have our days, and it's definitely not always easy, but she has been with me through thick and thin. We've both stood our ground, grown, laughed, and cried together. She knows her mamma so well it's downright scary sometimes! LOL. I love you, kiddo, more than you'll ever know!

September 26
- Don't let your pain set the tone for today. God has you in the palm of His hand. Lean into Him for love and encouragement. May God abundantly bless your day!
- If God is extracting something or someone from your life, let Him. You cannot come into your complete and perfect purpose in Him with roadblocks in your life.
- "Every test that you have experienced is the kind that normally comes to people. But God keeps his promise, and he will not allow you to be tested beyond your power to remain firm; at the time you are put to the test he will give you the strength to endure it, and so provide you with a way out." 1 Corinthians 10:13
- "Let all bitterness, wrath, anger, clamor, and evil speaking be put away from you, with all malice. And be kind to one another, tenderhearted, forgiving one another, even as God in Christ forgave you." Ephesians 4:31-32
- Don't settle for what you've always got because you don't know anything else. Trust God to bring HIS best into your life, and don't underestimate how wonderful it will be. God keeps HIS promises, so when He promises a wonderful blessed future, that is EXACTLY what you will get if you wait faithfully and obediently for your blessing.

- "Don't let the world around you squeeze you into its own mold, but let God remake you so that your whole attitude of mind is changed." Romans 12:1
- Love the Lord your God with all your heart, all your soul, all your strength, not just the leftover portions after the hectic day full of obligations is through. He is supposed to be our ALL in ALL, second to none!

September 27

- Faith is letting Jesus run your Entire life and not worrying how it is going to turn out.
- Do not neglect your physical health no matter what trials you are going through, no matter how busy and hectic your schedule. You are a valuable child of God who has responsibilities, and if you do not take care of yourself properly, you will not be able to take care of all that He has entrusted to you. Take time to replenish yourself physically, mentally, emotionally, and spiritually. God bless and keep you always!
- In the Old Testament, God gave very specific instructions as to how His temple was to be built and operated down to minute details. Did you also know that your body is His temple? Take care of his temple. Do not neglect or abuse it or allow anyone else to do likewise. You are a precious jewel of our King and are to always be treated as such!
- "Or do you not know that your body is a temple of the Holy Spirit who is in you, whom you have from God, and that you are not your own?" 1 Corinthians 6:19

September 28

- The worries of this world can physically ravage your body. Be strong in your faith, so as not to worry, and diligent in caring for your body so that you may fully walk in what our Lord has set before you. In this way, we will fully and energetically glorify our Father.

- When God calls you to do something, HE will equip you (if He hasn't already!). All you have to do is obediently walk into your future and rely completely on Him to give you the wisdom and strength to succeed. His plans are always perfect! ☺
- There is such an amazing, liberating feeling that comes from truly walking out in faith. God is in control. I truly have to do nothing but be obedient and watch Him work everything out for His good, and He'll bless me for my efforts. How AWESOME is that! ☺ God is so amazingly good to His children!

September 29
- God is faithful and just and KEEPS HIS PROMISES. ☺
- "A quitter never wins and a winner never quits . . ." 21:03
- "Train up a child in the way he should go, and when he is old he will not depart from it." Proverbs 22:6
- Don't always assume the worst about people. When you're walking in your faith and being wise in the ways of the Lord, He will bring you blessings. Enjoy them and stop waiting for the "other shoe to drop." You're in God's hands. ☺
- You cannot embrace your future until you come to terms with and accept your past for what it is. Let God walk you through it. Let Him show you how He has mastered it all and saved you from where you were headed, how He has healed you, watched over you, and never stopped loving you because you are Priceless in His eyes, and He wants to draw you closer to Him.

September 30
- If things aren't shaping up as you had envisioned, give Praise! Our vision is limited. God's is eternal. His plan is always better.
- In the corporate world, knowledge is power and means you're likely to have control over situations and people. In

the spiritual world, realize that the only One with complete knowledge is the only One who truly has the power. God is the only One who is in control. This is the key to actually understanding what it means to have faith. Once this is completely understood, spiritual maturity will blossom.

- When you realize just how little you actually know, you'll begin to realize how active your faith must be.

- "God makes people right with himself through their faith in Jesus Christ. This is true for all who believe in Christ." Romans 3:22

- "So the people asked him, saying, 'What shall we do then?' He answered and said to them, 'He who has two tunics, let him give to him who has none; and he who has food, let him do likewise.'" Luke 3:10-11
Give to someone in need today. Believe it or not, there is always someone out there who is worse off than you.
God bless and keep you always!

- Have you been in the Word today? Jesus is waiting to spend time with you.

- "Sing to God, sing praise to his name, extol him who rides on the clouds—his name is the Lord—and rejoice before him. A father to the fatherless, a defender of widows, is God in his holy dwelling. God sets the lonely in families, he leads forth the prisoners with singing; but the rebellious live in a sun-scorched land." Psalm 68:4-6

- Psalm 37 (I love this psalm! ☺))
by Single Parents Rock! When we lean on The Rock on Friday, September 30, 2011, at 5:52 p.m.
Psalm 37Security of Those Who Trust in the LORD, and Insecurity of the Wicked.
A Psalm of David.
¹Do not fret because of evildoers,
Be not envious toward wrongdoers.
²For they will wither quickly like the grass
And fade like the green herb.
³Trust in the LORD and do good;

Dwell in the land and cultivate faithfulness.
⁴Delight yourself in the LORD;
And He will give you the desires of your heart.
⁵Commit your way to the LORD,
Trust also in Him, and He will do it.
⁶He will bring forth your righteousness as the light
And your judgment as the noonday.
⁷Rest in the LORD and wait patiently for Him;
Do not fret because of him who prospers in his way,
Because of the man who carries out wicked schemes.
⁸Cease from anger and forsake wrath;
Do not fret; *it leads* only to evildoing.
⁹For evildoers will be cut off,
But those who wait for the LORD, they will inherit the land.
¹⁰Yet a little while and the wicked man will be no more;
And you will look carefully for his place and he will not be
there.
¹¹But the humble will inherit the land
And will delight themselves in abundant prosperity.
¹²The wicked plots against the righteous
And gnashes at him with his teeth.
¹³The Lord laughs at him,
For He sees his day is coming.
¹⁴The wicked have drawn the sword and bent their bow
To cast down the afflicted and the needy,
To slay those who are upright in conduct.
¹⁵Their sword will enter their own heart,
And their bows will be broken.
¹⁶Better is the little of the righteous
Than the abundance of many wicked.
¹⁷For the arms of the wicked will be broken,
But the LORD sustains the righteous.
¹⁸The LORD knows the days of the blameless,
And their inheritance will be forever.
¹⁹They will not be ashamed in the time of evil,
And in the days of famine they will have abundance.

[20]But the wicked will perish;
And the enemies of the LORD will be like the glory of the pastures,
They vanish—like smoke they vanish away.
[21]The wicked borrows and does not pay back,
But the righteous is gracious and gives.
[22]For those blessed by Him will inherit the land,
But those cursed by Him will be cut off.
[23]The steps of a man are established by the LORD,
And He delights in his way.
[24]When he falls, he will not be hurled headlong,
Because the LORD is the One who holds his hand.
[25]I have been young and now I am old,
Yet I have not seen the righteous forsaken
Or his [g]descendants begging bread.
[26]All day long he is gracious and lends,
And his descendants are a blessing.
[27]Depart from evil and do good,
So you will abide forever.
[28]For the LORD loves justice
And does not forsake His godly ones;
They are preserved forever,
But the descendants of the wicked will be cut off.
[29]The righteous will inherit the land
And dwell in it forever.
[30]The mouth of the righteous utters wisdom,
And his tongue speaks justice.
[31]The law of his God is in his heart;
His steps do not slip.
[32]The wicked spies upon the righteous
And seeks to kill him.
[33]The LORD will not leave him in his hand
Or let him be condemned when he is judged.
[34]Wait for the LORD and keep His way,
And He will exalt you to inherit the land;
When the wicked are cut off, you will see it.

[35]I have seen a wicked, violent man
Spreading himself like a luxuriant tree in its native soil.
[36]Then he passed away, and lo, he was no more;
I sought for him, but he could not be found.
[37]Mark the blameless man, and behold the upright;
For the man of peace will have a posterity.
[38]But transgressors will be altogether destroyed;
The posterity of the wicked will be cut off.
[39]But the salvation of the righteous is from the LORD;
He is their strength in time of trouble.
[40]The LORD helps them and delivers them;
He delivers them from the wicked and saves them,
Because they take refuge in Him.

OCTOBER 2011

October 1

- "For the Lord God is a sun and shield; the Lord bestows favor and honor; no good thing does he withhold from those whose walk is blameless." Psalm 84:11

- Encouragement from a friend: Don't worry if you're still single. God is looking at you right now, saying, "I'm . . . saving this girl for someone special." God will send someone to compliment you, not to complete you!
My response: ☺

- Encouragement from a friend: GOD IS FOR YOU. And if God is for you, who can move against you? God is sovereign, and He rules over everything. Whoever has tried to harm you could only go as far as God let them and not one inch further. And no matter what they did, no matter how horribly you have been used or abused, God will use it to make you like Jesus. This is His promise.
My response: I'm a living proof of this one. Amen. God is so very good to his children!

- "For the Lord God is a sun and shield; the Lord bestows favor and honor; no good thing does he withhold from those whose walk is blameless." Psalm 84:11

- I've Fallen into This Trap Sooo Many Times! Thank God He Is So Gracious and Patient with His Children . . . by Single Parents Rock! When we lean on The Rock on Saturday, October 1, 2011, at 2:18 p.m.
Psalm 73
BOOK 3
The End of the Wicked Contrasted with That of the Righteous. A Psalm of Asaph.
¹Surely God is good to Israel,
To those who are pure in heart!
²But as for me, my feet came close to stumbling,

My steps had almost slipped.
3For I was envious of the arrogant
As I saw the prosperity of the wicked.
4For there are no pains in their death,
And their body is fat.
5They are not in trouble *as other* men,
Nor are they plagued like mankind.
6Therefore pride is their necklace;
The garment of violence covers them.
7Their eye bulges from fatness;
The imaginations of *their* heart run riot.
8They mock and wickedly speak of oppression;
They speak from on high.
9They have set their mouth against the heavens,
And their tongue parades through the earth.
10Therefore his people return to this place,
And waters of abundance are drunk by them.
11They say, "How does God know?
And is there knowledge with the Most High?"
12Behold, these are the wicked;
And always at ease, they have increased *in* wealth.
13Surely in vain I have kept my heart pure
And washed my hands in innocence;
14For I have been stricken all day long
And chastened every morning.
15If I had said, "I will speak thus,"
Behold, I would have betrayed the generation of Your
children.
16When I pondered to understand this,
It was troublesome in my sight
17Until I came into the sanctuary of God;
Then I perceived their end.
18Surely You set them in slippery places;
You cast them down to destruction.
19How they are destroyed in a moment!
They are utterly swept away by sudden terrors!

²⁰Like a dream when one awakes,
O Lord, when aroused, You will despise their form.
²¹When my heart was embittered
And I was pierced within,
²²Then I was senseless and ignorant;
I was *like* a beast before You.
²³Nevertheless I am continually with You;
You have taken hold of my right hand.
²⁴With Your counsel You will guide me,
And afterward receive me to glory.
²⁵Whom have I in heaven *but You*?
And besides You, I desire nothing on earth.
²⁶My flesh and my heart may fail,
But God is the strength of my heart and my portion
forever.
²⁷For, behold, those who are far from You will perish;
You have destroyed all those who are unfaithful to You.
²⁸But as for me, the nearness of God is my good;
I have made the Lord GOD my refuge,
That I may tell of all Your works.

October 2

- It is so liberating to honestly be able to say my past does not own me anymore. I am walking confidently, completely, and entirely restored into my future. Praise God who never fails to heal and restore his children!

- You cannot change who you are, but when you embrace who you are in Christ, your perspective on the whole world changes radically. When you start looking at yourself through God's eyes, you are freed from your past, mistakes and skeletons in your closet, old ways of thinking, and destructive habits no longer have a hold on you. Hold on to Christ and let everything else go. He will never fail you.

- Praise God in all situations; trust in Him, and He will give you strength.

- "Flee from sexual immorality. All other sins a man commits are outside his body, but he who sins sexually sins against his own body. Do you not know that your body is a temple of the Holy Spirit, who is in you, whom you have received from God? You are not your own; you were bought with a price. Therefore honor God with your body." 1 Corinthians 6:18-20

October 3

- Please keep all McPherson High School students in your prayers this week. A high school junior passed away this past Saturday after the Homecoming dance. The unofficial word is suicide. There are a lot of hurting and confused students who need all the prayer and support they can get. I can't imagine what this young man's family is going through right now either. PLEASE keep them all in your prayers.
- Love and support each other. Let others know how valuable and needed they really are. You never know when or if you will see them again. God bless and keep you all, all of you are dearly loved by our Father!
- "My most cherished possession I wish I could leave you is my faith in Jesus Christ, for with Him and nothing else you can be happy, but without Him and with all else you'll never be happy." Patrick Henry

October 4

- Let the most difficult things in life bring you closer to Jesus and make you stronger in your faith. When you are called upon to help others through the storm, don't try to shoulder the burden yourself. Lovingly help them take it all to the feet of our Heavenly Father.
- "Let us therefore come boldly to the throne of grace, that we may obtain mercy and find grace to help in time of need." Hebrews 4:16

- "We have such trust through Christ toward God. Not that we are sufficient of ourselves to think of anything as being from ourselves, but our sufficiency is from God." 2 Corinthians 3:4-5
- I posted this song on my daughter's wall:—"Lean on Me" (2010) by Group 1 Crew (see Song Appendix for lyrics)
- In life, if it's not one thing, it's another. Something is always coming at ya full force! What the enemy doesn't realize is the more stuff he throws at me, the more I will rely on my Jesus, so the enemy is just compounding his troubles by pickin' on me! Bring It! My Jesus will make me stronger every day. ☺
- Encouragement from a friend: If at first you don't succeed, try, try again. God wants us to be relentless and to refuse to give up!
  My response: AMEN! A timely word, thank you. ☺
- Spend some time with your kids—REAL TIME—time with just you and them, time to listen to them, play with them, let them know you truly appreciate them for who they are, to let them know that they are valuable . . . that you truly love them enough to carve time out of the day especially for them. They are priceless, and they don't stay young long.

October 5

- Encouragement from a friend: Things can't get better. Yes they can, if you pray. But you don't understand. The only but is but God. You don't know what it's like for me. It doesn't matter, God is bigger.
  No one gets it. God does.
  "Yea, though I walk through the valley of the shadow of death, I will fear no evil; For You are with me; Your rod and Your staff, they comfort me." Psalm 23:4
  It's only a shadow of death, not ACTUAL death. Keep walking. No need to run.
  FEAR is

F.alse
E.vidence
A.ppearing
R.ight
God is with you. When? Sometimes? No. Now and then?
No. When He's awake? No. ALL THE TIME? YES!
His rod and staff are a comfort because they protect,
shield, guard. Be comforted.

- I said Bring It, and he's bringin' it. But he's NOT gonna
  win! My God is BIGGER!
  Victory last night: Sound sleep.
  Victory today: Truck wouldn't start, but it's only the
  battery, no problem; difficult people at work, got all
  worked out; funeral Friday, God will give all peace.
  My God gives me the VICTORY regardless of
  circumstances! ☺

- Walk in victory regardless of your circumstances. God's
  got your back. Just trust in Him and follow His guidance,
  and He will take care of you Always! ☺

- The right mate will love you, respect you, and treat you
  with kindness, patience, and honor. There won't be any
  "games" or wordplay. Honesty will define your relationship
  along with respect, generosity, kindness, and an urgency
  and priority to grow closer to Jesus together. Don't settle
  for less just because you have never seen it, felt it, or had
  the privilege of watching someone else attain it. God will
  provide. Be patient, keep the faith, and wait on His timing.

- You Already Have EVERYTHING You Need ☺
  by Single Parents Rock! When we lean on The Rock on
  Wednesday, October 5, 2011, at 3:35 p.m.
  By his divine power, God has given us everything we need
  for living a godly life. -2 Peter 1:3 NLT
  GUESS WHAT??? This means that you already HAVE
  EVERYTHING you need to live a Godly life. You
  already have EVERYTHING you need period. You do
  not need a mate to complete you. You are already totally

complete and completely loved and accepted just as you are in Christ. Powerful truth, if you'll embrace it. You are not the exception to the Word of God. This IS a biblical truth and yes . . . God does know and understand your circumstances. He knows exactly how difficult they are and has equipped you to handle everything with HIM. You only have to come to Him, totally surrender all of your life and walk in His ways and He WILL provide everything you need and will bless you with the desires of your heart. You'll be surprised at how He conforms your heart to match His and then pours on the blessings! It is an absolutely AMAZING process, I hope and pray that you get to experience it soon! You will Never forget it and will want everyone you know to be able to experience this kind of blessing and hope in their lives too! Be blessed dear friends . . . be Very Blessed!!!

- Peace: In the midst of the storm, no doubt, but peace is always welcome. ☺ It is completely amazing to me how God provides peace, even while the storm is still raging, when we walk out into what He has for our lives, when we are completely and wholeheartedly devoted to Him and His work. God is truly amazing. He truly loves us beyond all comprehension.

October 6

- Listen to God and He will not only show you your purpose, but will also give you abundant opportunity to actively pursue it. So fulfilling, such an amazing blessing! Thank You, Jesus. ☺
- Encouragement from a friend: Sometimes you just have to take that leap of Faith!
  My response: Leap . . . SPLASH! ☺
- Song: "Intimacy" by Trip Lee (see Song Appendix for lyrics)
- Song: "Cling to You" by Trip Lee (see Song Appendix for lyrics)

- Think about it: Ladies, if you allow your boyfriend to treat you like you're disposable, he will. If you keep taking him back when he mistreats you, don't expect him to magically change. NEWS FLASH: YOU ARE A DAUGHTER OF THE MOST HIGH KING! If your boyfriend does not treat you as such, bounce. Get out. God made a man for you who WILL treat you like the Royalty you are, but HE can't bring him into your life until you get rid of the riffraff.
- Wow . . . What a Week! Lord, Give Me Strength . . . by Cynthia Johnson on Thursday, October 6, 2011, at 8:12 p.m.

Trials and Blessings of this week:

Trial: found out that one of my daughter's friend's committed suicide last weekend

Blessing: have been able to guide her through this tragedy with God's help, wisdom and peace

Trial: encountered difficult people at work with very tight time lines to get things accomplished

Blessing: was able to work through all the issues, complete things on time and not lose my temper

Trial: battery in my truck gave up the ghost

Blessing: it was only the battery and it quit AFTER I got to work where I was able to borrow someone's car to take my daughter to school, then get a jump for my truck, take it to the mechanic, get a ride back to the mechanic to pick it up and all this for a relatively small amount of money and before I had to pick my daughter up for school

Trial: my washer hose just gave out, filling up my laundry room with water and causing stress

Blessing: my wonderful landlord came right over, helped me shut off the water, unhook the hoses and let me know where I could buy the hoses I need for a good price

Trial: had to work overtime tonight to get caught up at work so I can take off early tomorrow to take my daughter to her friend's funeral

Blessing: I was able to work while she was at work so I didn't miss any time with her and I actually got a good run in after I was done at work . . . little did I know I would NEED the stress relief tonight!

God is good all the time!!! Even when our world is spinning out of control, HE is in control . . . we just have to keep looking UP and not get caught up in the drama and stress of life . . . just keep looking for the blessings, because they're there. Our Father never fails to take care of our every need, even if it's not in the way we'd like Him to. He doesn't take the trials and heartaches of life away, but He is always there to walk through them with us.

Thank You Jesus for all you have done for me and my girl this week, I'd be lost without you Father!

- Encouragement from a friend: "I can trust the One who has my best interest in mind." A. W. Tozer
My response: Truth. ☺

October 7

- Song: "Courageous" by Casting Crowns (see Song Appendix for lyrics)
My comment on the song: I will recognize my man because my Heavenly Father made him courageous! ☺
- I am leaning back in God's grace and protection, taking a breather, recouping after a very trying week . . .
- Your situation is not yours to figure out. Quit trying to strategize, maneuver, and "work it" to your best advantage. Your job is to follow God's lead no matter how impossible things may appear. Our God specializes in impossibilities!
- I will recognize my man because my Heavenly Father made him courageous! ☺

October 8

- Following God during the most difficult times in life brings the greatest blessings.

- "As your faith is strengthened you will find that there is no longer the need to have a sense of control, that things will flow as they will, and that you will flow with them, to your great delight and benefit." Emmanuel Teney
- The Lord Is My Keeper, I Will Not Be Harmed . . . by Single Parents Rock! When we lean on The Rock on Saturday, October 8, 2011, at 10:50 p.m.
Psalm 121
I lift up my eyes to the hills -
where does my help come from?
My help comes from the Lord,
the Maker of heaven and earth.
He will not let your foot slip -
he who watches over you will not slumber;
indeed, he who watches over Israel
will neither slumber nor sleep.
The Lord watches over you -
the Lord is your shade at your right hand;
the sun will not harm you by day,
nor the moon by night.
The Lord will keep you from all harm -
he will watch over your life;
the Lord will watch over your coming and going
both now and forevermore.
Thank you Lord for your unconditional love and
everlasting protection.
Amen

October 9
- "Everyone wants to be an overcomer, but nobody wants anything to overcome." Joyce Meyer Ministries
- "Unless the Lord builds the house, its builders labor in vain. Unless the Lord watches over the city, the watchmen stand guard in vain. In vain you rise early and stay up late, toiling for food to eat- for he grants sleep to those he loves." Psalm 127:1-2

Who is building the house of your relationships?

- "May the words of my mouth and the meditation of my heart be acceptable to You, Lord, my rock and my Redeemer." Psalm 19:14

- Priority check: Couple questions: Where does your loyalty lie? What or who takes up most of your energy every day? What or who do you think about most during the day? What or who do you pursue most daily? What or who do you desire most? What is your deepest longing?

  Do you seek, desire, and long for a relationship with Jesus more than anyone or anything else in your life? What or who you are living for makes a BOLD and unmistakable statement to those around you. What are you teaching your children to live for? Something to think about . . . because more people are watching than you think . . .

- Defibrillator or Daily Vitamin?

  by Single Parents Rock! When we lean on The Rock on Sunday, October 9, 2011, at 10:20 a.m.

  Many people use Jesus as an emergency response defibrillator, strictly for emergency purposes when their hearts have already stopped and they are in eminent danger of spiritual death and sometimes only after they have had a close encounter with literal physical death. Defibrillation is a drastic measure taken to bring a person back from nearly dying. Here is a definition, to give you a reference: Defibrillation is a common treatment for life-threatening cardiac arrhythmias, ventricular fibrillation and pulseless ventricular tachycardia. Defibrillation consists of delivering a therapeutic dose of electrical energy to the affected heart with a device called a defibrillator. This depolarizes the critical mass of the heart muscle, terminates the arrhythmia, and allows normal sinus rhythm to be reestablished by the body's natural pacemaker, the sinoatrial node of the heart.

  Okay, now . . . have you seen a T.V. show where the doctor plugs in the machine after someone has had a heart attack, rubs the paddles together, screams "CLEAR!!!" and shocks the heck out of the person?? THIS is a defibrillator in action! So, when the definition says that it 'delivers a therapeutic dose of electrical energy to the affected heart' is doesn't quite convey the violence of this event. When a defibrillator must be used, it is violent, painful and does not always work.

This makes me wonder WHY??? would we ever put our heavenly Father in the same role as this emergency response machine? One major difference is that if a person actually LISTENS to Jesus, gives Him their heart and walks in His ways, this treatment will NEVER fail. However, we do have a choice . . .

It is up to us whether we run to Him and embrace His love, grace, peace and healing (although the healing process is very painful and difficult to work through . . . we have one added perk though . . . although this process of peeling all of the sin, pain, hurt and pent up anger out of our lives is very painful, Jesus will never leave us and is right there holding our hands all the way through it.)

We also have the option to chose to run away from our Lord and Savior and try to manage life on our own . . . in my experience this leads to OVERWHELMING feelings of loneliness, hopelessness, sadness, helplessness, and me getting myself into situations that were so horrible and so deep that I could NEVER dig myself out and no one else could say or do anything that eased the pain either.

Once I decided to let Jesus be my Daily Vitamin . . . a small dose (especially at first, as i could not handle anything more than a very small dose a day to start with) each morning to help start changing my perspective, ways of thinking, and eventually my heart and expectations of life and how others should treat me as a LOVED DAUGHTER OF THE KING (I didn't even believe I was loved for years and years, Jesus had to show me through many years of events in my life that He orchestrated especially for me to reveal His true real love to me. Everyone has their own process here and Jesus is in charge . . . you can't rush anyone to believe they are loved . . . all you can do is plant the seeds and let God grow inside their hearts . . . you may never see the results, but be obedient to His Spirit anyway, someone did the same for you . . . Remember??)

In this servant's humble opinion, one of the best ways to encourage others to rely on Jesus as their Daily Vitamin instead of strictly their emergency response Defibrilaltor, is to let them see you walking with Jesus every day. Be transparent, let everyone see you walking your walk daily with Jesus, let them see you relying on the Father for daily decisions, let them see you loving others like Jesus loves them regardless if you really like them at all . . . let them see you obeying Jesus even and especially when it is very difficult to do so . . . if you let them see all of this, they won't be able to miss seeing all of the blessings that God will bestow on you for being a good and faithful servant. They won't be able to deny that Jesus is REAL and really does LOVE His children more than the human mind can comprehend! They may never admit it to you, but you will make a much larger impact than you ever thought possible. Grace and Peace be with you always!

October 10

- My God has not forgotten me. He did not heal my heart to simply leave it vacant. My blessing is on the way, though my eyes have yet to see it. My Father will never abandon me.

- Never lose the lesson in your circumstances, remember what worked and remember what did not work, then only repeat what works! You'd think it would be easy to remember! LOL. lesson learned . . . again . . .

- I praise the Lord for my trials and heartaches, for without them, my faith would not be refined. My walk with Jesus would not be as close, My confidence in Him would not be as strong. I praise the Lord for my trials and heartaches.

- "The Lord is righteous in all his ways and loving toward all he has made. The Lord is near to all who call on him, to all who call on him in truth. He fulfills the desires of those who fear him; he hears their cry and saves them. The Lord watches over all who love him, but all the wicked he will destroy." Psalm 145:17-20

October 11

- Facades: Most people are more cultured and observant than you give them credit for. The facades you throw up are transparent. Be honest and real with people. They can see more than you think they can anyway.
- My life is not my own to worry about. I am not in control. Thank God!
- If you truly believe it, let your life reflect it. Lip service does more damage than silence.
- When God shows you things through situations in your life, pay attention. Otherwise, you will have to learn the lesson again later, possibly through an even more unpleasant situation. Pass the test the first time and move on to the next level! ☺ God bless and keep you always.

October 12

- Growth means that you must be willing and ready to leave behind things and situations that no longer fit to embrace change, give thanks for progress (even when it is painful), and wait expectantly for God's best.
- If someone will not happily invite you into their world, they don't want you there. Don't keep trying to "catch" someone's attention. When you meet YOUR mate, you will naturally catch their attention. You don't have to chase the right person. They will already WANT you to be in their life!

October 13

- The Golden Rule is not just a cliché. We are required to treat others as we would like to be treated, and more than that, we're called to treat others the way Jesus would treat them. Selfish motives are unacceptable options.
- It's amazing how we're abundantly blessed out of obedience to His will . . . absolutely Amazing!
- "God will fulfill all your needs, In Christ Jesus, as lavishly as only God can." Philippians 4:19

October 14

- Song: "What Love Really Means" by JJ Heller (see Song Appendix for lyrics)
- Song: "Strong Enough" by Matthew West (see Song Appendix for lyrics)
  My comment on the song: SO glad I don't have to be strong enough . . .
- So happy for my girl . . . and a little jealous! LOL. She has early access tickets and a meet-and-greet pass to actually meet each of the bands at the end of the concert—the David Crowder concert! Sounds like SO MUCH FUN! Take lots of pics, baby girl. ☺
- Never judge a book by its cover: If someone looks like a "good" person from the outside, hang around long enough, BEFORE you get in too deep, to find out what they are Really like. Does their lifestyle reflect what they say they believe? Do they treat you like you should be treated? If not, walk away.
- A Tree and Its Fruit: "Beware of the false prophets, who come to you in sheep's clothing, but inwardly are ravenous wolves. You will know them by their fruits. Grapes are not gathered from thorn bushes nor figs from thistles, are they? So every good tree bears good fruit, but the bad tree bears bad fruit. A good tree cannot produce bad fruit, nor can a bad tree produce good fruit. Every tree that does not bear

good fruit is cut down and thrown into the fire. So then, you will know them by their fruits." Matthew 7:15-20
- God loves us for us no matter what we've done.
- Let HIM be strong enough for you. None of us can do it alone.

October 15
- Strong woman: Despite all of the heartbreak, trials, tribulation, confusion, and mistakes in my life (which are too numerous to count!), I can finally say that I have learned to rely on the One who truly gives me strength. A person can be humanly strong, but no one can truly have peace in this life without relying on Jesus each and every day. I'm so glad I've finally got it and don't have to rely on my own strength alone anymore! ☺
- Do you still believe that you need someone else's help to make it through this life? Are you still relying on a person to bail you out or get you through your trials? God is our ALL IN ALL; God will provide EVERYTHING that you will ever need to not only get through this life, but to PROSPER as well! God will fight all your battles, if you only walk in His will and abide by His word. He will never take you into a trial that He cannot help you overcome. God bless you always!
- "Then Asa called to the LORD his God and said, LORD, there is no one besides You to help in the battle between the powerful and those who have no strength; so help us, O LORD our God, for we trust in You, and in Your name have come against this multitude. O LORD, You are our God; let not man prevail against You." 2 Chronicles 14:11
- Have a wonderful day. It looks like a Beautiful weekend out there! Get out of the house and have some fun! God bless you in all you do. ☺
- People who claim to be "Christians" can be much more dangerous and harmful than those who aren't even trying. Before you jump into a relationship of any sort with a

person, make sure their actions match up with what they say they believe. If they're all too willing to jump into bed with you, or do other unsavory things, or if they try to entice you into things you know you ought not be doing, run far, run fast! These are the people who can cause you to lose your faith, who cause others to believe that no one really truly walks with Jesus and lives an upright life. DON'T fall into their trap! Keep your eyes on the Lord. God bless and keep you safe always!

October 16

- Encouragement from a friend: God, when my sisters lose hope, help them to remember your love is greater than their disappointment, and your plans for their life are better than their dreams. Amen
- Song: "Rescue" by Newsong (see Song Appendix for lyrics)
- No matter what people do, remember they're only people. It is not for you to judge or seek revenge. It IS for you to do as YOU are called and leave the rest to our Heavenly Father.
- Be careful how you treat others. What you do and say may have longer term effects than you realize.
- Searching for a mate in today's society can feel like looking for a Godly person in Sodom and Gomorrah. If my choice is to either WAIT for God's best or settle for some lesser version of broken, I choose to WAIT! Broken means more broken hearts, more hurt, more devastation, more oppression. I don't know about you, but I want more blessing, more love, more happiness, more fulfillment. All of which come through God, and only God can lead us to the right person to share our lives with.
- Do NOT settle for less than God's best for your life. It will only lead to more devastation. Wait for your blessing!
- Don't let others derail you. Keep your heart and mind focused on the Lord and He will take care of you. It is not our place to judge or take retribution on those that have

harmed us. Judgment is only for the Lord. Keep your focus on the Lord, not on the deeds of others.

October 17

- Looking forward to some downtime out of pocket this weekend! ☺
- "Now hope does not disappoint, because the love of God has been poured out in our hearts by the Holy Spirit who was given to us." Romans 5:5

October 18

- Encouragement from a friend: You may be wondering if you will ever see your dreams come true, if you'll ever walk in victory over a specific area in your life, if you'll ever find freedom from your painful past, if you'll ever see light at the end of your tunnel, if you'll ever get past the limbo season you find yourself in.
  Don't lose heart, sweet friend. Don't lose faith. God delights in doing exceedingly, abundantly above all you could ask or think! Your "new thing" may be just around the corner, just a still small whisper away. But you've got to spend time with Him if you're going to hear Him say, "This is the way, walk in it."
- Walking in God's will is much more rewarding and fulfilling than sulking in your own troubles. Take a look outside of yourself, look around you, and help someone else today. You'll be surprised how much God will bless you for it. ☺
- "Blessed is the man who endures temptation; for when he has been approved, he will receive the crown of life which the Lord has promised to those who love Him." James 1:12
  Trust God no matter what. You will have to endure so many kinds of temptation, but the reward makes all the hard work worth it. God never lies. His promises are TRUE!

October 19

- Encouragement from a friend: When you get tired of life treating you wrong, Don't give up because you are closer to your Blessing than you think. Hold on.
  My response: I need this more than I can say today. Thank you.
- Lemme see . . . laundry, pack a bag, toss everything in the truck, one more day at work then I'M OUTTA HERE for the weekend! Can't wait to disappear for the weekend . . . seriously need to get away from all the craziness and just chillax with my girl!
- People are never what they seem. God, on the other hand, never changes. HE will never pretend to be something He is not. You can ALWAYS count on Him!
- If you have had a difficult day, if you're feeling down, if you're struggling with hard feelings toward someone, consider picking up your Bible and read Psalms or Proverbs. Funny thing, when I read Psalms and Proverbs, I always end up in a good mood and much more thankful for what I have. Give it a try.
  God bless you always.

October 21

- "Life is too short to be stressed over small stuff." A Smart Guy I know ☺

October 22

- Enjoying an amazingly blessed weekend! Hearing God remind me, "Keep seeking Me in everything you do and I will continue to bless you." What more can a girl ask for? ☺ Feeling blessed and secure in Him.
- I am still amazed at the way God works in my life. Everything happens for a reason. Many times, I don't understand why things must happen the way they do, but occasionally, I get to see why and that is always

a tremendous blessing! Hope everyone else has had a wonderful weekend as well. ☺

- Lean not on your own understanding. Truly, if you'll just trust in the Lord, He will lead you through all of life's troubles. You will never understand everything, but if you'll truly place your trust in Him, everything will work out according to His plan. It's not always comfortable, and it's often very difficult and confusing, but God never abandons His children. ☺ Have a blessed evening!

- There is always a lesson in what you're going through. Pay attention, learn it, and put it into practice in your life, or you will have another opportunity to learn it all over again.

October 23

- Never underestimate yourself. You are capable of so much more than you realize.

- Don't let your own desires get in the way of what God has in store for your life. Our own desires often times lead us to destruction, pain, and more suffering while God's desires and direction for our lives lead us to healing, restoration, and unbelievable blessing. We just have to see past the short-term work and seemingly undesirable circumstances to see the big picture that God is forming. Keep your gaze upon Him and He will lead you through the storm and give you the strength you need.

- Breathe in . . . Breathe out . . . Since God is in control and I am not, it does not matter how impossible things look. My Heavenly Father will take care of me.

October 24

- Deserving: Other people do not DESERVE our forgiveness. True. But we did not deserve HIS forgiveness either. Think about it . . . We are called to forgive not dispense justice. That is God's job.

- Consider this: If you choose not to forgive someone, you are choosing to block your blessings. Is the wrong they did to you really worth blocking your blessings? Christ forgave us when we were still sinners, not after we begged for forgiveness. Even if you never get an apology, you must forgive so you can be right with Christ.

- FYI: Growing closer to God means tackling your demons (whatever they happen to be for you individually) one by one, and HE doesn't skip the hard ones. HE will give you knowledge, strength, and discernment; but you must be willing and able to lean on Him and voluntarily take His path when the way looks impossible. The impossibility is an illusion. HE WILL make a way where there seems to be no way.

October 25

- You've made bad decisions in the past. Everyone has. STOP beating yourself up over it and simply start making better decisions. Berating yourself is Not going to help you make better decisions. In fact, it will keep you making bad decisions because you will convince yourself that you're not capable of better. You ARE capable of better! Own it!
- "Faith isn't faith until it's all you're holding on to." Author Unknown
- Being vulnerable isn't always a bad thing. It's the only way to truly let someone in, to let others see that you're not as strong as you seem.
- When it comes right down to it, do you Really rely on God? I find myself in a place where it is just me and God, no one else to rely on, no one else to comfort me, no one can offer the comfort that Jesus can. Are you relying on the Father to comfort you, or are you finding your comfort in other people, things, or situations? I Thought I knew how to totally rely on Jesus and no one else, but HE has yet again revealed to me another opportunity I have to grow with Him alone. Thank You, Jesus, for continuing to offer me growth and comfort from the pain.

- Some things are tragic. Sometimes life is just plain difficult and confusing, but God is there with us through it all. We just have to call His name and let Him walk through this life with us and usher us into the next with Him.

October 26

- If God has given you a dream deep in your heart that looks like a complete fairy tale of impossibility, it's NOT! HE has given you the dream you are supposed to have so that you will not settle for Anything less. Embrace it, BELIEVE HIM, and WAIT for your blessing.
- Encouragement from a friend: Jesus shows Himself in our lives time and time again. He saves us and keeps us, delivers us, feeds us, shelters us, comforts us, provides for us, heals our bodies. He loves us so much that He's given us the Holy Spirit so that we can be filled with Him, yet we know Him not! He's shown us in so many ways that we can trust in Him, that whatever He says will come to pass. All He wants is for us to have a closer relationship with Him. He would like to commune with us daily. He would like to use us in a way like no other, which comes through prayer, reading, praise, worship, but how can we do that if we won't even acknowledge who He is? Jesus is Humble, Gentle. He is not here to hurt us, but to save us. Begin to give thanks and praise to God even through the storms of life, for He is God, and He is worthy to be praised. He cries out for His children because those who won't acknowledge Him will be LOST. Those who have ears, let them hear.
  My response: Holding on to this truth . . . whatever He says will come to pass . . .
- Encouragement from a friend: Impatience can lead us to take actions on our own outside of God's will.
  My response: TOO TRUE!
- "Rejoice in the Lord always; again I will say, rejoice! Let your gentle spirit be known to all men. The Lord is near.

Be anxious for nothing, but in everything by prayer and supplication with thanksgiving let your requests be made known to God. And the peace of God, which surpasses all comprehension, will guard your hearts and your minds in Christ Jesus. Finally, brethren, whatever is true, whatever is honorable, whatever is right, whatever is pure, whatever is lovely, whatever is of good repute, if there is any excellence and if anything worthy of praise, dwell on these things. The things you have learned and received and heard and seen in me, practice these things, and the God of peace will be with you." Philippians 4:4-8

- Don't settle for a partial blessing; wait on your whole blessing. Just okay (well, that'll work, it's good enough, at least it's something NOW, etc.) is not what God has planned for you. Don't short change yourself because you are tired of waiting.

- "There is surely a future hope for you, and your hope will not be cut off." Proverbs 23:18

- It is absolutely Amazing how much helping someone else makes you feel better about your own situation. When you shift your focus from your own problems to helping others with their problems, a few major things happen: (1) You stop being self-centered and start being Christ-centered as Christ was always helping others. (2) You realize you are good at helping others, giving you a sense of satisfaction and purpose. (3) You show Christ's love to others, thereby receiving blessings by doing what you have been called to do. All in all, help someone else today. It is actually good for YOU too! God bless you in all you do. ☺

- Don't get mad at God for the lack of blessing in your life when you have blocked your own blessings by holding on to the destructive influences in your life. You must allow God to purge the destructive influences and heal you so that you are able to receive all of the blessings He has stored up for you. It's up to you. What are you waiting for?

- STOP focusing on the fact that you've been hurt and START focusing on the fact that IF you LET Him, God will heal you, restore you, and place you in an even BETTER place than you were before!

October 27

- True Love doesn't take. It gives. If people in your life constantly take and don't give, maybe it's time to examine your relationships.
- Believe it or not, sometimes when people turn their back on you, it is God's way of protecting you from even More pain. Let them walk away.
- No matter how badly we've been hurt or how deep the pain goes, we are called to forgive. Who are we not to forgive when Christ forgave us? God, please help me forgive like You have.
- Encouragement from a friend: We live in a broken world full of broken people. But isn't it comforting to know God isn't ever broken? He isn't ever caught off guard, taken by surprise, or shocked by what happens next. He can take our worst and add His best. We just have to make the choice to stay with Him and keep following Him through it all.
My response: Nothing is ever too bad for God to forgive. All we have to do is ask, receive, and obey.
- "An honest answer is like a kiss on the lips." Proverbs 24:26
- Nothing is ever too bad for God to forgive. All we have to do is ask, receive, and obey.
- Caught in the Crossfire . . .
by Single Parents Rock! When we lean on The Rock on Thursday, October 27, 2011, at 5:47 p.m.
Don't get caught in the crossfire! It is easy to fall for someone who is not in a good place, someone who has past pain that they have not dealt with, someone who is angry because someone before you hurt them deeply, someone who has pain that they must deal with before they are capable of being in a healthy relationship. PLEASE take

things slow enough to accurately assess where you and your partner are emotionally. Please realize that if you rush into things because there is a strong physical attraction or if the person appears to the the 'right' kind of person . . . that you WILL get hurt, possibly very deeply, if either one of you is not in a healthy place.

Even good people, godly people act out of past pain and sometimes even rebellion or vengeance because of some traumatic event in their past. They are not bad people, but they are not healthy people either. If you want the relationship that God has for you, I can guarantee you it's not with an unhealthy person. If this is really the person that you are supposed to spend the rest of your life with, God will bring you back together after everyone has healed and is capable of treating each other in a godly, supporting, loving, appropriate fashion.

God loves you dearly and does NOT want you to settle for less than His best, HE does not want you to keep entering into unhealthy, painful relationships over and over again. HE did give you the choice though . . . you can either learn from your past mistakes, take the time to let Jesus heal you and then seek out healthy relationships OR you can persist in bad relationships (I know they look easier from the surface, but they cause so much damage and pain that they actually make your life so much more miserable!!!) and bear the consequences over and over again. Please let God guide you and do not get caught in the crossfire of past emotional baggage.

If someone walks away from you because you insist in an upright relationship . . . they are not the right person for you, they do not have the capacity or desire to be in a healthy relationship . . . they may not be ready to do things right, which means, at least for now, they're not an option. If you're the person who needs healing . . . PLEASE be considerate enough of everyone around you to take the time you need to heal before selfishly diving into something and

hurting someone else . . . even though they may appear strong, you do Not know how much pain they have had to endure to this point and the damage you inflict may be much more detrimental to them than you realize. If their faith is weak, you could even make them fall away from the Lord . . . Please lean on the Lord to heal you . . . it is actually much less painful than repeating harmful cycles of pain, hurt, distrust and violating others' trust . . .
God bless you in all you do, in all the decisions you make . . .

October 28

- Encouragement from a friend: Being judgmental and requiring accountability are two totally different things. Judgment is not up to you or me. That's for God. Accountability requires having a relationship to assist one to maintain a set standard, which means those that set the "standard" must also meet their own "standard." Practice what you preach!
  My response: Amen!
- Don't be upset when God leads you in a different direction than you want to go. Just Trust that HE knows best and follow. If you always pull against Him because of your own desires, you will never know the peace He gives when you Totally surrender your will to His.
- Have ya ever wonder, since we are ALL so very messed up, how does anyone ever manage to get it right? I've seen people who are obviously in the wrong place and acting wrong, people who are seemingly in the right place and acting wrong, and people who want you to think they're in the right place but do the right things for the wrong reasons. Does anyone ever REALLY get it right (by that, I mean have a right walk with Christ and actually have HONEST relationships with those around them)?
- Song: "Miracle of the Moment" by Steven Curtis Chapman (see Song Appendix for lyrics)

- Even though I'm not where I wanna be, I'm exactly where I'm supposed to be.
- Embrace who you are, where you are. God knows EXACTLY where you are, and HE has a great purpose for your life. Look to Him and He will show you where to step next. When you stop hating where you are and start looking Up for advice and direction, not only will your attitude get better, but your life will get better too.
- Praise God for who you are and where you are. Nothing about you is an accident.
- You ever have those moments where Jesus steps in, fills you up, wraps you up in His arms, and reminds you of all the good things in your life? He's wrapped me up tonight . . . feeling SO BLESSED! Thank you, Jesus, for the many blessings in my life. ☺

October 29

- The strong are strong because they have been refined by fire. Strong people feel deeply. Just because they don't always show their emotions doesn't mean they're immune to pain. Don't wish for strength unless you are willing to go through what it takes to achieve it.
- It is a new day, shake off the worries of yesterday, and start new today. Smile, God has great things in store for you today! Look for your blessing. What you find will surprise you. ☺ God bless you always.

October 30

- Encouragement from a friend: There is no pit too deep that Jesus cannot reach.
  There is no sorrow too strong
  that will overtake his beloved ones . . .
  And He's brought me to the wilderness
  where I will learn to sing,
  And He lets me know my barrenness
  so I will learn to lean,

even in the brokenness.
I will sing,
even in this loneliness.

- Understanding something does not necessarily make it easier to go through.
- Your past does not have the authority to determine your future, unless you give it permission. Who do you wanna be?
- Why are we so attached to the things that Will destroy us? Why we don't let them go and cling to God?
- It's fairly easy to know what we Should do but so much harder to actually DO it.
- Encouragement from a friend: When life gives you a hundred reasons to cry, remember that God has given you a thousand reasons to smile.
- You are to be a "living sacrifice." Don't take that phrase lightly.
- Emotions always fade. Don't let them dictate your actions.
- "Let your conduct be without covetousness; be content with such things as you have. For He Himself has said, 'I will never leave you nor forsake you.' So we may boldly say: 'The Lord is my helper; I will not fear. what can man do to me?'" Hebrews 13:5-6
- Breathe in . . . Breathe out . . . It's a new day . . . Let's find something to be thankful for.
- If you're devastated when someone lets you down, could it be that you were relying on them too much in the first place? Be careful where you invest your heart. People will always let you down and disappoint you, but God will never leave or forsake you. Before you get into a relationship, make sure you have God's blessing. It will save you so much pain in the long run!

October 31
- Trust: If you have always been cheated on, lied to, mistreated, and betrayed; if you don't think you can trust anyone ever again, I can promise you one thing, Jesus IS

trustworthy, you CAN trust Him to keep His promises! Don't let people stop you from growing in your faith. Jesus is worth it all, and HE will Never use you or throw you away or betray you!

- When you allow God to grow you to the point where you will not accept poor treatment from others, don't let anyone convince you you'll die alone because of it (because they WILL try, trust me, I know firsthand!). Sure, everyone messes up, but you Should require others to treat you with Real respect and love.

- Encouragement from a friend: We're never so vulnerable than when we trust someone—but paradoxically, if we cannot trust, neither can we find love or joy."
  My response: I know that's right!

- Encouragement from a friend: Love means to commit oneself without guarantee, to give oneself completely in the hope that our love will produce love in the loved person. Love is an act of faith, and whoever is of little faith is also of little love.
  My response: You are so on point for me today. Wow . . . Thank you for posting . . .

- ON TIME: Funny thing, I've been struggling with forgiveness issues, so God has placed some people in my life who have had to forgive worse things than I am being asked to forgive, and placing them blatantly in front of me so I can't miss their stories. Funny how our emotions deceive us into thinking that our issues are more painful than others' issues . . . looking around and getting a better perspective today.

- Don't be scared or ashamed to let others see how far you have fallen, how many times God has picked you up, dusted you off, forgiven you, and told you HE loves you anyway. Your testimony speaks volumes to anyone who hears to know exactly how gracious, forgiving, and loving God really is. Everyone has fallen! God can heal any wound. We just have to let Him.

- Song: "Times" by Tenth Avenue North (see Song Appendix for lyrics)
- Song: "Let it go" by Tenth Avenue North (see Song Appendix for lyrics)
- God has brought you through your trials so that you can share with others what He has done for you. I don't know about you, but I don't really listen to people who haven't been through something. It means much more coming from someone who has "been there, done that." I'm not proud of the decisions I've made in my past, but I am so very thankful that God didn't hold it against me and loves me enough to heal and restore me. I surely don't deserve His love, but He gives it lavishly anyway!
- Love someone today. Is there anyone you know who could use a smile, a cup of coffee, a conversation between friends? Could you be the person to brighten their day?
- Candid thought: It shouldn't be a matter of "not letting him 'do it,'" it should be a matter of mutual respect, that both people respect and care for each other enough to Want to WAIT and make sure it's the right relationship before anything physical happens. I know it's easier said than done, but the pain that comes with rash decisions is too great not to say what needs said.

NOVEMBER 2011

November 1

- Thank you all so very much for all of the wonderful birthday wishes! I am so blessed to have such amazing people in my life! God has been astoundingly good to me this year. I can't even begin to explain. HE is truly my rock!
- TRUTH: I can personally attest to this one, seen it firsthand! Amazing!

  "I will lead the blind by ways they have not known, along unfamiliar paths I will guide them; I will turn the darkness into light before them and make the rough places smooth. These are the things I will do; I will not forsake them." Isaiah 42:16
- Try to concentrate on your blessings instead of being dragged down by all of the frustrating things in life. When we can find the good in a situation, when we can focus on what we can learn from a situation instead of how we have been hurt. Our outlook becomes much more God-focused, enabling us to do what HE has asked us to do with an attitude that HE finds pleasing instead of slipping into unforgiveness, grumbling, and harsh feelings.
- "Let love and faithfulness never leave you; bind them around your neck, write them on the tablet of your heart. Then you will win favor and a good name in the sight of God and man. Trust in the LORD with all your heart and lean not on your own understanding; in all your ways submit to him, and he will make your paths straight." Proverbs 3:3-6
- Don't be so serious. Take some time to laugh. It'll do ya good. ☺

November 2

- "Be sincere in your love for others. Hate everything that is evil and hold tight to everything that is good. Love each other as brothers and sisters and honor others more than you do yourself. Never give up. Eagerly follow the Holy Spirit and serve the Lord. Let your hope make you glad. Be patient in time of trouble and never stop praying." Romans 12:9-12
- When God uses other people and situations in your life to teach you a lesson, don't be angry with the people or situations. They were put there to HELP you. Sometimes pain is necessary to effectively teach us what we need to learn. Be thankful for the lesson and Learn it so you won't have to go through a similar situation again! ☺
- Things look easy for other people when all they see is the surface. It's never as easy as some make it look. For the real picture, stick around long enough to look deeper. What you will find will surprise you.
- If you don't know where you're going, you'll probably not wind up there.
- "There is not a righteous man on earth who does what is right and never sins. Do not pay attention to every word people say, or you may hear your servant cursing you—for you know in your heart that many times you yourself have cursed others." Ecclesiastes 7:20-22
- "He gives power to the faint, and to him who has no might he increases strength." Isaiah 40:29

November 3

- "Faith is not a sense, nor sight, nor reason, but taking God at His word." Arthur Benoi Evans
- Think about it: Funny thing about being a child of God, HE teaches us that we are royalty and deserve the BEST. So why should you settle for being someone's "option" when you deserve to be someone's ONE AND ONLY?

- Has a strong new building ever been built on the same plot of ground as an old dilapidated building without the old building being entirely torn down first? Why do we think it is any different with us? We can't expect to see drastic changes in our lives without experiencing the painful process of tearing down old ways first.
- Just because you Have options doesn't mean that you should take them.
- Forgiveness starts with forgiving yourself.
- The YOU that you haven't forgiven is more detrimental to you than anyone else in your life.
- The ultimate bad relationship starts with a negative view of yourself.
- Never settle for being someone's "option." You deserve to be someone's ONE AND ONLY! Don't settle for second best. Anyone who can't see that you deserve their absolute BEST is Not someone who will treat you with the amount of respect and love that you deserve.
- You cannot heal from your past and move on until you OWN IT. You must accept who you have been so that you can appreciate the miraculous transformation God is waiting to perform in you. No matter how horrible your past is, GOD IS BIGGER! Trust Him. He really does have Amazing plans for your future. Just let Him drive.

November 4
- Changing your lifestyle is one thing, but actually being able to see yourself the way God sees you, that can be exceedingly difficult.
- It is easy to blame others for undesirable situations in your life. It is much harder to assess yourself, take responsibility for your own issues, and take action to address those issues.
- Taking responsibility does NOT include beating yourself up! You have been forgiven. It means turning from past bad actions and taking steps to make better decisions in the future so as not to make the same mistakes again.

- I am thankful for my job and how God has blessed me with good people to work with, an attitude of gratitude (finally, it has been a struggle) and plentiful provisions for my little family. I am abundantly Blessed!
- "Learn to put aside your own desires so that you will become patient and godly, gladly letting God have his way with you. This will make possible the next step, which is for you to enjoy other people and to like them, and finally you will grow to love them deeply." 2 Peter 1:6-7
- Don't let it shake your faith when good people treat you poorly. They're fallen too. Just rely on Jesus.
- Don't give up on yourself because you've fallen for a game once again—better disguised this time, but the same game nonetheless. Don't beat yourself up or dwell on what has happened. Simply take responsibility for your part, learn the lesson, and walk on knowing that the next time this situation appears, you will be much better equipped to handle it. Learn, grow, and reach your purpose! God bless you in all you do and say.
- Encouragement from a friend: "Now faith is being sure of what we hope for and certain of what we do not see." Hebrews 11:1
  "I can trust the One who has my best interest in mind." A. W. Tozer
  My response: ☺ Absolutely True! ☺

November 5

- I'm tired of letting the bad stuff drag me down. I've made a million mistakes in my life and am guaranteed to make more, but I have been forgiven, and I claim it! I am living in my Blessing from right now forward. I refuse to feel lonely for choosing the right road anymore because God's got my back!
- You may think it's strange, but cleaning the house makes me feel good on the inside too. ☺ Love it when my girl and I have a productive day!

- Encouragement from a friend: Doing a quick heart check: "This people honors me with their lips but their heart is far from me." Matthew 15:8
My response: It amazes me sometimes that we don't realize that others treat God's people the same way they treated Christ when He was on earth. We get so baffled when people put on the illusion of Christ and still walk in the ways of the world. We shouldn't be so shocked. People have been doing this for centuries.
- "Knowing how to want what you need more than what you want, will prove life's maturities." Eric Maurice Clark, *The Experience (Near to Death)*
- I have often wondered what exactly God requires of me. This verse speaks to that point directly: "He has showed you, O man, what is good. And what does the Lord require of you? To act justly and to love mercy and to walk humbly with your God." Micah 6:8
- "What I want from you is your true thanks; I want your promises fulfilled. I want you to trust me in your times of trouble, so I can rescue you, and you can give me glory." Psalm 50:14-15
- Funny how we want God to rescue us from our troubled circumstances, yet we do not want to let go of certain things and people in our lives. If God is trying to remove someone or something from your life, LET HIM. It hurts terribly bad right now, but it will hurt much more in the long run if you don't let Him. HE knows what is causing you harm. Trust Him!
- Focus on Jesus and He will bless you in ways that you haven't yet dreamed of.

November 6
- Song: "Battle" by Chris August (see Song Appendix for lyrics)
- I'm thankful this morning for everything, good and bad ups and downs. If any of it was different, I wouldn't be

where I am today, and I've been abundantly blessed. Who could ask for more?

- Our society says, "It's all about me, my success (as defined by money and status), my desires, and my happiness." Our God says, "It's all about ME. You get the privilege of being my servant and laying down your life for my sake. In return, you can spend eternity with Me in glory." Which will I choose? I choose to sacrifice now and receive my Eternal reward! ☺
- "Your tears are your water for your blessings. Don't be afraid to water your blessings." Eric Maurice Clark
- "Letting go of people who mean you no good is very important. Learn how to not let anyone control your actions. Don't give up due to other people's judgment of what they think of you." Eric Maurice Clark
- If you step out into what God is asking you to do, He will replace your desires with His and fill you to the brim with His joy and contentment. Your circumstances do NOT determine your worth! God made you a priceless Child of the King. Claim your inheritance.
- "Give, and it will be given to you: good measure, pressed down, shaken together, and running over will be put into your bosom. For with the same measure that you use, it will be measured back to you." Luke 6:38

November 7

- I'm tryin' to walk by faith, not by sight.
- No one is above the struggles of this world. Don't hold it against anyone when they fall. Just do your best to help them up, encourage them, and get back on the right path. God's love has NO boundaries! For God so loved THE WORLD . . . ☺
- Cold outside, warm inside . . . It's a perfect night to be in my comfy clothes, curled up with a warm cup of coffee, and my Daddy's Book. ☺

- "Take your evil deeds out of my sight! Stop doing wrong, learn to do right! Seek justice, encourage the oppressed. Defend the cause of the fatherless, plead the case of the widow." Isaiah 1:16-17
- Never underestimate the impact that YOUR actions, words, and opinions have on others. You have the power to either lift someone else up or irreparably damage them. You may not think something is a "big deal," but to someone else . . . well . . . it could be absolutely devastating! God bless you in all you do and say.
- I needed this encouragement today, so I thought I'd pass it along to you: "Fear not, for I am with you; Be not dismayed, for I am your God. I will strengthen you, Yes, I will keep you, I will uphold you with My righteous right hand." Isaiah 41:10
- You know, it's okay to be broken. In fact, it's GOOD to be broken . . . (Broken before the Lord that is.) You see, God can't use people who are so full of themselves that they won't listen to Him. God can use people who are broken of their own will and selfish desires, people who are actively looking to Him and listening diligently for His guidance because they know that His ways are infinitely better than their own. LET God use you. You will be amazed at how He will bless your life!
- Know your worth. ☺

November 8
- Morning algebra: Life - Christ = no hope + death; Life + Christ = Hope + eternal life
- Ya ever get the feeling that you're on the edge of something So much bigger? Yeah . . . Feelin' a pull that I can't explain and dunno where it will lead . . .
- At one forty-eight tomorrow, my baby girl will officially be SIXTEEN years old! Wow . . . can't believe the time has gone by so Very Fast! Jaquilyn, you are my heart and have been since the day you were born. I hope you know

how very much you mean to me! I am so very proud of you I can't possibly put it into words. You have grown into a Beautiful young lady. I pray that God continues to bless you, keep you safe, and close to Him. LOVE YOU, BABY GIRL! I hope you have a Wonderful Birthday tomorrow. ☺

- At the request of my daughter, supper tonight is baked salmon and mixed veggies. YUM! I LOVE my girl!
- Song: "Where I Belong" by Building 429 (see Song Appendix for lyrics)
- Song: "Everything I Need" by Kutless (see Song Appendix for lyrics)
- Song: "That's What Faith Can Do" by Kutless (see Song Appendix for lyrics)
  My comment: Definitely worth listening to!
- Song: "Lose My Soul" by Toby Mac (see Song Appendix for lyrics)
  My comment: Awesome song!
- Purpose . . . Your purpose . . . Have you ever Really thought about it, prayed on it, diligently sought it out . . . and been ready for the answer no matter what it is . . . and ready to embrace it no matter what?

November 9
- Sometimes we are required to wait on God. TRUST Him.
- Maturity: As we mature, we're expected to slowly take more responsibility, accept and succeed at more difficult tasks, and help others learn what we have already mastered. Spiritual maturity is no different. It's time to take it to the next level.
- Overcome your past. Don't ignore it. Let it make you better.
- I am thankful for my beautiful daughter who turns sixteen years old today. I wouldn't change a thing because that might change who she has turned out to be, and I can't

possibly imagine a better young lady to be my daughter. I love you, girl!

- Just in case you're wondering, if God has given you a task, he has given you the ability to accomplish it. Trust Him and give yourself some credit. HE knows you're capable.
- If you have a gift, focus and use it. It's part of your blessing.
- Sometimes God wants us to be close to Him and walk with Him, only Him, hand in hand for a season. There are so many reasons for this, but the reasons He has shown me are to ensure that I am truly relying on Him (not some other person or situation), to grow my faith, to make me more firm in my convictions, and to clarify HIS purpose for my life. HE wants to show you who you were made to be in Him. Sometimes the best way to do that is to empty out our lives of everyone and everything else that is not in the right place.
- When the chips are down, who do you go to for help? Who's that first call, the one you go to ease your mind enough to think straight? Who do you truly rely on to pick you up when you make that huge mistake? Did God make it in the list?

November 10

- I am thankful to have another day of walking in His purpose for my life. I don't deserve the abundant blessings He has bestowed on me, I deserve death, but He gives me life. What a gracious God we have!
- I am thankful for a job that allows for sick days.
- Journals are wonderful things for those of us who need to express ourselves! If I have a thought, it Must come out. Sometimes it's just better if it doesn't come out in public.
- "The Lord can rescue you and me from the temptations that surround us." 2 Peter 2:9

- "Don't let the world around you squeeze you into its own mold, but let God remake you so that your whole attitude of mind is changed." Romans 12:1
- "Sexual sin is never right; our bodies were not made for that but for the Lord, and the Lord wants to fill our bodies with himself." 1 Corinthians 6:13
- Believe God's promises for your life and reject the world's lies. The lies are many and loud and come at us every single day, but God's promises are everlasting and cannot be diminished by anything that the world hurls our way. Lean on His promises. They are True.
- What can you do to help someone else? What can you do to share what you have learned through your experiences to help someone else avoid trouble? It only takes a minute to share a kind or wise word with someone. You never know how you could change someone's life just by lending them a hand. God bless you in all you do and say.
- When you let your fears motivate you, you let the enemy win.

November 11

- Don't judge others even if you are hurt by their actions. You have no idea what they are going through. Extend Grace to them. You would want them to do the same for you. No one likes to air their dirty laundry, and no one owes you any explanation. Go to God for your comfort and healing.
- To all my fellow veterans and all those currently serving in our country's active duty military, THANK YOU for your service and sacrifice! God bless you and yours always!
- I am thankful for every single horribly frustrating situation in my life. Without them, I wouldn't be nearly as motivated to keep running! Who knew frustration could keep a girl so fit? ☺
- We need to practice extending grace to others when they don't "deserve" it, when we know that we are not going

to achieve something on our own agenda by doing so. We should not show grace to others only when we know they will respond favorably and we will gain something out of the situation. Show grace when you have nothing to gain, but the knowledge that you are doing what you are supposed to do. God sees selfish motives.

- God is always with me. ☺
- "The LORD is righteous in all His ways, gracious in all His works. The LORD is near to all who call upon Him, to all who call upon Him in truth. He will fulfill the desire of those who fear Him; He also will hear their cry and save them." Psalm 145:17-19
- Love people for who they are, not what they are.

November 12

- I'm thankful that my daughter can drive. We're going to the beauty shop and I get to kick back and enjoy the ride. ☺
- I believe in the impossible. ALL things are possible through Him who gives me strength! ALL things . . . ☺ "He will fulfill the desire of those who fear Him; He also will hear their cry and save them." Psalm 145:19
- Don't be ashamed of your history. Without it, you would never have arrived at your present.

November 13

- Your story: YOUR story is Not intended to be your own. You are not to make your decisions with no consultation from your Father. The purpose of your life is to sacrifice it to Live for HIM. When we do this, our lives reflect HIS glory instead of our own mistakes. Will you let Him clean up your mess and bless you, or will you continue to walk in your own ways and leave a trail of destruction?
- "Do not be afraid or discouraged because of this vast army. For the battle is not yours, but God's . . . You will not have to fight this battle. Take up your positions; stand firm and

see the deliverance the Lord will give to you. Do not be afraid; do not be discouraged . . ." 2 Chronicles 20:15, 17

- Believe the revelations that God gives you about people. What you see with your own eyes can be deceiving.
- You are significant. You are important. You have a story to tell that someone else needs to hear. Don't be ashamed. Tell your story, ALL of it; God gave you a testimony to share with others to glorify HIM. God bless you in all you do and say.

November 14

- Things aren't always as they seem on the surface. Wait for God's guidance.
- "Stop giving someone else the job of making you happy." Joyce Meyer Ministries
- "Forget the former things; do not dwell on the past. See, I am doing a new thing! Now it springs up; do you not perceive it? I am making a way in the desert and streams in the wasteland." Isaiah 43:19
- Being single is not a sickness, a disease, or a malfunction; it does not mean that there is something wrong with you! Being single is simply a lifestyle. Seek out a relationship with Jesus first, and HE will fill all your gaps. Simply having a partner in life doesn't "fix" anything. Singleness is not something that needs to be "fixed" anyway. God made you COMPLETE just the way you are!
- No wonder so many single people think that they're not complete. So many mainstream songs have lyrics that enforce that thought or talk about sex and relationships like they're the end all to be all. Don't buy into the scheme. God is the only ONE who can truly complete you. If you are looking for someone else to complete you, you will always end up terribly disappointed. People just aren't made to complete other people. We are made to compliment, help, and love other people, and we all make

mistakes all the time. Without God's love and grace, no relationship stands a chance.

- "Know therefore that the LORD your God, He is God, the faithful God, who keeps His covenant and His loving-kindness to a thousandth generation with those who love Him and keep His commandments." Deuteronomy 7:9
- "Submit yourselves therefore to God. Resist the devil and he will flee from you. Draw near to God and he will draw near to you." James 4:7-8

November 15

- Retraining your mind to focus on the good instead of the bad is a constant battle. Forming healthy habits in place of defensive old habits takes time. Don't let frustration with slow progress derail you. It's impossible to make permanent changes overnight.
- I'm STOKED to be able to walk into the next phase of His will for my life! I've been blessed with another Wonderful opportunity to help others through the very things that God has helped me through in my life. What an amazing opportunity! I'm so very thankful I can't put it into words! Thank you, Jesus, for yet another opportunity to shine your light into the dark places, to show others what you have done for me and give them the glimmer of hope that they need to learn to lean on YOU. ☺ I couldn't feel more blessed right now!
- "The Lord Almighty has sworn, 'Surely, as I have planned, so it will be, and as I have purposed, so it will stand.'" Isaiah 14:24
- Consider this: If you got married right this minute, you would still have all the issues you currently have. None of them would magically disappear. So why not take advantage of the time and space you have while you are still single to work on your issues? Get it all worked out between you and God. That way, when HE does bring that special person into your life, you won't have to trudge

through a ton of past baggage before you can enjoy your lives together.

November 16
- In hectic moments, it can be difficult to feel God's love. Take a minute, find some silence, and just BE with God. You will feel His love when you're simply still in His presence.
- Song: "All of Me" by Matt Hammitt (see Song Appendix for lyrics)
- Song: "TRUST" by Matt Hammitt (see Song Appendix for lyrics)
  My comment: GREAT song . . . Don't forget how good God is
- Sometimes I wonder are teenage girls ever happy for more than five minutes at a time?
- If people in your world insist on playing games, let them keep on playin' with someone else. You deserve better! Let them walk away.
- When God says it, He will do it. Rest easy in Him. You're not in control anyway. ☺ God bless all you do and say. Cast all your cares on Him and keep your faith.

November 17
- There is no better way to get perspective than to read God's word. It is His love letter to us. ☺
- Be the person God created you to be. You are BEAUTIFUL!
- If you can do what you're passionate about full time, you are Blessed! Maybe I'll get there someday. ☺
- Overheard a conversation today about being single versus married . . . People still think that the main reason and perk for getting married is for physical gratification . . . Made me sad . . . It's NOT all about Sex! Wish more people understood God's Truth about marriage . . .

- Song: "UNCONDITIONAL" by Tedashii (see Song Appendix for lyrics)
  My comment: Relearn to love . . .
  UNCONDITIONAL . . . Great song!
- Song: "Beautiful Feet" by LeCrae (see Song Appendix for lyrics)
- KIDS: We all know that children of any age can be exceedingly difficult at times. It is much easier to be patient with our children when we realize how patient God has had to be with us (we are HIS children). God has been more patient with me than I can fathom. Show some grace to your children. They're a work in progress too. God bless you in all you do and say.
- Relationships take work, so why ignore your relationship with God?
- Dying is PAINFUL. Why should we expect dying to self to be easy? Christ never promised it would be easy. In fact, He asked us to take up our crosses and follow Him. Carrying a cross is HARD. The good news is that we don't have to do it alone. We can give our burdens to Him when we sacrifice ourselves and relentlessly pursue HIS will for our lives. Let Jesus be your soft place to fall. Let Him renew you daily so that you can continue to follow Him and receive His blessings.

November 18

- Just as soon as I get frustrated and short tempered, God reminds me to be kind and compassionate to others because HE has been kind and compassionate to me. God is so good!
- Unashamed: Even when the desires of your heart go against society's accepted "norms," when the path that God has planned for you causes your family and friends to raise an eyebrow and wonder why you're breaking out of what they expect of you and ridicule your choices, God has a plan for you. Embrace it. Don't let people make you

deny God's plan for your life just because it doesn't match their expectations of you. God works everything for the good of those who love Him. Trust Him. Follow Him UNASHAMED.

- Other people weren't made to meet your every need. It's not all about you. It is ALL about God

- LONELY: When your heart is broken and bleeding, longing to be truly loved, don't let the world convince you that you're not loved at all, that you're not worth loving. Let our Heavenly Father wrap you up in His love, in His word, His promises for your life. Lean on the truth that Jesus gave His very life for you, and His love means more than any humanly love in this world. Let our Creator comfort you with His everlasting love. Let Him wrap you up in His arms and bandage your heart to stop the bleeding. He will quell the aching of your heart's desire, and thwart the lies of this world. God bless and keep you always.

- When you relearn love God's way and stop believing the false "love" that the world describes and offers, it Will break your heart, and you will begin to see things more clearly from God's eyes. Your heart will yearn for real love and closeness with Jesus, and slowly, your relationships in this world will begin to reflect Christ's love for the church. This is the kind of love that is meant to be reflected in marriage.

November 19

- Being God-centered (focusing on what God is telling you to do in your life) = unexplainable joy, contentment, and peace in the midst of trouble
  Being Self-centered (focusing on what you want to do in your life) = frustration, stress, resentment, and a feeling that the world owes you something

- Backward? Nope. When I keep my eyes on the Lord instead of what I think I want, HE brings me in line with

His will and blesses me with the right things in the right way and the right time. I'm often like a thirteen-year-old who wants her license already, RIGHT NOW! LOL. It would be dangerous if God gave us everything we want right when we want it. Sometimes we're just not ready for our blessings yet. Learn the lessons and wait for your blessing. HIS timing is always best!

- God's love is UNCONDITIONAL! You don't have to earn it. God made you. HE loves you just the way you are.

- Attitude and Focus: Funny thing, my attitude gets much better about whatever situation I'm going through when I stay focused on Jesus. As easy as it is to slip back into negative thinking and self-pity because I don't like whatever is going on, if I stay focused on God's word and His promises for my life, my attitude improves. He has shown me so many times that my own motives aren't only selfish, but they're terribly short-sighted. God's plan for my future is so much more abundant than I can imagine (with my limited sight and constantly underestimating my capabilities) that I always end up shooting for a lesser mark than He has in mind. Trust God's plan for your life, let go of your perceived control, and let HIM guide you into the marvelous future He has for you. With God's help, we can do all that He asks of us, and we get to receive HIS blessings for walking in His will. Who could possibly ask for more? Be blessed in all you say and do. ☺

November 20
- I'm thankful for another beautiful day to spend with my daughter. Time is so very precious.
- Thought: Without the rough spots in life, the places you're embarrassed of, the things that you're tempted to leave out when you give your testimony because they're so ugly, without those events in your life, your testimony loses impact. God met you in those places. He didn't say, "I won't go there. That place is too ugly for Me." NO! He met

you there so He could rescue, heal, and restore you so you could fulfill His purpose for your life. Share ALL of your story. Someone else is in the ugly place you'd like to forget ever existed, and they NEED Hope! Just like you did . . .

- Song: "Faithful" by Brooke Fraser (see Song Appendix for lyrics)
- Powerful truth dear to my heart in this season of my life: "Learn to put aside your own desires so that you will become patient and godly, gladly letting God have his way with you. This will make possible the next step, which is for you to enjoy other people and to like them, and finally you will grow to love them deeply." 2 Peter 1:6-7
- The closer you get to Jesus, the less appealing the things of the world become.
- Why give thanks when the situation is bad? Because, as Christians, we know that God works everything for the good of those who love Him. Look for the lesson, put aside your own personal wants and desires, and embrace the blessings that God has for your life. Always give thanks for everything with full confidence that God knows what is best for us much better than we do.
- "Those who trust in the Lord are steady as Mount Zion, unmoved by any circumstance. Just as the mountains surround and protect Jerusalem, so the Lord surrounds and protects his people." Psalm 125:1-2

November 21

- God is loving, honest, and just. Do not make the mistake of attributing human traits to Him. HE is not deceitful, scheming, or cruel. HE truly Loves you.
- A quitter never wins, and a winner never quits.
- Never doubt your purpose. EVERYTHING happens for a reason, yes, even the bad things. God will make everything work for the good of those who love Him. Learn the lessons, listen to His leading, and He will show you how to

walk in the purpose for which HE created you! Trust Him, and you will receive abundant blessings!

"And we know that God causes all things to work together for good to those who love God, to those who are called according to His purpose." Romans 8:28

- Faith, Fallenness, and Grace . . . Not Disgrace . . . by Single Parents Rock! When we lean on The Rock on Monday, November 21, 2011, at 4:00 p.m.

If you have been around the church for any amount of time at all, you have probably figured out that leaders are NOT perfect people. In fact, some of you may have walked away from a church because of something a leader did or said that you saw as wrong . . . and they very well could have been wrong. You see . . . just like 'moms are people too,' leaders are fallen too. No one in this world is immune from falling, saying the wrong thing, doing the wrong thing, thinking evil thoughts, walking outside of God's will, etc . . . Everyone falls, some are in more of a public place when they fall, but EVERYONE FALLS! God flipped the script on me and showed me something very simple about this situation . . . He put me in the shoes of the 'leadership position' and then continued to show me all of my short comings and struggles . . . all the while, He had been growing me immensely, so I was able to guide other people through their troubles, help others rely on Him and even dispense the answers to my own struggles and issues, but . . . I couldn't manage to put them to practice entirely in my own life because of deep seed hurt and pain from my past. God is continuing to heal me, but HE has given me a whole new perspective on giving grace to other people, especially leaders in the faith. We ALL need God's grace, and we should ALL remember that no one is immune to the fall, no one should be put on a pedestal. In fact, I would encourage everyone to pray for those who are in leadership in the faith in ANY capacity. We ALL need prayer continuously to enable us to continue to walk in God's will for our lives.

Please extend grace to everyone instead of heaping disgrace on their shoulders when what they really need is prayer. God bless you in all you do and say.

- I was stressed until I realized just how blessed I am today . . . Seeing all the difficult times in the past begin to pay off, get to use those tough experiences to help others . . . God is good all the time. HE can bring good out of ANYTHING!

November 22

- I SO love my girl When she's not feeling well, she wants homemade chili, of all things. LOL. Oh well . . . homemade chili, it is. ☺
- Song: "More than a Friend" by Jeremy riddle (see Song Appendix for lyrics)
- Believe it. Receive it. You have WON already, WON through our Lord and Savior Jesus Christ! HE has already gained the victory. All we have to do is believe His word, obey His direction, and receive His blessings! Praise the LORD! With news like this, who can be sad? God has given us the VICTORY! ☺
- Don't look for your worth in the eyes of other people. Be confident and rest in the knowledge that you are so valuable and desired by God that HE sent His Son who made the ultimate sacrifice for you. HE relentlessly pursues you all the days of your life because He wants to spend ETERNITY with you! You couldn't possibly BE more LOVED.

November 23

- Crossing the chasm: To cross safely to the other side, stay focused on YOUR tasks at hand. The quickest way to fall to your death is to look at others and get distracted by what they are doing. When you're distracted, you WILL lose your footing and fall.

- "O give thanks to the LORD, for He is good; For His loving-kindness is everlasting." 1 Chronicles 16:34

November 24

- I'm enjoying a very blessed day, spending Thanksgiving with my sister and my daughter, precious time together with our Jesus. ☺
- Sometimes the smallest things have the greatest impact. Never underestimate your influence.

November 25

- When holidays are difficult, remember where your strength truly comes from. HE will never leave us alone even if we feel alone.
- Victory: "Don't hate the player, hate the game"? I don't think so . . . Rise above the game. The victory has already been won. Claim it!
- We had a very nice Thanksgiving. I'm so very thankful for my daughter! Jaquilyn, you make my heart burst, so proud of you! Thank you for being you. ☺

November 26

- Mind game: Don't let your mind be distracted. "You will keep in perfect peace him whose mind is steadfast, because he trusts in You." Isaiah 26:3
- Helping hands don't have to be especially talented; they just have to be willing to help. Small simple things, many times, mean more to people than grand gestures.
- Show someone a little extra love today. Holidays can be very difficult. Perk someone up today. Be their bright spot, their smile. Be that giggle that they need to break the monotony.

November 27

- Encouragement from a friend: All of us are affected by what other people think, say, and do in response to who we are. Yet if pleasing other people becomes the goal, you will spend the rest of your life chasing down your critics. If satisfying the critics becomes your goal, you'll never have peace. God knows you and loves you unconditionally. Remember that you serve the Living King and not the critics.

- Encouragement from a friend: The truth of the matter is no one knows your destiny except God. Other people may see your potential or have some idea about the direction you are headed to, but no one can get you there except God. Therefore, you must seek God for your predestined purpose and make your decisions line up with His will.

- Removal of unrealistic expectations + accepting and caring for someone regardless of their faults = the beginning of an honest relationship

- Observation: When I'm busy doing what God has called me to do, it is much more difficult to be frustrated or grouchy about what I do not yet have.

- YOU have great things to offer to others in this world. No matter how small or insignificant you think your talents are, GOD knows that you and your talents are VERY IMPORTANT to HIS work. Never underestimate how your contribution will affect others in the name of Jesus. God bless you in all you do and say!

- What you are going through is not in vain! Our Father will make you better through it, stronger for it. God will give you a strong testimony and renewed purpose for your life if you let Him lead you and don't give up.
"Surely it was for my benefit that I suffered such anguish. In Your love You kept me from the pit of destruction; You have put all my sins behind Your back. For the grave cannot praise You, death cannot sing Your praise; those who go down to the pit cannot hope for Your faithfulness.

The living, the living—they praise You, as I am doing today; fathers tell their children about Your faithfulness." Isaiah 38:17-19
Praise God always; HE brings us closer to Him through all of our trials.

- "Why do you say, O Jacob, and complain, O Israel [meaning God's people], 'My way is hidden from the Lord; my cause is disregarded by my God'? Do you not know? Have you not heard? The Lord is the everlasting God, the Creator of the ends of the earth. He will not grow tired or weary, and his understanding no one can fathom. He gives strength to the weary and increases the power of the weak. Even youths grow tired and weary, and young men stumble and fall; but those who hope in the Lord will renew their strength. They will soar on wings like eagles; they will run and not grow weary, they will walk and not be faint." Isaiah 40:27-31

November 28

- Thank You, Jesus, for all of the blessings in my life! You are so much more than I deserve. You blow my mind every single day with your kindness, love, and grace!
- Encourage those around you. Be kind, thoughtful, and put the feelings of others above your need to be right. Show God's love in all you do and say. May God bless you always!
- "I took you from the ends of the earth, from its farthest corners I called you. I said, 'You are my servant'; I have chosen you and have not rejected you. So do not fear, for I am with you; do not be dismayed, for I am your God. I will strengthen you and help you; I will uphold you with my righteous right hand. All who rage against you will surely be ashamed and disgraced; those who oppose you will be as nothing and perish." Isaiah 41:9-11
- How does God feel about you? This just struck me as I was reading in Isaiah. God is addressing His people, and He

says, "Since you are precious and honored in my sight, and because I love you . . ." Isaiah 43:4 and "Bring my sons from afar and my daughters from the ends of the earth—everyone who is called by my name, whom I created for my glory, whom I formed and made." Isaiah 43:6-7. Not only are we precious and honored in His sight, but we're loved and we were each individually crafted, limited editions, made especially to glorify God. So the next time you think you're not worth it, THINK about it for a minute. The Creator of the universe took the time to specially craft you, make you just exactly like you are for HIS glory and to call you by name. I'd say you're worth more than you realize! God bless you always!

November 29
- Daily giving up my desires to pursue HIS plan for my life . . . Not easy, but I must remember it brings abundant blessings . . . #gottastayfocusednsacrificeself
- Warning Signs: Don't ignore warning signs when you see them, regardless how much you wish they weren't there! Working through a bad situation is much harder than heeding the warning signs in the beginning. #been2hurt2settleagain
- Live your life. Pay attention. Learn the lessons. Grow in your Faith. Don't waste time repeating the same mistakes over and over. Claim your blessings, Receive the Joy and Peace that come with knowing Jesus better. Be Blessed!
- Encouragement from a friend: "And now, in these final days, he has spoken to us through his Son. God promised everything to the Son as an inheritance, and through the Son, he created the universe." Hebrews 1:2 NLT
Jesus was God's agent in creating the world. As followers of Christ, we may give easy assent to this truth but deny it in practice. We may believe that Christ knows and controls the laws of heaven (pertaining to salvation and spiritual growth), but we may act each day as though our financial,

family, or medical problems are beyond his reach. If Jesus could create the universe, then no part of life is out of control. Do not exclude Jesus's wisdom and the Bible's guidance in your complex problems of life. No expert, professor, doctor, lawyer, or financial advisor knows more about your ultimate security and well-being than Jesus does.

Go first to God for advice. Talk to him in prayer and listen to him in his Word. He can sustain you in times of stress. From that perspective, you can evaluate all the other wisdom and help made available to you.

My response: Something to think about . . .

- Only heart change brings life change.
- Thank You, Lord, for another day to make a difference.
- If you're so tired of being alone that you're willing to let someone treat you poorly, step back! You are God's child, a child of the KING, and you deserve to be treated with full love and respect. Don't settle for anything less because you're tired of facing each day alone. You are Not truly alone. God is with you. I know it doesn't seem like enough sometimes, but that is just the lie that the enemy wants you to believe. If you realize your REAL worth in Christ, the devil would be in big trouble! Don't be deceived by the deceiver, hold on to your worth in Christ, and HE will see you through. #persistinChristHELovesU
- It is absolutely amazing how free you feel when you stop carrying your past around with you everywhere. You are NOT bound by who you have been in the past. Forgive yourself; God has already forgiven you. Just claim it!

November 30

- God wants to bless us in EVERY area of our lives. If we're holding back, trying to maintain control or trying to justify immoral actions in Anything, we are blocking God's blessing for our lives. And Since others are always watching us, as Christians, if we're not walking the walk we profess in Every part of our lives, we could easily cause others to turn away from Jesus. Give it ALL to Him!

- Nontraditional . . . odd? I don't think so! ☺ Those of us who are traveling a nontraditional road know how people look at us sometimes, like we're just a bit "odd" to say the least. LOL. I've come to realize that God is in charge of the road I have ahead of me, and if people think it is "odd" . . . well, that's okay with me. I'd much rather live to please my Heavenly Father than to please people. #livin4myeternalreward

- Origin of my confidence: "For You are my hope; O Lord GOD, You are my confidence from my youth." Psalm 71:5

- Hey, guess what? Yes, I'm talking to YOU! YOU are priceless, you deserve the best, you are worth the effort! Let Jesus take your hand and bless your life Abundantly! God bless you always.

- God NEVER lies. God has called YOU to be a light in this world. Meet Him and answer His call, and HE will heal you and bless your life beyond what you can imagine.
  "I, the Lord, speak the truth; I declare what is right." Isaiah 45:19b
  "See, I have refined you, though not as silver; I have tested you in the furnace of affliction." Isaiah 48:10
  "Before I was born the Lord called me; from my birth he has made mention of my name." Isaiah 49:1b
  "For I am honored in the eyes of the Lord and my God has been my strength . . ." Isaiah 49:5b
  "I will also make you a light for the Gentiles, that you may bring my salvation to the ends of the earth." Isaiah 49:6b

DECEMBER 2011

December 1

- REALLY? Walking in God's will for my life is more fulfilling than Any human relationship? REALLY! Being obedient and living God's will for your life truly IS more fulfilling than Any human relationship! I didn't believe it either until I tried it. God truly does supply our every need when we set our minds on Him.
- If you're looking for a meaningful way to give this Christmas, please consider giving to a wonderful local ministry serving single women and their children. ☺
- Don't get distracted. Stay focused on the ONE relationship that matters more than any other, the relationship between you and your Heavenly Father. If we do not maintain a healthy active relationship with Jesus, every other relationship in our lives will suffer. Without Christ's grace, love, forgiveness, and kindness in our hearts, we cannot treat others as we should. Christ shouldn't just be in the middle of Christmas. HE should be right smack in the middle of our everyday lives! God bless and keep you always.

December 2

- Even when you have grown and moved past a destructive phase in your life, it will try to recapture you. Stand firm. Don't revisit past mistakes. Keep your eyes on Jesus and let Him lead you into your future.
- No matter how hectic today has been, just remember GOD IS IN CONTROL! No need to worry or stew. You are in our Heavenly Father's loving hands. ☺"
- Song: "Bout Time Full" by Tedashii (feat. Cam) (see song Appendix for lyrics)

My comment on the song: Never works the other way . . . 'bout time we do this thing right.

- Song: "Kingdom People" by Tedashii - He Cares Feat. Keynon Akers (see Song Appendix for lyrics)
- Always maintain your integrity. Don't let others aggravate you into acting poorly. Take a minute, compose yourself, and treat people how you would like them to treat you, even when they're out of line.
- When someone tries to pull you into a destructive conversation, opt out! God cannot be glorified in a conversation that was meant to destroy. God calls us to build each other up, not tear each other down.
- Check your thoughts: Destructive thoughts quickly turn into destructive actions.

December 4
- We are to love others and plant the seed of God's love in their hearts and lives, then step back and allow God to work as HE sees fit. We are to show God's love in the world. HE is the SAVIOR. God, please help us recognize our place, perform what you have called us to do in humility, and not try to occupy a role meant for the ONE who truly saves.
- "God wants to give us the power to overcome wrong motives and intentions if we'll humble ourselves to ask and receive it rather than trying to handle it on our own." Joyce Meyers Ministries
- WONDERFUL to have actual PRAISE and WORSHIP in a Sunday morning service! ☺
- Sitting in the VIP section of the Crowder concert with my girl and they're playin' LeCrae while we wait! How cool is that! ☺☺☺
- Try to always look at others through God's eyes. Try not to project your expectations on other people. It's not your measuring stick that they must live up to, and it's not your job to measure. Give everyone grace and remember

you're just as messed up as they are and God still loves you!
#stayhumbledandforgivedaily

It's not about Rules. It's about your heart. To have a real
Relationship with our Heavenly Father, HE has to have
your heart. Ask yourself: Where is my heart. What do I
value most? What do I allow to cause me the most pain?
What do I do everything to protect? What or who do I
TRULY love more than anything else? Is there anything
that would "devastate" me if it collapsed? Examine yourself
honestly, just between you and Jesus, and give it ALL to
Him. HE will heal you if you let Him. God bless and keep
you close to His heart always!

- Opposite day? Funny thing, the more you give God, the
  more He blesses you! In the world, the more you give, the
  more other people take. God is not like that! The more
  you surrender your life to Him, the more HE heals you
  and blesses your life and legacy. Thank you, Jesus, for
  being so gracious to us. We could never deserve it, but You
  desire us. We will never fully understand why you love us
  so much. Please keep touching our hearts and lives and
  pulling us closer to You.

December 5

- Job Uncertainty: We can be secure in Jesus's arms. Trust
  His guidance, security, and protection no matter what
  happens with your job. God works everything for good for
  those who love Him.
- Saying NO is easy? Guess what? I found something out
  that you all should know. When you get yourself to a
  healthy place spiritually, it actually becomes much easier
  to make the right decisions and tell people who "only want
  one thing" NO! ☺ The hard work DOES pay off. Stay on
  course. Brighter days are ahead, and things really DO get
  easier! It's never going to be a cakewalk, but when we rely
  on Jesus to lead us and truly trust Him, it's not hard to say
  NO to destructive habits of the past. The habit no longer

has a hold on you, so you're free to have Faith and move forward with a healthy life. ☺ Praise God!

- Breathe in . . . Breathe out . . . The day is just about done . . . Time to relax for a minute, decompress, and hit the sack . . . God bless you all . . . Sleep well.

December 6

- Praise God for the situation you're in. It's exactly where you need to be to do what He has called you to do! There is infinitely more blessing in His will than there would be in what you wish for in your own will.
- Be inspired. Let the Holy Spirit inspire you and WALK IN IT. ☺ Whatever it is, HE will never lead you astray. Trust Him.
- Have you ever been so excited about where you are that it's hard to concentrate on the day-to-day stuff? I'm so very excited! GOTTA focus though . . . okay . . . Gotta get back to work . . . Yeah, okay . . . Seriously . . . LOL.
- Love yourself enough to make healthy choices for your life. Don't let anyone convince you that you're not good enough or that your goals are "out of reach for you." Allow yourself to see your own potential and strive for your goals. YOU CAN DO IT! God bless you in all you do.

December 7

- "I believe it, I receive it, it is done . . . already done. ☺" 21:03
- God is moving. HE is mighty! He has answered prayer for me so powerfully today it is amazing! HE will do the same for you. Believe it, receive it, it is done . . . already done (inspired by a song by 21:03). God has completed His good work. We must have faith and walk closely with Him. HE has already won the victory for us. We just have to claim it! Praise God!

December 8
- My God is my Guide.
- Only have one errand to run . . . then I get to enjoy a nice quiet evening at home . . . ☺

December 9
- Just because you've never seen it or felt it doesn't mean it is impossible.
- One more month and my girl should be done with her braces! Yea!
- When one lifestyle is all you've ever known, it is incredibly difficult to break out of it and form healthier habits. Show those around you some grace today.
- Man, life is messy!
- When you fall down, don't beat yourself up. Simply get back up, dust yourself off, and start again. Just try not to let the same bump trip you up again.

December 10
- Thank You, Lord for, another day and yet another chance to get it right that I surely do not deserve.
- God is good, God is strong, HE is MIGHTY, and HE is amazingly forgiving of all our shortcomings and mistakes. Fall into HIS arms. Let Him comfort you and pick you up. HE will never leave or forsake you. God is LOVE. ☺
- "Depart, depart, go out from there! Touch no unclean thing! Come out from it and be pure, you who carry the vessels of the Lord. But you will not leave in haste or go in flight; for the Lord will go before you, the God of Israel will be your rear guard." Isaiah 52:11-12
- Action - Consequence:
  Action: Abiding in Christ's love for us, living by His standards, dying to our own will and desires.
  Consequence: Receiving the true love of Christ, being filled with the Spirit, and recognizing our true worth in Him.

Action: Giving in to lust, living in our own desires, doing things our way, and justifying that everyone else does it, why should we be held to a higher standard.

Consequence: Reducing our own worth to our physical abilities and traits, believing the lie that we're not good enough to ever deserve true love, carrying guilt, and self-loathing and treating others in the same manner because of the hurt we are carrying around in our own hearts. WHICH WILL YOU CHOOSE?

- No matter what happened today or yesterday, Jesus still LOVES you. You are priceless to Him because He made you. He will Always love you.

December 11

- I was blessed by another inspired sermon this morning. When we listen to God, go where He leads us and do as He tells us. We are abundantly blessed!
- Song: "Broken but I'm Healed" by Byron Cage (see Song Appendix for lyrics)
- Choices: Everyone has a choice. What will yours be? "Therefore everyone who hears these words of Mine and acts on them, may be compared to a wise man who built his house on the rock. And the rain fell, and the floods came, and the winds blew and slammed against that house; and yet it did not fall, for it had been founded on the rock. Everyone who hears these words of Mine and does not act on them, will be like a foolish man who built his house on the sand. The rain fell, and the floods came, and the winds blew and slammed against that house; and it fell—and great was its fall." Matthew 7:24-27
- I am so thankful that my Lord and Savior has my back when the storm overwhelms me. HE is truly my strength!
- Something to ponder: Who do you turn to in the really tough times, I mean really turn to? Who do you call first when there is a crisis? Who do you rely on to wipe away your tears, pick you up off the ground, and restore you

when you're devastated? I ask because I've observed in my own life that I tend to rely on PEOPLE way too much. Instead of taking all of my deepest desires, hurts, and needs to my Heavenly Father, I tend to rely on human beings to fill some gaps for me. I've come to realize that this is one major reason I've had so much heartache in my life. I need to rely on my Heavenly Father for those needs instead of people. Hopefully, you will not make the same mistake, but if you have, please consider taking EVERYTHING to Jesus first and truly relying on Him to provide for you, heal you, restore you, and make you whole. People are just not made for such things. These belong exclusively to the Father.

God bless and keep you always.

- Look for the fruit: Don't rush into any relationship. Just because someone knows what to say and do does not mean that they are practicing what they preach. Take your time and look for the fruits of their labor. Make sure that the fruit of their life matches up with their professed beliefs before you assume they are what they seem. If it is a right relationship, they will want to take the time to get to know you too.

God bless and keep you in all you do and say.

- If you're wondering if you're really loved: The Lord speaking to his children: "With deep compassion I will bring you back . . . with everlasting kindness I will have compassion on you . . . Though the mountains be shaken and the hills be removed, yet my unfailing love for you will not be shaken nor my covenant of peace be removed, says the Lord, who has compassion on you." Isaiah 54:7b, 8b, 10

December 12

- If you don't respect yourself, no one else will either. Respect yourself enough to insist on healthy relationships.
- When you've made the wrong decision enough times, you finally realize what the right decision actually looks like.

- God doesn't force us to obey His instruction, but neither does He remove the consequences of our actions. Whatever choices you make, be sure you are prepared to deal with the consequences. God loves us Always, but I know from experience He is not opposed to tough love!

December 13

- Quote: "Would you dare, would you dare to believe . . . that you still got a reason to sing? Cuz pain you've been feeling is just the dark before the morning."
- Encouragement from a friend: "Remember, God will never give you more than you can handle." People repeat this frequently. It is meant to be a source of encouragement, and it would be if I believed it were true. But I don't. I believe that God totally, absolutely, intentionally gives us more than we can handle because this is when we surrender to Him and He takes over, proving Himself by doing the impossible in our lives. God does give us more than we can handle, not maliciously, but intentionally in love, that His glory may be displayed.
My response: FINALLY, someone I agree with on this! Thank you so much for putting this out there in this context! God bless you for speaking candidly in love and truth. ☺
- Holiday blues: Please remember just how very much Jesus loves you during this holiday season. With so much focus on family, it can make us single folks sad. Don't concentrate on what you don't have. Concentrate on all of the blessings God has blessed you with this year. Singleness itself is actually a blessing if you let it be. God bless you in all you do and say.
- "If anyone loves me, he will obey my teaching. My Father will love him, and we will come to him and make our home with him." John 14:23
Praise God my Father is with me always! ☺

December 14

- God is good! God is so very good to me! Raises me above the muck and lets me walk in His light! ☺ Such an amazing and undeserved blessing . . .
- I'll take a long day doing what I'm meant to do over a lazy day doing nothing any time. Very blessed to be walking in God's purpose, very rewarding! ☺
- I used to be petrified of being alone. Now I relish the quiet time I get to spend with my Jesus. HE has quieted all my fears and gives me comfort every day. ☺ It's so much more than I deserve.
- Give praise to the Lord in all things. Truly, HE's got your back! All you need to do is walk in His ways and He will bless your life Tremendously more than you can imagine! Truth! ☺ Be blessed in all you think, say, and do.
- Let Jesus take your burdens. Let Him teach you His ways and He will give you rest. ☺ Thank you, Jesus, for loving us all so very much!
- You have a responsibility to God, your family, and yourself to make good decisions, even and especially when they are very difficult decisions. TRUST that God will carry you through even when you know the right road is exceedingly difficult. God will ALWAYS be by your side, get you through the hard times, and use them to make you better and stronger. You just have to LET Him. HE never forces us to rely on Him but waits on us patiently to realize HE is the only way to Life. God bless you in all you say and do.
- Repeat after me, "I refuse to be bitter about how other people have done me wrong. I will rise above it, keep my eyes on the Lord, and walk in HIS purpose for my life." ☺ God bless you in all you do and say.

December 15

- When we show others grace, we expand the kingdom of God.

- You know you've grown when HE completely flips the script and you're okay with that. ☺ Wow . . . Never thought I'd be here in a million years . . .
- "So the people asked him, saying, 'What shall we do then?' He answered them and said to them, 'He who has two tunics, let him give to him who has none; and he who has food, let him do likewise.'" Luke 3:10-11
  When we give of ourselves to others, we receive TREMENDOUS blessings from our Father. GIVE of yourself today (time, money, food, a smile, anything, doesn't have to be big) and receive your blessing! God bless you in all you do and say.
- You know God has been working in your life when the things that you used to think you couldn't possibly live without are no longer a driving desire. HE has rearranged all of my priorities, and now I'm walking in such blessing I can hardly believe it! Tripping over HIS goodness every single day, it is astounding. The funny thing is I still do not have the one thing I used to desire above all else—a mate—but it really doesn't matter now. God has filled my every need and desire. I'm completely at peace with the knowledge that HE holds my future in His hands, and He will bring me my mate when the time is right. I'm content to stay in His will and receive all that HE has planned for my life. God bless and keep you always!

December 16
- Do not be hard-hearted toward those who have hurt you. You are not blameless either.
- "Jesus said, 'Assuredly, I say to you, if you have faith as a mustard seed, you will say to this mountain, "Move from here to there," and it will move; and nothing will be impossible for you.' Matthew 17:20
- God really does have it all under control. Remember, you don't know how to get to where you're going. All you know is heaven is your Final destination. Trust the Father to lead

you through this life, follow in blind faith, trusting that HE really does have the road map and will never lead you astray. HE loves you so much and knows better than you do what is best for you and your life. God bless you in all you say and do always!

December 17

- Waiting is a gift. When God asks us to wait, HE is giving us the opportunity to back up off our situation, take a breath, and see things through His eyes. We have the opportunity to adjust our thoughts, attitudes, and actions to come in line with His will for our lives instead of plunging headlong into yet another grueling lesson from which we'll need to heal and recover. What an Amazing gift waiting can be!
- Getting ready to spend the day with a wonderful group of ladies and do some Christmas baking. ☺
- "I live in a high and holy place, but also with him who is contrite and lowly in spirit, to revive the spirit of the lowly and revive the heart of the contrite . . . I have seen his ways, but I will heal him; I will guide him and restore comfort to him . . ." Isaiah 57:15b, 18
- Think about it: You don't have to be anyone else but yourself. God made you just exactly the way you are for a purpose, and His purposes are always good! You are amazing because our loving, all-knowing, amazing God made you for His purpose. HE took the time and effort to make YOU exactly the way you are! ☺

December 18

- Love yourself enough to pull away from those who don't truly Love you. Everyone deserves to be loved for who they are, not for what they can offer.
- God has the final say. No one else has HIS authority. No matter what your world looks like right now, if God has told you something, it is TRUE! ☺

- "The Lord will guide you always; he will satisfy your needs in a sun-scorched land and will strengthen your frame. You will be like a well-watered garden, like a spring whose waters never fail. Your people will rebuild the ancient ruins and will raise up the age-old foundations; you will be called Repairer of Broken Walls, Restorer of Streets with Dwellings." Isaiah 58:11-12

- Craving a close, true, intimate relationship? One that will never let you down or break your heart? The ONLY place you will ever find such a relationship is with our Heavenly Father. People are not capable of filling your desire for the most intimate needs in your life. Jesus is the only ONE who can complete you. HE put others in our lives to help us, encourage us, and compliment us—NEVER to complete us. No person will ever be able to fill the God Spot in your life. If you put them there, you will be disappointed and hurt every time. Never allow anyone or anything, except God, to occupy the God Spot in your heart. God bless and keep you always.

- Rest in God's grace and peace. HE is able to do immeasurably more than you can think or imagine. You are in the best hands possible when you rest and leave your troubles in God's hands. God bless and keep you always!

- Ministry isn't about a particular church, religion, congregation, race, building, pastor, etc. Ministry is about spreading the word of God at His direction, in whatever form HE deems necessary. Don't think you're not useful to God just because you don't have a certain title or position. HE gifts, uses, and blesses ALL of His children uniquely.

- When people are divisive and try to stir up trouble, take the high road. Do not let them suck you into the "discussion" when it is intended to be destructive or demeaning to anyone. We are called to love, support, encourage, and admonish each other in LOVE. If you let them bait you into this conversation, you will find yourself in the middle of a mess! God bless and guide you in all you do and say.

December 19

- God will show you the good in the midst of the bad. He will show you the beauty in the midst of the rancid. You must simply allow Him the opportunity to speak to you and heed His words, even when they're not what you want to hear.
- We are all broken, and God knows it, but He is gracious enough to use our brokenness to show us and those around us His light.
- When the Holy Spirit leads you to do something, do it and keep walking. Do not stew about, wonder what others will think of you because of it, or try to see the results. Simply trust Jesus that HE will use it as He intended and walk in your blessing. Even if you never see the results of what you have done in His will for yourself, trust that HE has it all under control. Your reward is knowing that HE will bless you for being obedience. Yours is not to know the Master plan. That is for the Master alone! Be blessed.
- I enjoyed a relaxing evening filled with funny faces from giggly children, girl talk with some wonderful ladies and my daughter, and making chocolate pretzels. ☺
- "Poverty and shame will come to him who disdains correction, but he who regards a rebuke will be honored." Proverbs 13:18
- "When my soul fainted within me, I remembered the LORD; and my prayer went up to You, into Your holy temple." Jonah 2:7
- "He who covers his sins will not prosper, but whoever confesses and forsakes them will have mercy." Proverbs 28:13
- Sometimes when God is ushering a new season into your life, HE wants to separate you from your current influences, good or bad, so that you will fully focus and

rely on HIM. Embrace this season of closeness with the Father; it is preparing you for the next phase in your life. The closer you are to HIM, the easier He is to hear when the world gets crazy hectic. Get in tune with Him so He doesn't fade off into the noise when things pick up again. God bless you in all you do and say.

- John 5—The Healing at the Pool
by Cynthia Johnson on Monday, December 19, 2011, at 10:06 p.m.

"Some time later, Jesus went up to Jerusalem for a feast of the Jews. Now there is in Jerusalem near the Sheep Gate a pool, which in Aramaic is called Bethesda and which is surrounded by five covered colonnades. Here a great number of disabled people used to lie - the blind, the lame, the paralyzed. One who was there had been an invalid for thirty-eight years. When Jesus saw him lying there and learned that he had been in this condition for a long time, he asked him, "Do you want to get well?" "Sir", the invalid replied, "I have no one to help me into the pool when the water is stirred. While I am trying to get in, someone else goes down ahead of me." Then Jesus said to him, "Get up! Pick up your mat and walk." At once the man was cured; he picked up his mat and walked. The day on which this took place was the Sabbath. and so the Jews said to the man who had been healed, "It is the Sabbath; the law forbids you to carry your mat." But he replied, "The man who made me well said to me, 'Pick up your mat and walk.'" So they asked him, "Who is this fellow who told you to pick it up and walk?" The man who was healed had no idea who it was, for Jesus had slipped away into the crowd that was there. Later Jesus found him at the temple and said to him, "See you are well again. Stop sinning or something worse may happen to you." The man went away and told the Jews that it was Jesus who had made him well."

Jesus continually amazes me . . . HE will meet us right where we are, paralyzed in our own mess, unable to get to

Him, HE willingly comes to us and simply asks . . . "Do you want to get well?" He doesn't force us to look to Him, but simply gives us the choice. Then, if we say "Yes, I want to be healed", he willingly heals us with no expectation of any payment . . . but He does offer us the choice and advice as we go . . . "See you are well again. Stop sinning or something worse may happen to you." He points us in His direction, then gives us the option to do as we please. If we are wise, we will continually follow Him and continually receive His blessing and healing. Don't judge people in their mess . . . simply point them to Jesus and treat them with grace, kindness and compassion and help them the best you can. Love everyone, judge no one . . . and give God all the glory for the good he has done and will continue to do in our lives!

May God bless and keep you always . . .

December 20

- Trust in our Heavenly Father. Don't let the noise and lies of this world distract you. Jesus holds your best future; let Him lead you to it. ☺
- Been moving into my new office space today at work, YEA! More room and more privacy. ☺
- Song: "Boasting" by LeCrae (feat. Anthony Evans) (see Song Appendix for lyrics)
- Letting God change your heart is not a painless process. You must let Him extract all of the old sinful desires, motives, emotions, and past pain that you've been holding on to for years. It IS worth it though! If you let Him, Jesus will restore you and renew your life and purpose in ways that you could never begin to imagine! Trust Him. Let Him guide you. HE IS THE WAY.
- Sometimes the best thing to do is find a nice quiet place and just be for a while.
- Love my God, Love my girl, Love my life . . . been blessed indeed! ☺

December 21

- Don't be so focused on being with, seeing, loving the "right" person. It's not about people. It's about God. Maybe things aren't going as you'd like because you're focusing on the wrong things.
- Need help with a situation? Need encouragement? Need a friend, a confidant, someone to really hear you and understand what you're going through? Stop looking in the mirror. Stop looking to other people and look UP. Look to our Heavenly Father, and you will find relief and rest.
- Ya ever been absolutely tired and truly happy at the same time? ☺ It's been a good day, long but good ☺
- I used to think it was impossible for me to be alone and happy at the same time. Now I know it's just impossible to be alone. God is always with me. ☺ Now I am truly happy. ☺ Amazing how HE changes our hearts and minds when we let Him!
- Jesus loves you. I know it sounds cliché, but it is the truth! Our Heavenly Father longs for us to draw closer to Him. He pursues us our entire lives, never giving up no matter how far away from Him we stray, no matter how many mistakes we make or how many times we turn our back on Him. HE truly desires to be with us every single day of our lives. There is no love relationship on this earth that can even mildly compare to the way our Heavenly Father loves us! Look to HIM to fulfill all your needs and desires because HE will. God bless you in all you say and do.
- God bless you all this evening. I pray you all find peace and rest so you will have the energy to do what you need to do tomorrow.

December 22

- God can and will give you joy in the midst of an undesirable situation. Sometimes we need to stay in the situation we abhor so there is no doubt Who is in control.

HE doesn't always take us out of what we don't like, but He never leaves our side.

- Song: "Spoken For" by MercyMe (see Song Appendix for lyrics)

December 23

- Tremendous blessings for my holiday season: (1) serving in a woman's ministry that is dear to my heart, (2) reading the Christmas story out of Luke with my girl on Christmas morning, (3) going on a mother-daughter shopping trip with my girl (who warms my heart beyond belief!) (4) spending time with family and dear friends, and last but NOT least (5) knowing that no matter what situation I'm in, God has it all under control. ☺ Here's hoping everyone has a tremendously blessed Christmas and a safe New Year!
- I must confess I hadn't been feeling the Christmas spirit this year. I'd been so busy, just got shopping done yesterday. But tonight, I get to work with and for some very special ladies. I've seen such an outpouring of love for these ladies that it's blessed my heart! People do still genuinely care for those in need around them. Thank You, Jesus, for this blessing! I know I needed some encouragement tonight. ☺
- We are promised a good future, one that will prosper us and not harm us. Believe it and leave the past behind. There is a reason it is the past. Trust in your promised future enough to walk into it blindly, expecting God's best!
- Focus on the things that truly matter this Christmas: Our Lord and Savior, Jesus Christ; family; true friends; and all of the blessings that Jesus has bestowed on you this year. If you don't think you're blessed, take a look around. How many people are homeless, jobless, on their death bed, are burying their loved ones, are starving, are being abused, don't know the Lord, and are hopeless? Even if you're going through a rough patch, just the fact that you know Jesus and are allowing HIM to help you through the mess means

you are TREMENDOUSLY BLESSED this Christmas season. God bless and keep you always!
- Take a deep breath, sit down, and relax for a minute. It's time to rest a bit and get some "sane time." ☺

December 25
- Merry Christmas, everyone! ☺
- My daughter truly touched my heart this morning. God has truly filled all the gaps for her; she has such a profound understanding of what it means to love someone no matter what. She is certainly my biggest blessing from God. What a tremendous gift that I could never be thankful enough for!
- If you're in ministry, remember it's GOD'S ministry, NOT yours. Let HIM lead you, and HE will take you to places beyond your wildest imagination! HE has to get you out of your comfort zone so HE can heap blessings on you beyond your comprehension! Let HIM stretch you. Stay blessed.
- I have enjoyed a wonderful day with my family: listened to my father read the Christmas story before the presents; got to pray with my mom, dad, sister, and daughter; enjoyed a marvelous meal; watched the Nativity Story with everyone; and spent some quality time playing games, snacking on sausage and crackers, pie and coffee; and playing board games. ☺ Couldn't ask for a better Christmas! Thank you, Jesus, for being the center of our day. ☺
- Family: No matter how much drama and hurt happens in our families, we are called to have grace and forgive our family members who have wronged us, to do our best to draw near to them, and show them God's love in spite of themselves. This goes for our brothers and sisters in Christ too. We are supposed to treat the family of God with respect, love, grace, and forgiveness at all times. God bless you in all you choose to say and do in the Mighty Presence of our Lord and King. (HE is with us always!) ☺

- Wishing everyone a very Merry and Blessed Christmas! Thank you, Jesus, for all You have done for us. We are unworthy and more grateful than we can say.
- If you had a nice Christmas meal today, you are blessed. There are many with no food. If you had the privilege of spending the day with family today, you are blessed. There are many with no one to share this holiday with. If you got to hug your children today, you are blessed. There are many who have no children or have had to bury them and say goodbye forever. If you had the privilege of worshiping our Lord today, you are blessed. There are many who would be imprisoned or put to death for such an act. Remember you are blessed. be Grateful for your blessings, and if you have the means, SHARE your blessings with others. God be with you in all you do and say.

December 26
- Encouragement from a friend: God called you to be a king. Even if you don't recognize it or believe it, God still calls you a king. David was the first person God called to be a king while he was still a youth. God said of David, "I have found a man after my own heart." Why did God call David a man when he was still a boy? It's because God knew that He had the power to make the boy become whatever He called him.
My response: Powerful word! Thank you.
- I finally know who I am because I know Whose I am.
- Guard your heart, for there is MUCH evil in the world! R ECIPE FOR GUARDING YOUR HEART: "Rejoice in the Lord always; again I will say, rejoice! Let your gentle spirit be known to all men. The Lord is near. Be anxious for nothing, but in everything by prayer and supplication with thanksgiving let your requests be made known to God. And the peace of God, which surpasses all comprehension, will guard your hearts and your minds in Christ Jesus." Philippians 4:4-7

- Relationship LOVE: When you have an intimate relationship with Jesus, you give Him your heart. When He has your heart, you want to please Him. Why? BECAUSE YOU LOVE HIM! There is no other love that goes as deep as the Love He has for us, and no other pull nearly as strong when we truly give Him our hearts.
- Permission: Being kind to someone who has hurt you does not give them permission to hurt you again. It IS possible to love someone with Christ's love without being in a relationship with them (as in dating, etc.). We are called into relationship with EVERYONE in God's name, but we need to be cautious with who we let into our hearts. If another person's heart is not seeking after Jesus, we need to love them and be a good influence for them, but not allow ourselves to be pulled into a man-woman relationship with them. A healthy relationship requires two healthy people who are both seeking after and actively trying to be like Christ. God bless you in all you do and say.
- Married couples do not have fewer issues than single people. They just have DIFFERENT issues. Being single doesn't mean that you're broken or that something is wrong with you. It simply means that you are not currently married. Don't limit your identity to your marital status. God made you for so much more!

December 27
- In the middle of the chaos that is life, find and cherish the precious moments. I got to spend the better part of the day with a very precious little one-year-old man . . . Brought back memories of when my girl was little . . . So innocent at that age . . . Gifts from God.
- Do not believe the enemy's lie that there are no upstanding Christian singles left out there. If God started a work in you, HE will complete it. HE will never leave you hanging! Believe what He has shown you, follow where HE leads you, and let HIM complete you. God bless you in all you do and say.

December 28

- When someone says all the right things but refuses to actually practice them in their own life, WALK AWAY! These people are dangerous! They can easily and quickly cause you to doubt your faith.
- If God has given you a ministry, if He has given you something to say for His glory, HE doesn't just want you to say it. He wants you to LIVE IT! Stay blessed by being obedient.
- No matter how many times you've messed up, guess what? JESUS STILL LOVES YOU! HE will never stop loving you because YOU are worth loving.
- Show everyone God's love, but be very careful who you let in your inner circle. Some who know your weaknesses will try to exploit them to your detriment. Be careful not to get too close to those people or things who will make you stumble.
- You can tell you've completely worked through and grown past an issue when old bad habits aren't even appetizing anymore. ☺
- Who do you trust more, God or people? God tells us we are dearly loved, relentlessly pursued, and priceless in HIS eyes. So when people treat you poorly or walk out of your life, don't believe the lies the enemy would have you believe. Do NOT believe that you are worthless or inferior to anyone else or that you're so messed up that no one else will ever want you. Believe what God says about your worth! Believe that our Creator made you exactly like you are for HIS purpose, and HE loves you and pursues your heart FOREVER! The TRUTH of the matter is that you ARE LOVED and ARE WORTH LOVING, our Creator said so!

December 29

- Today and tomorrow are set aside just to spend some quality time with my girl. LOVE mother-daughter time!

- Never lose faith no matter how impossible things seem.
- Enjoy the day with your loved ones. Let God bless you how He desires today. Be open to His will. Have a blessed day! ☺

December 30
- I will be thankful for all God has done for me today. I will not let my own desires for things I do not yet have blind me to the abundant blessings, healing, and restoration that God has mercifully given me.
- Song: "I Believe" by James Fortune (FIYA) (see Song Appendix for lyrics)
- Encouragement from a friend: "[1] I patiently waited, Lord, for you to hear my prayer. [2]You listened and pulled me from a lonely pit full of mud and mire. You let me stand on a rock with my feet firm, and you gave me a new song, a song of praise to you. [3]Many will see this, and they will honor and trust you, the Lord God." Psalm 40:1-3 CEV
My response: This is Exactly what the Lord has done for me.
- Choices: Love is a choice, faithfulness is a choice, obedience is a choice, respecting others is a choice, being blessed is a choice. We can choose to do what we are supposed to do and actively receive our blessings every day, or we can choose to do what WE wanna do and choose not to receive our blessings every day. Choices, they're EVERYWHERE.
- Went to get a Ted Dekker book tonight and ended up buying a trilogy instead . . . Looking forward to a relaxing and enlightening read. ☺
- I'm getting ready to clean house today, literally. But it always reminds me of how I need to clean house spiritually and emotionally . . . using this time to reflect of what I need to do to make sure my will is in line with God's

will . . . praying for the same clarity for you . . . God bless you in all you think, do, and say today.

- Green-eyed monster: When God brings that special person into your life, they will have eyes ONLY for you. You will not need to always WORK to keep their affection. They will WANT to get to know you, respect you, and love you the way that God directs us to love each other. If you're constantly threatened by their wandering ways, let them go. You trying to "keep" them will not stop them from doing what they're determined to do. Use discretion instead of relying on emotions. Use God's word as a filter for human behavior and heed His word even when it is painful. It is MORE painful not to heed His word. You will have much more pain if you let things continue outside of His will. God bless and keep you in all you choose to say and do.

- Heartbreak: If you think that no one can possibly understand how brokenhearted you are over your situation, consider this: God's chosen people disobeyed Him, rejected Him, were unfaithful to Him OVER AND OVER AND OVER AND OVER, and it broke His heart (If you doubt this, pick up your Bible and read just about any book in the Old Testament. It's filled to the brim with Israel's unfaithfulness and God's forgiveness.), but He STILL sent His Son as a sacrifice for all of their sins and ours because He loves us so very much! HE understands heartbreak, and HE is the only One who can truly heal the brokenhearted.

December 31
- "Let us step into the darkness and reach out for the hand of God. The path of faith and darkness is so much safer than the one we would choose by sight." George MacDonald
- If the enemy is coming at you hard on all sides, you Must be on the right path. He wouldn't have to try so hard to derail you if you weren't! Hold tight to what God has

promised you and trust in His faithfulness. You are very close to a blessing. ☺

- Here's wishing everyone a very blessed and safe New Year's celebration tonight! God bless you all and stay safe. ☺
- (NOTE: My page got hacked . . . LOL) "Mwahahahha!! u left your page open!! XD You know not to do that someone could write on it!!" ~Your loving daughter
- 2011 was a year of more difficult lessons, tremendous growth and recovery, and restoration from a monumental amount of past pain! 2012 is going to be a year of blessings, and I'm READY! ☺

January 2012

January 1

- Today is a new day. Praise God HE is ALIVE and so are you! Walk in His grace and peace. Let Him lead and protect you always.
- I have escaped the clutches of my past and am walking into my future with FULL confidence that my Jesus, my Lord and Savior, has my back, that HE LOVES ME DEARLY. HE is providing for all my needs and granting the deepest desires of my heart! PRAISE GOD our Jesus is SO good to his children! ☺
- Pastor said to me today, "I've never seen a stationary storm." No matter what you're going through, it WILL pass! God has already won the victory. We just have to stay on course, be obedient, and believe. God bless you always!
- Everyone struggles. We all need to cling to our Father during life's storms. Show each other some grace today.
- Have you talked to God today? It just takes a minute to let Him know how you feel, to send up a praise, to ask for direction, to receive your blessing. Please make time to spend with our Father. He wants to bless and guide you, but He won't force Himself on you. He will wait patiently for you to come to Him. Let him bless you today. HE loves you.

January 2

- THE WORD: God is showing me that when I tuck His word deep in my heart, read it every day, strive to understand it, pray on it, and allow Him to lead me, I not only understand God better. HE makes my heart line up with His desires. He allows me to understand myself better (why I've made all the bad decisions I've made, etc.), which allows me to understand His nature and my nature more and more, which in turn allows me to actually FORGIVE myself for all I've done. What a wonderful evolution. I never would have made it to this magnificent place of forgiveness and grace without Him. Thank you, Jesus, for ALL You have done for me! God bless and keep you always.

- Side note: Once you are able to forgive yourself, forgiving others by recognizing God's grace applies to EVERYONE is much easier!

- LADIES' FAITHFULNESS: You know how ladies are FIERCELY loyal to their man? You know, when they have his back no matter what, no matter how bad things look, they still follow him because they Love him? Now just imagine a relationship with Jesus so intimate and dear to your heart that you follow HIM like that. Our relationship with Jesus should trump every other relationship in our lives; we should let our Father teach us how to treat our men.

  Think about it: Love Jesus first, and HE will bless your heart so that you're capable of loving an earthly, flawed, and totally human man like God called you to love your man. God bless you in all you do and say always.

January 3

- Strongholds: Don't let the enemy have strongholds in your life! If you're feeling bombarded and overwhelmed, feeling like you're frustrated and about to make a mistake or slide back into a bad habit or wrong decision, surround yourself with positive input (uplifting music, scripture, positive Christian friends who know how to encourage you, etc.). Give yourself every possible opportunity to hear God through the mess, over the storm of life with all its noise and clapping thunder. God is there. HE wants to get through to us. Sometimes we must strain to hear His still small voice in the midst of the storm.

- Energy: Believe it or not, giving of yourself to a cause or ministry that you believe in or have a passion for will actually give you more energy. God blesses those who share their gifts with others. God has given you a gift to share, whether your gift is a skill or talent, compassion for a particular situation, money, time, or conversation over a cup of coffee. You'd be surprised how much energy you have, even after a very long day, when you've given of yourself. Try it. You will be amazed.

January 4

- Look to God for your strength. Do not rely on your own strength or understanding. Trust that God has a plan for you and will see you through. God bless and keep you always.

January 5

- Something to think about: Ladies, if you are single, the safest place for you to be is married to God. I know it sounds strange, but God refers to Himself as our husband in the Bible in several places. And the truth of it is, in the Garden of Eden, after woman was made, she only knew where God was. Man was not complete without her because he had lost a rib. She was not complete without him because she came from him. But God did not give man a wife until he was doing the work God had called him to do, and God did not give woman a husband before she knew where HE (God) was. So if you are without a husband, look to our Heavenly Father for guidance, for He will love and protect you and teach you what you need to know until the time HE sees fit to put you together with your earthly husband.
  God bless you always.
- Know that God loves you and be blessed. ☺
- "Therefore this is what the Lord says: 'If you repent, I will restore you that you may serve me; if you utter worthy,

not worthless, words, you will be my spokesman. Let this people turn to you, but you must not turn to them. I will make you a wall to this people, a fortified wall of bronze; they will fight against you but will not overcome you, for I am with you to rescue and save you,' declares the Lord. 'I will save you from the hands of the wicked and redeem you from the grasp of the cruel.'" Jeremiah 15:19-21
- PRAISE GOD Who will save us from the wicked and redeem us from the grasp of the cruel if we truly repent and follow Him!

January 6
- "Remember that if you are a child of God, you will never be happy in sin. You are spoiled for the world, the flesh, and the devil. When you were regenerated there was put into you a vital principle, which can never be content to dwell in the dead world. You will have to come back, if indeed you belong to the family." Charles Spurgeon
- "We know we're coming full circle with God when we stand at a very similar crossroad where we made such a mess of life before, but this time we take a different road." Beth Moore
- Godly men do NOT look like the "men" you see in sitcoms! Godly men have true character and excel at leadership and compassion.
- If you want a good picture of a real Godly man, look at Job 29. If you want a good picture of a real Godly woman look at Proverbs 31.
- KNOW WHAT YOU'RE LOOKING FOR!
  by Cynthia Johnson on Friday, January 6, 2012, at 8:31 p.m.
  Don't settle for Mr. or Ms. RightNow when God has your soul-mate in His hands. Trust in Him, let Him mold your heart into the heart of a truly Godly person so you can be a blessing to your spouse when HE sees fit to bring him or her into your life.

PICTURE OF A GODLY MAN:
Job 29
Job's Past Was Glorious
1And Job again took up his discourse and said,
2"Oh that I were as in months gone by,
As in the days when God watched over me;
3When His lamp shone over my head,
And by His light I walked through darkness;
4As I was in the prime of my days,
When the friendship of God *was* over my tent;
5When the Almighty was yet with me,
And my children were around me;
6When my steps were bathed in butter,
And the rock poured out for me streams of oil!
7"When I went out to the gate of the city,
When I took my seat in the square,
8The young men saw me and hid themselves,
And the old men arose *and* stood.
9"The princes stopped talking
And put *their* hands on their mouths;
10The voice of the nobles was hushed,
And their tongue stuck to their palate.
11"For when the ear heard, it called me blessed,
And when the eye saw, it gave witness of me,
12Because I delivered the poor who cried for help,
And the orphan who had no helper.
13"The blessing of the one ready to perish came upon me,
And I made the widow's heart sing for joy.
14"I put on righteousness, and it clothed me;
My justice was like a robe and a turban.
15"I was eyes to the blind
And feet to the lame.
16"I was a father to the needy,
And I investigated the case which I did not know.
17"I broke the jaws of the wicked
And snatched the prey from his teeth.

[18]"Then I thought, 'I shall die in my nest,
And I shall multiply *my* days as the sand.
[19]'My root is spread out to the waters,
And dew lies all night on my branch.
[20]'My glory is *ever* new with me,
And my bow is renewed in my hand.'
[21]"To me they listened and waited,
And kept silent for my counsel.
[22]"After my words they did not speak again,
And my speech dropped on them.
[23]"They waited for me as for the rain,
And opened their mouth as for the spring rain.
[24]"I smiled on them when they did not believe,
And the light of my face they did not cast down.
[25]"I chose a way for them and sat as chief,
And dwelt as a king among the troops,
As one who comforted the mourners.

PICTURE OF A GODLY WOMAN:
Proverbs 31
The Words of Lemuel
[1]The words of King Lemuel, the [a]oracle which his mother
taught him:
[2]What, O my son?
And what, O son of my womb?
And what, O son of my vows?
[3]Do not give your strength to women,
Or your ways to that which destroys kings.
[4]It is not for kings, O Lemuel,
It is not for kings to drink wine,
Or for rulers to desire strong drink,
[5]For they will drink and forget what is decreed,
And pervert the rights of all the afflicted.
[6]Give strong drink to him who is perishing,
And wine to him whose life is bitter.
[7]Let him drink and forget his poverty

And remember his trouble no more.

⁸Open your mouth for the mute,

For the rights of all the unfortunate.

⁹Open your mouth, judge righteously,

And defend the rights of the afflicted and needy.

Description of a Worthy Woman

¹⁰An excellent wife, who can find?

For her worth is far above jewels.

¹¹The heart of her husband trusts in her,

And he will have no lack of gain.

¹²She does him good and not evil

All the days of her life.

¹³She looks for wool and flax

And works with her hands in delight.

¹⁴She is like merchant ships;

She brings her food from afar.

¹⁵She rises also while it is still night

And gives food to her household

And portions to her maidens.

¹⁶She considers a field and buys it;

From her earnings she plants a vineyard.

¹⁷She girds herself with strength

And makes her arms strong.

¹⁸She senses that her gain is good;

Her lamp does not go out at night.

¹⁹She stretches out her hands to the distaff,

And her hands grasp the spindle.

²⁰She extends her hand to the poor,

And she stretches out her hands to the needy.

²¹She is not afraid of the snow for her household,

For all her household are clothed with scarlet.

²²She makes coverings for herself;

Her clothing is fine linen and purple.

²³Her husband is known in the gates,

When he sits among the elders of the land.

²⁴She makes linen garments and sells *them*,

And supplies belts to the tradesmen.
²⁵Strength and dignity are her clothing,
And she smiles at the future.
²⁶She opens her mouth in wisdom,
And the teaching of kindness is on her tongue.
²⁷She looks well to the ways of her household,
And does not eat the bread of idleness.
²⁸Her children rise up and bless her;
Her husband *also*, and he praises her, *saying*:
²⁹"Many daughters have done nobly,
But you excel them all."
³⁰Charm is deceitful and beauty is vain,
But a woman whofears the LORD, she shall be praised.
³¹Give her the product of her hands,
And let her works praise her in the gates.
DON'T SETTLE . . . WAIT PATIENTLY FOR THE
RIGHT PERSON . . . IT WILL BE WELL WORTH
THE WAIT AND MUCH LESS PAINFUL THAN IF
YOU STRAY OFF ON YOUR OWN LOOKING FOR
A SUBSTITUTE.

January 7

- Love is NOT lust! Love = true relationship, honesty,
  compassion, constantly forgiving, forever encouraging,
  sacrificing self for the benefit of another, receiving their
  gifts to you with a gracious heart, giving of yourself when
  you just don't feel like it, Truly and diligently seeking
  Jesus, and doing your best to love others as He loves you
  and as He directs you to selflessly love, not so you get
  "credit," but in order to reflect Christ's love for us all in this
  fallen world. God bless you in all you do and say always.
- Jesus said, "I'll stay with you, I'll be with you, I'm never
  gonna leave you." ☺ Couldn't ask for better news! ☺

January 8

- If you want to learn more about something, pick up a book, do some research, and educate yourself.
- The blessings God has for you He has for you specifically and personally. No one can take them away.
- Me: Sitting on sofa with a large headache, kinda leaned back.

  My girl: Comes over and gives me a big hug. "You need a hug, and no offense, Mom, but you look like crap."

  I LOVE my girl! So caring AND honest. ☺ Wouldn't trade her for the world!
- Roles: I must do my part to grow and move forward in my life. Part of my job is to recognize what God's role is and to let Him do it; no one is capable of doing God's part, except the Creator Himself. I must simply trust and obey. Amazing how something so very simple can be so difficult at times.
- Something to think about: Love each other. Respect each other. Support each other. Speak to everyone as though they were Jesus. I wonder how much our world would change if everyone did this.
- After more than sixteen years of being a single parent in this cruel world, I can honestly tell you today that I am abundantly blessed by our loving God and Father. He never promised us an easy road. In fact, it is clear in His word that our road is sure to be steeped with difficulties, but He did promise never to leave us, and I can testify to that today no matter how difficult my path, no matter how lonely I feel at times. My Father has never left me alone. Praise God in ALL circumstances, for He is faithful and merciful to His children.
- Your blessings are YOURS! Claim them today! God wants to shower you with blessings. All you have to do is be obedient and claim them every single day. God loves you; let Him show it in ALL the ways He has planned, even when it's not what you have planned. God bless you

abundantly and may you accept His blessings, even when they come in forms you never imagined!

- Take care of your body (stay in shape, eat healthy, continue learning and growing, etc.) out of respect for what God gave you. Don't just use your Godly gifts (body, talents, abilities, etc.) to try to impress others and gratify the flesh.

January 9

- Encouragement from a friend: The Word of God tells us that we have been given favor from the Lord, it's our inheritance as a child of God (Psalm 5:12). You may not be experiencing it at this very moment, but you can if you will focus on the total truth and begin to expect favor instead of lack and trouble. Remember this truth: If things can go wrong, they can just as easily go right! Psalm 139:14 reads "I will praise you, for I am fearfully and wonderfully made; marvelous are your works, and my soul knows very well."

- "When you treasure things that are eternal, your mind becomes stable and your heart secure." James Robison

- Encouragement from a friend: Following Jesus means following Him alone. Fans don't want to put Jesus on the throne of their hearts. Instead, they keep a couch on their hearts and, at the most, give Jesus a cushion. But Jesus makes it clear. He is not interested in sharing your heart.

- Encouragement from a friend: BE ADDICTED TO HOPE! Why? God is for you (Romans 8:31). All things work for good for you (Romans 8:28). Christ will finish what He started (Philippians 1:6). God can't lie (Numbers 23:19). Miracles can be and will be done (Hebrews 13:8). The same power Christ has is for you, in you, and through you (Ephesians 1:19). Nothing can take God's love from you (Romans 8:39). He will never leave you (Hebrews 13:5). You have a Helper (John 14:26). Christ lives in you (Galatians 2:20).

- Pain and Forgiveness: People strike out and hurt others when they have been hurt themselves. Stop the cycle of pain by forgiving those who have hurt you instead of striking back at them or others.

- "God is faithful. He's got it. Trust Him." Tony Evans
- Sometimes God tells us "no" or "not right now"' because if we receive our promised blessing too soon, we will not be properly equipped to handle the blessing. Sometimes, if we receive a blessing too soon, it becomes a curse. Don't rush your blessings. Trust God's timing. HE ALWAYS knows best! Don't stubbornly proceed and push to get what you "want." Wait for what God has for you in His time, and your life will be exponentially better! God bless you in all you choose to do and say.
- Jonah or Job . . . Which Will You Choose??

by Cynthia Johnson on Monday, January 9, 2012, at 1:17 p.m.
Jonah or Job?: Are you Jonah or Job, which do you want to be??

Jonah: ran away from God's calling for his life because He wanted to dictate consequences for others and would not let go of prejudice, he wanted things his way instead of God's way.

Job: praised God through the toughest trials anyone has ever endured without knowing why God had allowed all these horrendous things to happen to him. He had been a tremendously faithful servant of the Lord.

Results: Jonah ended up getting swallowed by a big fish, spat out on the land, finally delivered the message he was told to deliver, then pouted and grumbled as God showed mercy when Jonah wanted to see destruction and judgment. We never hear from Jonah again in the bible. The last we hear from him, he is mad at God, grumbling in disagreement with God's mercy and grace.

Job: Job endured the storm against all advice from his well-meaning but much less than helpful, friends and wife. Through all of the terrible trials, He never lost his faith. Job was restored to greater glory than he had before the trials began. The last time we see Job, God had blessed him abundantly and rewarded him for his faithfulness.

I don't know about you, but I don't want the last anyone hears from me to be grumbling and disagreement with God because I couldn't let go of my own prejudices and wanted things my own way. I want to be like Job. No matter how many trials and tribulations this life holds for me, no matter how little I understand of God's perfect will for my life . . . I want the abundantly blessed ending, so I will press on and fully trust that my Lord and Savior will work everything for the good of those who love Him. I will do my best not to complain and simply be obedient to His will for my life.

Which will you choose??? Will you choose to be like Jonah or like Job?

May God bless you abundantly in all you do and say . . .

January 10

- "Do not conform to the pattern of this world, but be transformed by the renewing of your mind. Then you will be able to test and approve what God's will is—his good, pleasing and perfect will." Romans 12:2
- Christian Community: I am so very thankful for all of my friends who encourage me in the faith simply by speaking and living how God has called them. When I am down, they encourage me with scripture, affirmation, and truth. Thank you all so very much! This is what Christian Community is all about! ☺
- Encouragement from a friend: If you're looking for love today, call on God! For God is LOVE!
- Sometimes I think God allows us to go through trials to humble us, so that we realize that we cannot do it alone. We are called to walk in community and not do things under our own power. We must always draw on God's strength and not rely on our own strength or understanding. Embrace the humbling experiences when

you must reach out for help, allow them to help you grow and draw closer to Jesus and His community of followers.

January 11
- "No matter how things may look, when you obey the voice of God somebody, somewhere is being blessed by your obedience." Eric Maurice Clark
- "God is the strength of my heart and my portion forever." Psalms 73:25-26 NIV
- Have you lost your direction? Look to the Son.
- God made you exactly who you are for a reason. He cares nothing for prejudice or other's perceptions of who they think you should be. In fact, Jesus broke all social norms when He was on earth. Believe the vision He has given you and rely on His strength and ability to bring it to fruition in your life. Simply obey His direction always.
- When something as small as a virus can literally Take Me OUT for a solid week, I shudder to think what a spiritual virus could do to my walk with Jesus. CAUTION: Make sure you're right with the One (Jesus) that truly matters!
- Encouragement from a friend: As you get ready to crawl into bed tonight, may you hand Jesus your worries and grab hold of His peace and perspective. May you lay down your judgments and hold close His fresh mercies. As you crawl under the covers, remember you're not under your circumstances. You are under the shadow of His wing. Take hold of what you possess in Him. Sleep well.

January 12
- Prayer Request: Please pray for my mother's health. She has an abnormally large cyst on her liver and cannot get in to see the specialist until the twentieth. She is in increasing discomfort every day. Please pray for God's healing hand and protection over her health. Any and all prayers are greatly appreciated.

- Instead of focusing on what you don't have, try concentrating on how you can show the Light of Christ inside you to everyone around you. Even the strong in the faith need encouragement, affirmation, and guidance. Be a Light for others instead of grumbling about the things you want and don't yet have.
- Encouragement from a friend: Jesus doesn't expect followers to be perfect, but he does call us to be authentic.
- Encouragement from a friend: A little #realtalk on prayer that's been on my heart today. In fact, I feel like putting quite a bit out there tonight, but let's start here. I am a prayer warrior. Now. For a while, I got very discouraged with prayer, praying, and generally anything having to do with asking God for or about ANYTHING! I felt like He either didn't care or wouldn't answer ME SPECIFICALLY! For a season, I felt like the most sure way to MAKE SURE something wouldn't happen was to pray about it almost like the enemy was snatching my prayers and crapping on them on their way up to Heaven. I'll admit it. I used to think praying was a huge waste of air and energy. My knees were even getting older, and I didn't need the pain! But the TRUTH is this: Every prayer is heard. Every prayer is answered! And here's the most exciting thing about it: Every prayer of mine that the LORD has answered might have taken Him ten times longer to respond to than I wanted, but His answer was ten times better than what I was asking! Basically, nothing beats sincere and patient prayer. Pray today! He cares, and He answers. Even if you're facing what feels like a mountain of problems, just be honest with Him and see how He begins to move in your life. I'm a witness.
- "My God shall supply all your needs according to His riches in glory. Trust Him." Tony Evans
- If you are frustrated with being single, please remember it could always be worse. Being single should not define who you are; it is merely your marital status. You are much

more than that, and there are much worse situations to be in than simply being single. Seriously, look around you and take stock of your blessings. There are more than you realize.

January 13

- Left to my own devices, I am weak and irreparably broken. I am strong because my Heavenly Father gives me strength.
- "The minute you expose darkness to the light, the light begins to defeat it. The darkness then loses its power over you." Joyce Meyer Ministries
  My response: Absolute, Truth!
- "God knows what you need. Trust him." Max #GreatDayEveryDay
- When your physical body is pushed beyond its max, pull back and trust that God will fill all the gaps that need filled. Get rest and recoup so you can continue His work. Sometimes it is necessary to rely on others to help us out, though it is always a humbling experience. God bless and keep you always.
- No one will ever love you as much as Jesus, but there are times you will feel lonely because we're all human and we all desire to be loved by others. When this feeling threatens to get the best of you, please remember that emotions are fleeting, God knows your deepest desires and pains and works Everything for the good of those who love Him. Hang in there. Our Father knows your heart's desires, and He loves you way too much to give you less than the very best. It's all in HIS timing. Hold on. Your blessing's coming!

January 14

- Homecoming for my girl tonight . . . Good grief, she's growing up too fast! Couldn't be more proud though . . .
- Encouragement from a friend: If your plan is also God's plan, no one can sabotage it.

- Encouragement from a friend: Sometimes it takes more faith to sit still than it does to move!
- Encouragement from a friend: There is a plan for your life that is predestined and ordained for you from heaven. You don't have worry because what God has planned and purposed for your life, HE promises to see it to its completion.
- An upstanding man with self-control is definitely more attractive than a player. Just sayin' . . . If he has no self-control now, how's he ever gonna be faithful to anyone?
- Think about it: When you treat yourself with respect, others have no choice but to reciprocate.
- No matter how "HOT" he or she is, looks are only temporary. Character is WAY more important!

January 15
- A double-minded man is unstable in all his ways.
- Trust: If we really Trust Jesus, why do we stress so much? When you truly trust someone, there is no reason to be stressed.
- Listen and Pray: God changes your heart so you will live your purpose. When He lays someone or something on your heart, PRAY. He makes you aware of things He needs you to act on. Be obedient and pray it through until He gives you peace about it.
- When Jesus tells you that He loves you, He's not lying. When He tells you He has good things in store for you, plans for hope and a future, that is Exactly what He means. Stop stressing and TRUST HIM.

January 16
- It doesn't matter what things look like today. God has seen your tears and loves you dearly. He will work everything for your good.
- Standing on the promises of God!

- "God has a plan for you. And it is a good plan. Seek Him and walk in it." Tony Evans
- Understanding: Don't rely on preconceived prejudiced opinions when you're struggling to understand something! Ask intelligent questions and be open for an honest answer.
- No matter what anyone does to me or what anyone takes away from me, they can never take away my Jesus.
- I don't need to know what tomorrow holds; all I need to know is the One who holds tomorrow.
  Lord, I put in Your hands my past, present, and future.
- Gift (squandered or appreciated?): Life is a gift (truly stop think about it for a minute). What did you do with yours today?
- I am happy because my God has already conquered all of my problems and made me victorious over All of my situations. I just have to trust and obey. A tremendous weight has been lifted off my shoulders! I don't have to figure it all out. He already has. ☺
- When you allow God to rearrange your priorities, those who knew you before will not understand your new frame of mind. They will wonder what caused this big change, and many may not accept it gracefully. Trust that God has your best interest in mind, believe what HE shows you, and pray for everyone who touches your world. They are witnessing a great change too and are grappling for understanding. Give them grace and pray for them always!

January 17
- Complete healing and restoration come only through complete surrender. Whatever you're holding on to is hurting you. Give it all to the Healer and let Him heal you. Would you go to the doctor and let him repair your broken pinky finger and refuse to let him treat your pneumonia?
- Faith isn't automatic. It comes through obedience and growing reliance on God as we actively live as He tells us to live. It's an Activity, not a mental exercise.

- Progress: You know you're making progress when you no longer crave destructive habits, people, and lusts of your past.
- Show people love because you love them, not because you get something in return.
- Love is to be freely given. Trust is to be earned.
- "Trusting in God will teach you how to be an overcomer . . ." Eric Maurice Clark
- "Regret looks back. Worry looks around. Faith looks up." John Mason
  Where are you looking?
- Even after a Very Long Day, do yourself a favor and take a few minutes before bedtime to spend with Jesus. HE will calm you down from your day. HE wants to hear all about your day, wants to comfort you and assure you that He still has everything under control, and that you can rest easy this evening. Take a few minutes to relax in His arms to rejuvenate your spirit before drifting off to sleep. God bless and keep you always.

January 18
- Anyone who has knowledge of the Word of God should share it, for many have no understanding.
- Encouragement from a friend: Prayer is relational communication with God.
- No matter what's comin' atcha, remember God is BIGGER.
- Encouragement from a friend: I speak peace to all that may be going through something. There is a peace that passes all understanding. PEACE, PEACE, PEACE, GOD PEACE!
- The cool thing about realizing your purpose in life is realizing that NOTHING is an accident! God uses everything you have ever done and everything that you will ever do to accomplish His mission. HE is truly Amazing!

Hard to believe He uses even the bad to bless His children, but He does it every day.

- Being a victim in a situation does NOT make you a victim for life! God has already won the victory for you. You are a VICTOR. Humble yourself, lay everything at the Father's feet, let Him heal you, and walk in Victory. Shake off defeat. You're a King's kid!

- Start your day with a word from the Lord. His word will keep you focused on Him and will allow you to better deal with all that comes your way. God bless and keep you always . . .

- There is no substitute for integrity. No matter how anyone else has mistreated you, you are never justified in mistreating them back. God tells us to love everyone, to leave vengeance to the Lord, to pray without ceasing, and to make amends with others so we can come before the Lord with our pleas. Make amends to the best of your ability, act with love and integrity at all times, and lay everything else at the feet of the Lord. Our Father is more than capable of handling the load; HE does not need our help doing His job.

January 19

- Encouragement from a friend: It is when we come to the Lord in our nothingness, our powerlessness, and our helplessness that He then enables us to love in a way which, without Him, would be absolutely impossible.

- You'll never be truly free if you keep holding on to ANYTHING from your past. You must give EVERYTHING to God, and if it is good and wholesome and meant to be in your life, God will give it back. If it's not meant to be in your life, THANK God for taking it, even when it hurts, because it will hurt you MORE if you don't let it go.

- Think about it: So many people say they are Christians, yet so few actually read the Bible. How can we follow Christ if we don't read His Word?
- Single ladies, don't let the devil convince you that real, honest, Godly men aren't out there. Why does he have to try so hard to convince you if it is true? There would be no need because there'd be no options. Wait for the right one, he IS out there, and God will bring him into your world at the right time.
- HE has healed me from beyond recognition or repair. Why wouldn't I trust HIM with my future?
- To tell an intellectual mind not to lean on her own understanding . . . well, it's an EXCEEDINGLY difficult task, but I'm still tryin'! God made this overactive little brain of mine. HE knows how to harness it. ☺
- Don't wait for your world to get crazy busy before you truly rely on God. Even when all is going well and you have plenty of time to spend with your loved ones, concentrate on surrendering your will to God and letting Him guide you through. He wants to be there for you in the good times and the bad times. PLEASE don't wait for the bad times to actually have a relationship with Jesus. Relationships are beautiful things in the good times. Allow Jesus to spend some beautiful time with you too!
- As a single mom and sole provider for my daughter, I have many responsibilities at any given day: first job, second job, ministry involvement, raising my teenage daughter, church involvement, household chores, bible study, financial obligations, family obligations (helping my parents when I can), finding SOME sane time (social time with my daughter and friends), and I'm not even dating anyone right now. Eventually, that'll be in the mix too. ☺ The POINT of me telling you all this is If I didn't allow Jesus to guide my world and hold it all together, I would NEVER be able to manage half of what I squeeze into a day. Jesus looks after me every day and blesses me

tremendously! I couldn't do it without HIM! Praise the
Lord we have such a loving Savior. ☺ PLEASE let Jesus
lead, help, and guide you as well.

- When you do, you'll be AMAZED at what all HE will
help you accomplish! ☺

January 20

- I am thankful for all I have, for I realize that many have
nothing.
- Prayer: Used to be, when I prayed, it was strained, like
I was trying to speak to someone in another world and
hear through industrial-strength earmuffs . . . Now
I'm simply speaking to my Best Friend who is always
closer to me than anyone else. It is Amazing how God
meets us right in our space when our hearts are sincere.
#moreblessedthanIcldevrexpress!"
- Encouragement from a friend: Our experiences and
environment may be a factor but do not determine who we
are. You are not your past or your surroundings.
- If you're acting wrong, STOP IT! God is forgiving, but
knowing you're acting wrong and continuing in it says a
Lot about your character. It takes a BIG person to admit
their faults, accept the consequences, repent and turn away
from bad actions, and try to do better in the future. Be the
Big person, not the lazy, selfish person.
- Encouragement from a friend: God doesn't want to just fix
our problems. He wants to transform our hearts.
- If the one you love is in the middle of a mess, step back and
let them work it out with God. Then give control of your
heart to our Maker and let Him change, heal, and mold it
how He sees fit. HE will make you victorious in the end.
- Take Stock: You'll appreciate where you are now, all the
blessings you have received, if you remember and take
stock of where you came FROM. God has already brought
you through so very much. HE will never abandon you.

Praise God for all you have and keep trusting in Him for your future. God bless you always.

- Discernment: Just because someone KNOWS the right way does not mean that they are willing to LIVE the right way. Be very careful who you let in your innermost circle.

January 21

- "Don't copy the behavior and customs of this world, but let God transform you into a new person by changing the way you think. Then you will learn to know God's will for you, which is good and pleasing and perfect." Romans 12:2
- What people think of me affects the present. It can affect my comfort level and stress level if I let it, but it will Not affect my eternal future. #choosingtofocusonGodnotpeople
- Encouragement from a friend: "Some people think they have discernment when, actually, they are just suspicious. There is a true gift of the Spirit called the discerning of spirits (1 Corinthians 12:10). It discerns good and bad, not just bad. Suspicion comes out of the unrenewed mind; discernment comes out of the renewed spirit." Joyce Meyer Ministries
- FINDING HIM: Finding God is not something someone else can do for us. We can't rely on the pastor to take us to HIS feet once or twice a week and expect to be able to hear Him clearly all week long. Would you expect to be able to have a friend spend all her time with your best friend and then expect to be able to talk to that best friend as though it was you (sharing inside jokes, bonding experiences, reminiscing about all the funny and meaningful things that happened during their time together, etc.)? I don't think so. We must all build our own relationships with the Father. Spend time with Him. There is NO substitute.
- God loves us no matter what we've done. His grace and forgiveness FAR surpass any person's abilities to forgive. Jesus wants a relationship with each and every person on earth. He pursues us always. All we have to do is truly

look to Him (in the Bible, Christian relationships and
fellowship with each other, and prayer) for guidance, true
Love, and to teach us how to truly forgive (ourselves and
others).

- Look for something real. Don't settle for something
because it's available.

January 22
- No one is perfect. We all make mistakes.
- Seek God with your whole heart and you will find Him.
HE will hear your prayers, but you MUST seek Him with
your WHOLE heart, not just the convenient part, not just
the part that's easy to surrender, but with your whole heart.
"You will seek me and find me when you seek me with all
your heart." Jeremiah 29:13
- Today was one of those days when God used
EVERYTHING to speak to me. ☺ Love that He loves us
so much that He'll repeat things over and over until we
truly and fully understand. Love His promises!
- Song: "Loose Change" by Andrew Peterson (see Song
Appendix for lyrics)
- Observation: Our society tells us that it's all about us, that
we should get everything we ever strive for and desire,
and we should get it right now. It's all about instant
gratification and self-entitlement. Jesus calls us to live a life
of self-sacrifice and self-discipline for eternal gain, for His
glory not our own. We're so very short-sighted and selfish.
No wonder most of us find following Jesus so very hard.
- Everything you've gone through in the past and everything
you're going through now is going to work together for
your good if you let God work in your life. God will use
all of the trials, tribulations, heartaches, headaches, and
seemingly impossible situations to grow you into the Godly
person you were meant to be. All you have to do is open
your heart completely to Him and let Him drive. Follow
the guidance in His word, pray every single day (even if it's

just for a few minutes to start), and be obedient to what He tells you. You will see a remarkable change in your life. God doesn't do things small. He's into big, flashy, and REMARKABLE! ☺

- Always care more about what God thinks than what people think. You CANNOT please people and God at the same time.

- God has shown me something that I never thought I'd say in a million years. It is the following: Being single is an abundant blessing! You could be locked into a marriage with an ungodly spouse, and that road is Much more difficult than simply being single. I've had the privilege (I guess you could say it's a privilege, for lack of a better word) to see both Godly marriages and people stuck in marriages with very ungodly spouses. I can say with Total Conviction that I'd MUCH rather be completely single FOREVER than to be in a tough situation like that. So even if you don't think you can ever be happy being single, be Thankful that you're not in a worse situation because you easily could be . . . God bless and keep you always!

- TOUGH Trials! But With an Eternal Purpose . . .
  by Cynthia Johnson on Sunday, January 22, 2012, at 10:18 p.m.
  C onsider this, if you have been far away from Jesus . . . He just gave me this powerful word to contemplate: "I will surely gather them from all the lands where I banish them in my furious anger and great wrath; I will bring them back to this place and let them life in safety. They will be my people, and I will be their God. I will give them singleness of heart and action, so that they will always fear me for their own good and the good of their children after them. I will make an everlasting covenant with them: I will never stop doing good to them, and I will inspire them to fear me, so that they will never turn away from me."
  Jeremiah 32:37-40

Consider that the trials you are going through right now are meant to bring you in closer relationship with the Father . . . they are intended to help you grow and gain the 'singleness of heart' that the Lord is speaking of in this passage. Imagine what your life will look like when your faith grows to the point where you will never turn away from Jesus again! Wow . . . What an Amazing and loving God we have!!! He loves us so much that He allows us to go through exceedingly tough trials for our eternal benefit instead of letting us suffer the wrath we deserve.

January 23

- I have had a long week ahead of her this week. The Lord is my strength and my shield.
- "The Christian does not begin with what the human intellect has discovered. The Christian begins with what God has revealed." William Barclay

January 24

- "Faith is acting like God is telling you the truth." Tony Evans
- SONG: "Before the Morning" by Josh Wilson (see Song Appendix for lyrics)
- Any good you see in me is not me. It's HIM. God is everything good in me!
- "We are all faced with a series of great opportunities brilliantly disguised as impossible situations." Charles R. Swindoll
- Encouragement from a friend: "A Virtuous Woman serves God with all of her heart, mind, and soul. She seeks His will for her life and follows His ways." Psalm 119:15
  God has a time for everything, a perfect schedule. He is never too soon, never too late. The when of His will is as important as the what and the how.
- Encouragement from a friend: If you are not being treated with love and respect, check your "price tag"! Perhaps you

have marked yourself down. It's you who tell people what you are worth by what you accept. Get off the "clearance rack" and get behind the glass where they keep the valuables. The bottom line is value yourself more.

- Encouragement from a friend: Clearing old debris is not easy and, like success, must be intentional. If you cleave to what you've been through, it remains impossible for those around us to perceive our true selves. To let go of the past takes great courage. But if you believe, like I do, that the reward is worth the effort, let the work begin.

- If you truly love someone, the best thing you can do for them is to put them directly in the Lord's hands and back off so HE can work in their lives with no interference from you.

  My comment on my status: It can break your heart to let them go, but I know I would be completely devastated if I thought that I had done anything to inhibit their spiritual growth. That has Eternal consequences, and I love 'em way too much to compromise that!

- There's no other way to know the Word than to be IN the Word.

- Scripture God put on my heart today: "Brothers, if someone is caught in a sin, you who are spiritual should restore him gently. But watch yourself or you also may be tempted. Carry each other's burdens, and in this way you will fulfill the law of Christ. If anyone thinks he is something when he is nothing, he deceives himself. Each one should test his own actions. Then he can take pride in himself, without comparing himself to somebody else for each one should carry his own load. Anyone who receives instruction in the word must share all good things with his instructor. Do not be deceived: God cannot be mocked. A man reaps what he sows." Galatians 6:1-7

  My comment on my post: The rest of the passage: "The one who sows to please his sinful nature, from that nature will reap destruction; the one who sows to please the

Spirit, from the Spirit will reap eternal life. Let us not become weary in doing good, for at the proper time we will reap a harvest if we do not give up. Therefore, as we have opportunity, let us do good to all people, especially to those who belong to the family of believers." Galatians 6:8-10

- There is no easy way to get to where you want to go, to get to a truly healthy place, especially when you're coming from an unhealthy place. Don't blame others and don't make someone else hold you accountable. The best way for you to make progress is to take an HONEST look at your own actions, hold yourself accountable, and make the necessary adjustments. Love yourself enough to insist that you act appropriately, especially when it is the most difficult thing to do. God will bless you for it. Stay strong in HIM. HE is your strength and your shield, not you!

- The more you're in the Word (the Bible), the easier it will be for you to recognize God's will for your life. Don't leave your spiritual growth up to the pastor's message once or twice a week. Take an active role and spend some time with Jesus every night. God bless and keep you always!

January 25

- STOLEN? I THINK NOT! Godly people canNOT be stolen by another person outside of a committed relationship. To be in a Godly relationship, we must Always get HIS permission before entering into it, we must make sure we keep the relationship on the right level at all times, and we must stay committed and treat our partner how God tells us to treat our partner. Both people must be striving to do God's will and have God first in their heart and life. Otherwise, we're just headed for another relationship disaster. Let's all get in the Bible and find out how God would mold our hearts so we will know how He wants us to treat others in general and those special people we love most in our lives. God bless and keep you always!

- Sometimes the best thing to do is just get alone with God, just HIM and you, to have a heart-to-heart. Rely on Him always and He will never fail you. God bless and keep you always.
- Don't lose heart. Even when EVERYTHING seems totally out of control, God's still got ya! Just take His hand. Let Him carry you through. Close your eyes to all the craziness around you, don't listen to any of Satan's lies, and rely completely on Jesus to carry you through.
- SONG: "Forever Reign" by Hillsong (see Song Appendix for lyrics)
- YOU BE INSPIRING! I've heard so many times, "You really know the Word, please come back to join our Bible study [Sunday school, small group, etc.] again!" How about we ALL get in the Bible, study it, soak it in every day, THEN when we get together for Bible study, we will ALL have something from HIM to bring to the table, and we can ALL grow. Don't rely on one or two key people to pull you along. Get close to Jesus. Let HIM inspire you so that YOU can inspire others! God bless you always.
- WOW! Check This Out . . .
  by Single Parents Rock! When we lean on The Rock on Wednesday, January 25, 2012, at 9:15 a.m.
  This is what the LORD says about how He will treat His people after after they have suffered the consequences of their sin. He says that He will not banish them forever, that He will restore them to the land that He promised them and make them prosperous. The AMAZING thing to me is the words that HE uses . . . check this out:
  Jeremiah 32:36-41 "You are saying about this city, 'By the sword, famine and plague it will be handed over to the king of Babylon'; but this is what the Lord, the God of Israel, says: I will surely gather them from all the lands where I banish them in my furious anger and great wrath; I will bring them back to this place and let them live in safety. They will be my people, and I will be their God. I will give

them singleness of heart and action, so that they will always fear me for their own good and the good of their children after them. I will make an *everlasting covenant* with them; *I will never stop doing good to them*, and I will inspire them to fear me, so that they will never turn away from me. *I will rejoice in doing them good* and will assuredly plant them in this land *with all my heart and soul*."

WOW! That is POWERFUL! Think about it . . . God has made an EVERLASTING covenant with us, that means it is eternal, it will NEVER be broken. As long as we bring our hearts to Him and truly repent (are sorry for and turn away from) of our sin HE will ALWAYS forgive us. He says that He will never stop doing good to us. The verse that tells us that God will work everything for the good of those that love Him reinforces this message. Keep in mind that God CANNOT lie, it is impossible. Not only will he never stop doing good to us, He will REJOICE in it. God REJOICES when He does good for us, He loves us that much!!! It doesn't just make Him smile, He doesn't just get a sense of accomplishment over it, HE REJOICES!! That's full blown, all out REJOICING! Wow . . . Our God is THAT excited to do GOOD to us! Amazing . . . BUT the MOST AMAZING part to me is the last part. The Lord says that He will assuredly plant them in this land "WITH ALL MY HEART AND SOUL". Now think for a minute . . . This is the God that gave His only Son for our sins when He already knew ALL the sins that we would ever commit, He knew how many would turn away from Him, He knew all the destruction and evil that we would do to each other every single day of our lives. This is a Righteous Savior that abhors the site of sin, yet . . . He gave His ALL to save us in spite of ourselves and he says that He will "assuredly plant them in this land (the promised land) with all my heart and soul" . . . WOW . . . I can't even fathom the depths of His love for us and He wants to bless us and establish us in His will with all His heart and soul.

What an Amazing God we serve, one who loves the very least of us so very much to give His all, one who pursues a real relationship with us our entire loves, one who always sacrifices and gives grace and love even when He is mistreated, lied on, denied and rejected. One who keeps loving us with ALL HIS HEART AND SOUL!

My heart longs to be like Him, to be able to show others love and compassion like He does, to be able to walk in His light even when others mistreat me, lie on me, deny and reject me . . . to be able to keep loving HIM and loving others as He calls me because that is what He calls me to do.

God please help us all to shine YOUR light in this world, to not get so jaded and hurt over our trials and tribulations that we lose site of the goal. Please help us keep our eyes on You so that we will not lose site of what You have called us to do, to walk with You in this world and shine Your light so that all may be saved.

To God be all the glory! Amen

May God bless and keep you always!

- Encouragement from a friend: I've come to realize that the only people I need in my life are the ones who need me in theirs, even when I have nothing else to offer them but myself.
- Encouragement from a friend: Just because someone hurt you yesterday doesn't mean you should start living life today in constant fear of being hurt tomorrow.
- Self-discipline does not come naturally. It takes practice.
- Encouragement from a friend: End of Day Blessing: May God heal you, lift you up, and restore you fully. May you see glimpses of His glory everywhere you turn. May He show you wonders of His love that overwhelm you and make your knees weak. May He put a new song in your heart and a new dream in your spirit. May you walk forward unafraid and full of faith that your future will be far greater than your past. Rest well tonight. He's got you.

- Guard your heart. When illusions are shattered by the Light, you must remember they were just illusions. They were never real. Your real worth is found in Jesus. Never forget that.

January 26

- Sometimes we need our friends to remind us where our strength comes from. Today was one of those days for me. I have a faithful friend who kindly reminded me to look UP and that I'd be okay because God always makes sure that I'm okay. ☺ I hope and pray each and every one of you has at least one friend close enough to you to be able to gently remind you to look to Father God for your strength and encouragement when you need it most. God bless and keep you always!
- Patience, patience, patience . . . Be patient with people and show them God's love, ESPECIALLY when they treat you wrong. By showing them God's love, you let His message shine through instead of letting your hurt and bitterness give them more of a reason to act poorly in the future. When someone is acting very poorly and they're met with Godly love, it's disarming. Where the light is, the darkness must flee! TRUTH! God bless and keep you always.
- Men that use women and women that use men are not acting within God's will for their lives. One day, if they wake up, they will realize that they have allowed themselves to be used and degraded by their own desires. Don't hate them, pray for them because they are exceedingly lost!
- "Why are you cast down, O my soul, and why are you in turmoil within me? Hope in God; for I shall again praise him, my salvation and my God." Psalm 42:11
- Encouragement from a friend: Everything is going to be okay. God is here!
- God is not bound by our realm of possibilities and impossibilities. Don't let your disillusionment with your

situation make you lose heart. God WILL make a way where there is no way!

- Encouragement from a friend: People are often unreasonable, self-centered. Forgive them anyway. If you are honest, people may cheat you, but be honest anyway. What you spend years to build, someone could destroy overnight. Build anyway. The good you do today, people will often forget tomorrow. Do good anyway. You see, in the final analysis, it is between you and God; it never was between you and them anyway.

- I am thankful for dear friends in whom I can confide knowing that they'd never hold anything I said against me no matter how rough a day I'm having. You know who you are . . . Sincerely, THANK YOU!

- Encouragement from a friend: God's Light shines most brightly through believers who trust Him in the dark. That kind of trust is supernatural—a production of His indwelling Spirit.

- Liked a friend's status: Ask and you shall be given; Seek and you shall find; Knock and it shall be opened unto you!

- Encouragement from a friend: Don't punish the man in front of you for the mistakes made by the man behind you.♥

January 27

- Praise God in EVERYTHING! His plan is always the best, even when it doesn't seem like it to us right now. Does the five-year-old throw a fit when you tell him he can't reach on top of the hot stove to get the freshly baked cookie? Yes, he does! Would he get hurt if he reached up there? Yes, he would! We're God's children. We don't always understand why he gives us the answers and direction that He gives, but it is ALWAYS for our good. God bless and keep you always.

- If you need to square up with anyone, settle any debt or dispute. Do it now. Do not delay. Don't let it fester or

stew. Don't let it grow into an item of contention. Don't
let it divide you from anyone. Be properly reconciled
with everyone. Show God's love. Forgive what you need
to forgive. This will work to your benefit so that you can
receive your blessing, for if you have anything against
anyone, it builds a barrier between you and God. Be
reconciled with your brothers and sisters so that you may
take your burdens before the Father. God bless you always.

- When God gives you a deep compassion for a certain
group of people, walk in it, serve that group of people.
There will be heartbreaking moments, moments that bring
you to your knees. Don't be discouraged though. God has
everything under control.

- Encouragement from a friend: When you smile, you prove
to Jesus you're trusting in him. "Smile."

- Maybe God is using the pain in your life to help you
better understand what Christ gave for you. He calls us
to forgive without judgment of others, what we've done
is just as bad as what others have done to us. There is no
sliding scale of "better" or "worse" sins. Sin is sin, and it's
ALL ugly to the core.

- Maybe, just maybe, God's keeping you so busy to keep you
from making Terrible decisions that you'd make if left to
your own devices with an abundance of time . . . Ya think?
God loves us so much!

- Sometimes when we're asked to abstain from something,
it's to build our self-discipline. Be obedient, the reward
is far greater than the pain of the sacrifice. We cannot be
Christlike without self-discipline.

- Encouragement from a friend: Thinking: Five years ago,
my life was an absolute mess, and if someone would have
told me then that would I WILLINGLY stop fornicating,
WILLINGLY stop drinking alcohol, WILLINGLY stop
ALL THE MADNESS and surrender my life to God, I
would've said, "Yeah, right!" If they would've told me this
three years ago, I would've said "Child, boo! Whateva!"

Today, if someone was to say are you willing to die for Jesus? My answer is "YES! If my serving Jesus costs me life, that's a price I'm WILLING to pay! I WILL NEVER STOP WORSHIPPING JESUS!" I'm FREE! NO MORE BONDAGE! I'm 'bout to run a lap.

- Encouragement from a friend: What's the purpose of believing on JESUS? Picture yourself drowning in a big sea of sin. Now picture JESUS CHRIST being That ROPE for you to Grab, hold on to, and be pulled to safety. No Need to even touch the ROPE if you want to drown (keep sinning). The Purpose of THE ROPE is to Rescue you from sin. IN JESUS'S LOVING NAME. AMEN.

January 28

- Let us thank God for another day to spend with our families, another day He has given us to glorify Him and show others His love so that they too might be saved. Thank you, Father God, for loving us so very much and watching over us always!
- Obedience is required to receive your blessing. Always be obedient to God's will, even when you don't understand it. HE does not harm His children. He loves and watches over them always! God bless and keep you always.
- Love everyone just as they are. Show them all God's love. HE bestowed His love and forgiveness on us even before we were born. If we judge others, we show them condemnation. This world shows everyone enough condemnation for two lifetimes. Do not judge, for it is not our place. That is to be left to God. We are called to love like Christ loves us. We cannot reason or push people into the Kingdom. We must LOVE THEM IN! God be with you always.
- Encouragement from a friend: Never will He leave or forsake you.
- Love serving the Lord on Saturday! Thankfully, today He has given me a reprieve to get caught up and spend some

quality time alone with Him as I serve. Our Father truly takes care of our every need. ☺

- Stop focusing on yourself. It's not all about you. Start focusing on what God is leading you to do instead of being so wound up in your relationships, your happiness, your wants, your desires.

- Something to ponder: What if we all loved one another simply because God has called us to truly love one another? What an amazing change our world would see!

- If a man is not willing to seek God's heart to find you, He's not worthy to win your heart.

January 29

- EVE: The only thing Eve knew before God brought her to Adam was where God was. The text says, "But for Adam no suitable helper was found. So the Lord God caused the man to fall into a deep sleep; and while he was sleeping, he took one of the man's ribs and closed up the place with flesh. Then the Lord God made a woman from the rib he had taken out of the man, and he brought her to the man." Genesis 2:20b-22

  My thought: If you are a single woman looking for your man, you're looking in the wrong place. If you do not know which man is yours, the only thing you can look for is God. HE is the only one who can bring you to your husband. God didn't create Eve then to just leave her stranded in the garden, not knowing where to go or what to do, thinking, *Yeah . . . she'll find him eventually . . .* NO! God "brought her to the man." Be patient, and God will bring you to your man too. Be obedient and patient and allow God to bless and keep you always!

- Curl up with the Bible tonight. God may just show you something surprising! ☺

- A lil algebra: forgiveness + God's love + obedience = increased faith + tremendous blessings

Makes it possible to have Joy in the midst of the storm when you truly understand what awaits you on the other side. ☺

- Problem: Worried? Want some peace of mind?
  Answer: Read the Book (as we sang in Sunday school as children, "The B-I-B-L-E, yes, that's the book for me. I stand alone on the Word of God, the B-I-B-L-E." ☺

January 30

- "I call on the Lord in my distress, and he answers me." Psalm 120:1
  "I lift up my eyes to the hills—where does my help come from? My help comes from the Lord, the Maker of heaven and earth. He will not let your foot slip—he who watches over you will not slumber; indeed, he who watches over Israel will neither slumber nor sleep. The Lord watches over you—the Lord is your shade at your right hand; the sun will not harm you by day, nor the moon by night. The Lord will keep you from all harm—he will watch over your life; the Lord will watch over your coming and going both now and forevermore." Psalm 121
- Encouragement from a friend: Some women want you to be attracted to them with their mean and hateful ways. You must Really think men are Really Desperate. It's Not that serious. When a man learns his value, he knows to accept Only what's Good. Change your thinking. You can't seduce Every man. I have to See the Love of CHRIST and the holiness of GOD Flowing through you. Don't mistake desire for desperation. You still must meet Certain Righteous Demands. Humble yourself! IN JESUS'S NAME. ☺ AMEN.
  My comment: This one cuts both ways. Both men and women need to know their worth in Christ. If they did, neither would accept inappropriate behavior from the other. Men and women both need to back up off our "culture's accepted behavior" and quit excusing

COMPLETELY INAPPROPRIATE AND UNGODLY behavior because it's "normal" and using the excuses that "everyone does it," "it happens to good people all the time." We ALL need to be more respectful of each other and accept full responsibility for our actions.

- Encouragement from a friend: Mostly every woman I meet is sexually active. It has become the norm to claim to be single yet having a sex partner. A man who saves himself wants the same in a woman. And don't lie about how long it's been or say you're a virgin if you're really not. Sexual Purity is Commanded of us. So save yourselves for your husband. IN JESUS'S LOVING AND FAITHFUL NAME. AMEN.

  My comment: Truthfully, when a woman is walking in the Spirit, a sexually impure man—who continues in that path—is VERY UNATTRACTIVE, to the point of repulsive really. If more men and women realize this, maybe they would do a better job of remaining pure as God commands us.

- Encouragement from a friend: With the help of the lord, I will keep moving forward!

- Encouragement from a friend: Let's keep everyone in prayer that's going through a storm right now. Jesus will never leave us or forsake us. Keep praying.

- Encouragement from a friend: Our imperfect relationships with people should make us appreciate God's perfect relationship with us.

- Encouragement from a friend: Get Your Joy Back! Whatever situations are going on in your life right now, you need joy. The joy of the Lord is your strength. To think of Him and all that He has done so far and is still doing should bring you joy.

- "I tell you the truth, if anyone says to this mountain, 'Go, throw yourself into the sea,' and does not doubt in his heart but believes that what he says will happen, it will be done for him. Therefore I tell you, whatever you ask for in prayer, believe that you have received it, and it will be yours. And when you stand praying, if you hold anything against anyone, forgive him, so that your Father in heaven may forgive your sins." Mark 11:23-25 NIV

January 31

- ALL is well! All is well, all is well with my soul! We serve such an AWESOME God!
- Thank you, all my friends and family, who are so supportive when I need you. I love you all very much!
- All I can say tonight is PRAYER WORKS! Wow . . . God is good. ☺
- GOD ANSWERS PRAYER! Situation: My mom has had two breast biopsies, four pounds of tumors removed when she had female surgery years ago, had a sixteen-year-old cousin die from liver cancer, has a cousin who died from cancer, my grandpa on one side and grandma on the other side of the family died from cancer, all this to say my mom had surgery today to remove a cyst from her liver. It was abnormally large (size of a tennis ball) and was growing where all the cancerous cysts grow on the liver AND was between two major veins and an artery. The cyst was NOT cancerous, and after a very long day of surgery, she is resting comfortably at home in her own bed tonight CANCER FREE! GOD TRULY DOES ANSWER PRAYER! Be encouraged. HE is listening and performing miracles DAILY.

February 2012

February 1

- I apologize for not posting anything yesterday. It was a very hectic day. I took my mom to the hospital to have surgery. She had a cyst on her liver in the place where most cancerous cysts grow. We also have a VERY bad history of cancer in our family. (Mom had a cousin die of liver cancer when he was sixteen; another cousin died of cancer a couple years ago; my grandpa on one side and grandma and grandpa on the other side died of cancer; and my mom has had two breast biopsies, four pounds of tumors removed when she had female surgery years ago; and now this.) I say all this to let you know that the cyst was removed, and it was NOT cancerous! God has greatly blessed my family this week! HE DOES ANSWER PRAYER! God bless and keep you always.
- Sometimes we just need a soft place to fall to recoup from the day. Let Jesus be your soft place. No one else is more reliable or knows how you feel and just how to comfort you than our Savior. Let HIM hold you tonight. Lean back and know how much He loves you and is protecting you all through the night.
- Mastery not Torture: Mastery is using what has knocked you down to advance. God is not punishing you when you're called to keep walking in something that has knocked you down. He is giving you an opportunity to master it so that you will be able to move on. Embrace the opportunity, master the situation, and move on to your next blessing!
- Because I said so: Growing up, when our parents said "because I said so," it usually meant "I don't have time to explain it to you." But when our Heavenly Father says "because I said so," it means "because I love you too much

to let you settle for what you think is best for you right now. I have bigger and better plans for you, my Beloved." ☺

February 2

- No matter what you're going through, no matter what you're facing, if you have given your heart to Jesus, HE is with you, watching over you, protecting you. Never forget that HE LOVES YOU! God be with you tonight . . . close to your heart to protect it dearly . . .
- Rest in Jesus's arms. He loves you more than you can fathom.
- Seek justice, love mercy, and walk humbly with your God. Someone reminded me tonight that when we do these things, God is with us. He has not forgotten about our heart's desires. He loves us very much and still has wonderful things planned for our future. Sometimes the journey is daunting, but HE has already won the victory. He knows what breaks our hearts and will heal our every hurt. We just have to trust Him. Good night, all.
- Sometimes you gotta literally wrestle with issues. It's not pretty, and it ain't fun, but sometimes you gotta do what you gotta do. God never said we had to be graceful about it. He just tells us to be obedient.
- Deep-seeded pain takes time to heal. Give it time.

February 3

- When you give your whole heart to Jesus, it is HIS heart to protect. So when HE protects your heart, don't let yourself slip into feeling like you're in prison. Jesus is guarding your heart and keeping it safe so that you'll be able to give it to the right person when He shows them to you. Praise HIM for keeping your heart safe from you and others who would give it away too quickly or hurt it if they got their hands on it. Jesus is your protector and the lover of your soul. HE will never do you wrong. May you let God bless and keep you always.

- "Because of the Lord's great love we are not consumed, for his compassions never fail. They are new every morning; great is your faithfulness . . . The Lord is good to those whose hope is in him, to the one who seeks him." Lamentations 3:22-25
- If you are a single woman, the Holy Spirit is your covering, your protector, your husband. Surrender your will and LET HIM cover you. You cannot do this on your own.
- Sometimes the only thing left to DO is to rest in God's love and wait on His timing.
- There's just something about soft rain in the morning before the sun comes up. Beautiful . . . Peaceful. ☺ Thank You, Jesus, for this nice peaceful morning.

February 4

- Have some FUN today! No matter what else you have to do, take some time out of your hectic day to just have some fun. You deserve a lil break from all the craziness too. ☺)
- Spend a little time with Jesus tonight. It'll soothe your soul to read His word and spend a few minutes letting Him touch your heart. ☺
- A friend's status: It's very difficult, once certain patterns are established, to change our conditioned default settings. We all have had incidents, altercations, accidents, and inhibitions that have left us scarred and unsteady on our feet. As you submit to God, He will show you the real you and line you up with the original purpose and destiny for your life.
- When I am weak and weary, worn down from this hard and tumultuous road, Jesus is my strength and my light. He picks me up and carries me when I have no strength left. He protects me from my foes. Thank You, Father God, for watching over and protecting me.

February 5

- Going to praise the Lord this morning! ☺ Whether you have a chance to go to church or not, put on some jammin' praise music and spend some time simply and honestly praising the Lord for all of the blessings He's given you and for all the things and places that He has brought you out of. Give Him PRAISE today!

- Whatever God is taking you through is making you into the person HE meant for you to be. It may be painful now, but if you let God grow you, let Him show you the way you are meant to take, let Him change and mold your heart into the beautiful Godly heart He meant for you to have. You will be tremendously blessed! Don't let the pain you're going through blind you to God's grace, goodness, and blessing for your life. Often times, God must bring the pain to the surface so that He may heal us and grow us, so that we will have to lean on Him and put Him before everyone and everything else in life, so that He may teach us in His ways. He does this to shine through us and bring all to salvation. Please let God continue to use you through the pain and tough situations, for in our weakness, His strength and glory shine the brightest.

- Something to consider before giving in to frustration: God is making you into Exactly who you were meant to be. Thank the Lord for blessing you with what you need in order to grow into the person He created you to be. You may not be who you want to be or have what you want to have, but HE sees the big picture we do not. HE loves you more than you can imagine and wants the BEST for His children. Be patient and trust in Him. Jesus is much wiser than we are.

   God bless and keep your mind and actions so that they are pleasing to Him.

- Sometimes we must endure a certain phase of our life or undesirable situation for a prolonged period so that when God delivers us from that phase or situation, HE gets all the credit, so that we will Never forget where He has delivered us from and what He has brought us through.

- So grateful it's Sunday! I get to go to God's house, rest in His presence, and let all the worries and cares of this world fade away. Resting in His arms brings me peace. ♥

February 6

- Lord, thank you for showing me my worth in You. Thank YOU for not allowing me to underestimate myself any longer, to abide in my worth in You. You make my life INFINITELY better. I give You all the glory for what you have done for me and where You have brought me from. I could Never have done it without you. To God be the glory. Amen.

- You Are What You Eat (Heart Food)
  by Single Parents Rock! When we lean on The Rock on Monday, February 6, 2012, at 9:29 p.m.
  The old saying 'you are what you eat' is accurate in so many ways. The things we allow in our lives, or have no choice but to allow in our lives (in the case of how we were raised, no one gets to pick how they are raised . . . all they can do is try to use their upbringing for the best after they are old enough and independent enough to strike out on their own) play a huge part in how our hearts are formed and how we treat others.
  I was reading in Ezekiel and it struck me . . . I have a problem with hard heartedness . . . While contemplating this, I realized that while growing up I was ALWAYS around certain people who were (and still are to this day) very hard hearted. To look at the lives of the people in my life I Must realize that these people have been carrying around some Serious emotional baggage their entire lives and have therefore become hard hearted. They did this so that they wouldn't be hurt by other people, and the world in general, any more. They did not rely on Jesus when they were in pain, they instead tried to do it all alone and failed

(because we ALL FAIL when we try to do anything on our own for we can do nothing without Christ).

I did not realize that I was forming habits in my life that mirrored those of these influential people around me. I did not realize how much I was influenced by them and began to pattern my life with habits gained from them. To this day, I have a hot temper and have to watch it closely or it gets the best of me. Jesus is showing me that the only way I can permanently conquer this aspect of my life is through TOTAL SURRENDER of my ENTIRE heart to HIM, to my Lord and Savior. HE wants to heal my heart, soul and life completely. HE wants to restore me to the wholeness HE has destined and planned for me.

The passage in Ezekiel is very encouraging: Ezekiel 11:17-20 "Therefore say: 'This is what the Sovereign Lord says: I will gather you from the nations and bring you back from the countries where you have been scattered, and I will give you back the land of Israel again.' They will return to it and remove all its vile images and detestable idols. I will give them an undivided heart and put a new spirit in them; I will remove from them their heart of stone and give them a heart of flesh. Then they will follow my decrees and be careful to keep my laws. They will be my people, and I will be their God."

Even though Israel had been so very despicable in the Lord's sight, He still loved them and promised to restore them to give them a new heart and to be their God. HE wants to do the same for you and me today. If you struggle with this issue as well, I encourage you to not mirror those hurt and hurting people in your life. Mirror Jesus, lay your heart completely open before the Father and let Him heal you completely and bring you into your true purpose.

• Just because no one has ever loved you with a Godly love doesn't mean that no one ever will. It just means that you haven't found the right one yet.

February 7

- God is taking you through what He is taking you through for a reason. Many times, we do not understand His divine purpose, but everything will work out for your good in the long run. Stay in the race. Don't give up. Our God is a good and loving God. TRUST HIM! He is growing you into the amazing person He created you to be. Hang in there and trust that His plan is better than how things appear in the short term.

- Marriage requires self-sacrifice. If you are not willing to sacrifice yourself for God, how do you expect to be able to sacrifice what needs sacrificed for a spouse? Hummm . . .

- Something to think about: Maybe, just maybe, you are called to walk the road you're walking so that you will realize it's not all about you. Maybe you need to acknowledge and walk in the truth that, though you are Fiercely loved by our Father, you are called to live for Someone else and not for yourself.

February 8

- Something to think about: GOOD NEWS! If you're a single parent with teenage children, they get to watch how you conduct yourself when you date.
  BAD NEWS! If you're a single parent with teenage children, they get to watch how you conduct yourself when you date.
  Which is true for you?
  May God bless and keep you always.

- Don't let your situation defeat you. Stay grounded in the Word (the Bible), pray often, and know that God is holding you in the palm of His hand. He loves you dearly, has not forgotten about you, and will always be there for you. All you have to do is call on His name and He will answer. God bless and keep you always!

- Personal Experience: God will take your least desirable situations and experiences and use them to bless you tremendously! Be patient in your current situation and disappointments. Trust that God will use them for your good. Let Him grow and bless you because He will.

February 9
- Let Jesus be your strength.
- God cares about what's in your heart. He cares about your deepest hurts. Don't reserve your deepest pain all for yourself; you'll never get rid of it if you do. Trust God enough to lay it ALL open to Him so that He can heal you. He desires to heal you completely so you don't have to walk in so much pain. It breaks His heart when you choose to stay hurt to keep the resentment, anger, frustration, and heart pain. Let it go.
  May God bless and keep you always!
- Pray, pray, pray, and pray some more. Never stop praying. Listen to God's guidance and pray how He directs you. You don't have to understand why. Just do as He says because he is your Father.
- Encouragement from a friend: If God is powerful enough to take you to heaven, He's powerful enough to have your back on earth. Trust Him.
  My response: Amen! ☺
- When you finally get to the place where you are resting at ease in God's grace and have complete confidence in His plan, it makes obeying Him so much less stressful! Hard to get there, but so worth it!
- Ask and you shall receive: We tend to think if we mind all the rules, we'll get what we want, not so. It's not about rules. It's about relationship with Jesus. The closer we get to Him, the more He molds our hearts to look like His. So when we pray for the desires of our hearts, they're the desires God has for us and He blesses us tremendously. It is a process, like all relationships. It takes time.
- Encouragement from a friend: My heart belongs to Jesus!

February 10

- Make it a priority to spend some fun time with your family tonight. ☺ You can never show your family how much you truly love them enough! Love them dearly every day you have them.

- Trust God more than you trust anyone or anything else. If HE tells you to move on, do it. If He tells you to stay and pray when things look completely impossible, do it. Obeying our Heavenly Father will save you so much heartache! Allow Him to protect you and heed His word. Without His protection, we are all headed for disaster as our vision is terribly limited.

- NEVER give anyone else the power to make you feel worthless. Know your worth in GOD, ground yourself in His word, give Him your heart, and let Him protect you. You're WORTH IT! You're a King's kid, and HE loves you more than you can imagine! God bless and keep you always.

- Pain comes in all shapes and sizes. Never assume anything about anyone from appearances. They may be carrying more pain inside than you could possibly imagine.

- Don't take the role that YOU want to take. Take the role that God directs you to take. Everything will work out much better if you go with His plan and abandon your own.

- Don't be ashamed of the story God has given you. Share it proudly! There is purpose in it. You've been brought through it to share it with others so that they may be encouraged by the amazing works God has done for you.

- No matter what you do, you're never going to please everyone. Make sure you're square with the Lord. Everything else is gravy.

- Encouragement from a friend: Be yourself no matter what other people think. God made you the way you are for a reason. Besides, an original is always worth more than a copy.

February 11

- Open Heart Surgery—Don't Do It Without the Anesthetic!
  by Cynthia Johnson on Saturday, February 11, 2012, at 9:18 a.m.
  As I've been walking through this journey of healing something occurs to me . . .In Ezekiel the Lord tells us the following:
  Ezekiel 11:17-20 "Therefore say: 'This is what the Sovereign Lord says: I will gather you from the nations and bring you back from the countries where you have been scattered, and I will give you back the land of Israel again.' They will return to it and remove all its vile images and detestable idols. I will give them an undivided heart and put a new spirit in them; I will remove from them their heart of stone and give them a heart of flesh. Then they will follow my decrees and be careful to keep my laws. They will be my people, and I will be their God."
  Upon listening to others speak of the pain that has been involved in their healing process and reflecting on my own process that God has been gracefully and faithfully taking me through, I've been given a revelation. God has revealed to me that this process is a LOT like physical open heart surgery and the only anesthetic is God's love and grace. During my healing process it has been physically excruciating at times due to the amount of spiritual and emotional healing that have taken place.
  See, in order for God to 'give them an undivided heart and put a new spirit in them, I will remove from them their heart of stone and give them a heart of flesh'. In order for God to do this He must first EXTRACT all the old junk that is so deeply embedded in our hearts, spirits, minds, bodies and souls. HE has to tear us open and we have to LET Him take these things that we hold onto so fiercely. Not only does the actual surgery hurt with an agonizing pain, the thought of letting these terrible things

go is mortifying to us because, like it or not . . . they have become our comfort zone, they have become our normal and we don't know how to cope without them.

We MUST be willing to let God take us COMPLETELY out of our comfort zones, to extract all the destructive junk (old abusive and destructive mind frames, negative self image, feelings of worthlessness, anger, hatred, bitter grief, selfishness, envy, pride, etc . . . the list is endless) in our lives and teach us how to rely on HIM. This means we must be humble enough to admit that we've been so terribly wrong and we must be open to His instruction and be willing to obey.

If we want to quell the pain as much as possible during this possible, the solution is simple . . . First understand we must feel the pain in order to realize how destructive our old ways, habits and mind-frames have been for us, we must walk through it to understand how deeply these things have been embedded into our spirits, so that we can understand what a miracle it is that God is able to extract these things out of us in the first place. This process needs to be allowed to bring us closer in relationship with our Jesus. In order for this to happen, we must allow His love and grace to overwhelm us. We must get in the Word (Bible) and search out just how much Jesus loves us and hang onto what HE tells us for dear life.

Getting into the Word has revealed His love for me on a level I never before thought possible. The amazing thing is that if we allow God to speak to us every single day (through Bible reading, prayer, devotions, etc . . .) we keep the GOOD NEWS going in and the devil has no choice but to flee! PRAISE GOD!!! This is our anesthetic for the pain. THIS is the way God holds us close to His heart while in surgery. Take the anesthetic, without it your heart may stop on the table and you may not survive the surgery! Let GOD LOVE you through the pain. It does get better on the other side. Please let God bless and keep you daily dear friends.

SUMMARY

The first post that started this whole thing was "Be true to yourself . . . don't just do what you think others expect of you . . . forge your own path . . . ," and that is where I was at that time. I was convinced that I needed to be true to myself, use my own judgment, and find my own way. In truth, that is the worst place any person can possibly be. Yes, it shows a little self-confidence, which had taken me *years* to formulate, but the thought is completely self-centered and misdirected. I don't care how strong a person you are. If you try to tackle this world with that mentality, you'll be beaten down every single time. There is only one way to survive this world and have a good outcome in the end, and that is to completely and totally rely on Jesus Christ.

The Bible teaches us that there is only one name by which a man can be saved, and that name is Jesus Christ. Until we submit our lives to Him and let Him heal and restore our hearts, we will never be able to see the world as He does, do the work that He has for us to do, and ultimately make it to glory with Him. The only way a person truly knows that they are ***totally and completely loved*** is to open their heart to the Lord. If you do this, He will heal your heart and open your eyes to who He created you to be. I pray that coming along with me on my journey from self-centeredness to God-centeredness has blessed you as much as it has blessed me. This journey has truly changed my life permanently! I will never look at the world, or myself, with the same cynical, unloved, jaded eyes ever again. God has given me a new passion to share His word and do His work, and I pray that you'll let Him change your heart too.

When I was thinking back on where I was emotionally during this journey, there are a couple of things that struck me: First, I am not a Bible scholar now nor was I when I started this book. In fact, I still have not yet read the Word completely through cover to cover. I am working on it and am going to finish it this year, but I have not yet read it all cover to cover. Lest you think that I knew the Bible like the back of my hand when I started this journey, I didn't and still do not. I am learning more and more every day. God gave me all the inspiration in this book. He guided me and put scripture in my hands, mind, and heart. He is the one who was driving, I am **not** that talented! The second thing that really struck me is I know where I was emotionally. I know what I was thinking, and there were *many* days that I was emotionally drained, spiritually bankrupt, mentally tapped, and totally stressed out. When looking back on the content of this book, I was *astounded* at how much information God kept giving me ***every single day***! He didn't take a break. He didn't get frustrated with me. He just kept teaching me, loving me, being right there with me through it all. HE *never* left me, ***ever***! *No one* on the planet has *ever* shown me that kind of love before. *No one* has ever stuck by my side through thick and thin, no matter how I felt, acted, or treated them. *No one* is capable of showing us true *agape* love like God can.

In my case, the only love I've ever known before this process was conditional, judgmental "love" and "love" by a worldly standard that was always tied to what I could do for someone else. Now I know what *true Love* is. God has truly healed my heart. I must say the following is heavy on my heart, and I *must* share this last message: *You do not have to be married to be complete. God completes you, God truly loves you, and God will see you through everything and provide for all your needs. Until you have a right relationship with Jesus, it is not even possible to have a completely right relationship with any human person. Please rely on God for all your needs, grow your relationship with Him, and let Him heal all of the relationships in your life. There is no other way to actually be a complete and fulfilled person.*

This book started with a message that I thought was the right one, "Be true to yourself," but in reality, we don't even know who we are until we let Jesus into our hearts on a real relationship level. In order to really understand what we're to do while we're here on earth and to be complete, we must find our identity in Christ. When we draw near to Him, in a deep, intimate, every-minute-of-every-day relationship with Him; when we let Him mold and shape our damaged hearts and make them into the beautiful Godly hearts that

HE created them to be, then we stop searching for something else to fit into that God-shaped hole in our hearts. We stop searching for love in all the wrong places because we've finally realized that the answer has been right there all the time. The old time Sunday school song says it best, "Jesus Loves Me." *It's true!* The scripture tells us that "God is love" (1 John 4:7-12, 16), and when we realize that it is absolutely true, then we realize that God is Love, so God is the source of *all* real love, and only God can love us with *agape* love.

We are called to love each other as God loves us, and we need to do it to the best of our feeble abilities. We must also recognize that we are human, and we're never going to be perfect at it like HE is; but in order to do this, we must also realize that we must continually forgive each other and show each other God's grace. He has forgiven all of our sins and shown us grace countless times. We are called to do the same for others. My burdens have been taken away; my heart is whole (albeit still a little sore, since the healing process is so fresh, but I know, without a doubt, that the soreness will fade with time). God has truly taken me from **Loneliness to LOVE,** and it has been nothing less than a miracle in my life. I could never have done this on my own. God bless and keep you always!

1 John 4:7-12: "Dear friends, let us love one another, for love comes from God. Everyone who loves has been born of God and knows God. Whoever does not love does not know God, because **_God is love_**. This is how God showed his love among us: He sent his one and only Son into the world that we might live through him. This is love: not that we loved God, but that he loved us and sent his Son as an atoning sacrifice for our sins. Dear friends, since God so loved us, we also ought to love one another. No one has ever seen God, but if we love one another, God lives in us and his love is made complete in us."

1 John 4:16: "And so we know and rely on the love God has for us. **_God is love_**. Whoever lives in love lives in God, and God in him."

B90X Reading Schedule

21 Aug - Day 1 - Gn 1:1—Gn 16:16
22 Aug - Day 2 - Gn 17:1—Gn 28:19
23 Aug - Day 3 - Gn 28:20—Gn 40:11
24 Aug - Day 4 - Gn 40:12—Gn 50:26
25 Aug - Day 5 - Ex 1:1—Ex 15:18
26 Aug - Day 6 - Ex 15:19—Ex 28:43
27 Aug - Day 7 - Ex 29:1—Ex 40:38
28 Aug - Day 8 - Lv 1:1—Lv 14:32
29 Aug - Day 9 -Lv 14:33—Lv 26:26
30 Aug - Day 10 -Lv 26:27—Nu 8:14
31 Aug - Day 11 - Nm 8:15—Nm 21:7
1 Sep - Day 12 - Nm 21:8—Nm 32:19
2 Sep - Day 13 - Nm 32:20—Dt 7:26
3 Sep - Day 14 - Dt 8:1—Dt 23:11
4 Sep - Day 15 - Dt 23:12—Dt 34:12
5 Sep - Day 16 - Jo 1:1—Jo 14:15
6 Sep - Day 17 - Jo 15:1—Jgs 3:27
7 Sep - Day 18 - Jgs 3:28—Jgs 15:12
8 Sep - Day 19 - Jgs 15:13—1 Sm 2:29
9 Sep - Day 20 - 1 Sm 2:30—1 Sm 15:35
10 Sep - Day 21 - 1 Sm 16:1—1 Sm 28:19
11 Sep - Day 22 - 1 Sm 28:20—2 Sm 12:10
12 Sep - Day 23 - 2 Sm 12:11—2 Sm 22:18
13 Sep - Day 24 - 2 Sm 22:19—1 Kgs 7:37
14 Sep - Day 25 - 1 Kgs 7:38—1 Kgs 16:20
15 Sep - Day 26 - 1 Kgs 16:21—2 Kgs 4:37
16 Sep - Day 27 - 2 Kgs 4:38—2 Kgs 15:26
17 Sep - Day 28 - 2 Kgs 15:27—2 Kgs 25:30
18 Sep - Day 29 - 1 Chr 1:1—1 Chr 9:44
19 Sep - Day 30 - 1 Chr 10:1—1 Chr 23:32
20 Sep - Day 31 - 1 Chr 24:1—2 Chr 7:10
21 Sep - Day 32 - 2 Chr 7:11—2 Chr 23:15

22 Sep - Day 33 - 2 Chr 23:16—2 Chr 35:15
23 Sep - Day 34 - 2 Chr 35:16—Ezr 10:44
24 Sep - Day 35 - Neh 1:1—Neh 13:14
25 Sep - Day 36 - Neh 13:15—Job 7:21
26 Sep - Day 37 - Job 8:1—Job 24:25
27 Sep - Day 38 - Job 25:1—Job 41:34
28 Sep - Day 39 - Job 42:1—Ps 24:10
29 Sep - Day 40 - Ps 25:1—Ps 45:14
30 Sep - Day 41 - Ps 45:15—Ps 69:21
1 Oct - Day 42 - Ps 69:22—Ps 89:13
2 Oct - Day 43 - Ps 89:14—Ps 108:13
3 Oct - Day 44 - Ps 109:1—Ps 134:3
4 Oct - Day 45 - Ps 135:1—Prv 6:35
5 Oct - Day 46 - Prv 7:1—Prv 20:21
6 Oct - Day 47 - Prv 20:22—Eccl 2:26
7 Oct - Day 48 - Eccl 3:1—Sg 8:14
8 Oct - Day 49 - Is 1:1—Is 13:22
9 Oct - Day 50 - Is 14:1—Is 28:29
10 Oct - Day 51 - Is 29:1—Is 41:18
11 Oct - Day 52 - Is 41:19—Is 52:12
12 Oct - Day 53 - Is 52:13—Is 66:18
13 Oct - Day 54 - Is 66:19—Jer 10:13
14 Oct - Day 55 - Jer 10:14—Jer 23:8
15 Oct - Day 56 - Jer 23:9—Jer 33:22
16 Oct - Day 57 - Jer 33:23—Jer 47:7
17 Oct - Day 58 - Jer 48:1—Lam 1:22
18 Oct - Day 59 - Lam 2:1—Ez 12:20
19 Oct - Day 60 - Ez 12:21—Ez 23:39
20 Oct - Day 61 - Ez 23:40—Ez 35:15
21 Oct - Day 62 - Ez 36:1—Ez 47:12
22 Oct - Day 63 - Ez 47:13—Dn 8:27
23 Oct - Day 64 - Dn 9:1—Hos 13:6
24 Oct - Day 65 - Hos 13:7—Am 9:10
25 Oct - Day 66 - Am 9:11—Na 3:19
26 Oct - Day 67 - Hb 1:1—Zc 10:12
27 Oct - Day 68 - Zc 11:1—Mt 4:25

28 Oct - Day 69 - Mt 5:1—Mt 15:39
29 Oct - Day 70 - Mt 16:1—Mt 26:56
30 Oct - Day 71 - Mt 26:57—Mk 9:13
31 Oct - Day 72 - Mk 9:14—Lk 1:80
1 Nov - Day 73 - Lk 2:1—Lk 9:62
2 Nov - Day 74 - Lk 10:1—Lk 10:19
3 Nov - Day 75 - Lk 20:20—Jn 5:47
4 Nov - Day 76 - Jn 6:1—Jn 15:17
5 Nov - Day 77 - Jn 15:18—Acts 6:7
6 Nov - Day 78 - Acts 6:8—Acts 16:37
7 Nov - Day 79 - Acts 16:38—Acts 28:16
8 Nov - Day 80 - Acts 28:17—Rom 14:23
9 Nov - Day 81 - Rom 15:1—1 Cor 14:40
10 Nov - Day 82 - 1 Cor 15:1—Gal 3:25
11 Nov - Day 83 - Gal 3:26—Col 4:18
12 Nov - Day 84 - 1 Thes 1:1—Phlm 25
13 Nov - Day 85 - Heb 1:1—Jas 3:12
14 Nov - Day 86 - Jas 3:13—3 Jn 14
15 Nov - Day 87 - Jude 1—Rv 17:18
15 Nov - Day 88 - Rv 18:1—Rv 22:21
16 Nov - Day 89 - Grace day
17 Nov - Day 90 - Grace day

The two grace days may be used at any time during the reading schedule. It also helps if you look at it as only twelve pages per day instead of looking at the task of reading the entire Bible in ninety days as a whole. I know that God blesses all who seek earnestly after Him. Keep the faith, and God bless!

Song Appendix

ORGANIZED BY DATE

- January 13, 2011
    "God Is Enough" by LeCrae

- January 30, 2011
    "The Best in Me" by Marvin Sapp
    "Never Would Have Made It" by Marvin Sapp
    "I'm Not Perfect" by J Moss

- February 13, 2011
    "Note to God" by Charice

- February 19, 2011
    "Crazy Love" by Hawk Nelson
    "You Can Have Me" by Sidewalk Prophets
    "This is the Stuff" by Francesca Battistelli

- March 7, 2011
    "Tonight" by Toby Mac
    "Lose My Soul" by Toby Mac

- March 10, 2011
    "Blessings" by Laura Story

- March 13, 2011
    "He Has His Hands on You" by Marvin Sapp

- April 4, 2011
    "Please Don't Let Me Go" by Group 1 Crew
    "Captured" by Toby Mac

- April 11, 2011
  "Stronger" by Mandisa
  "Does Anybody Hear Her" by Casting Crowns

- April 14, 2011
  "Background" by LeCrae

- June 8, 2011
  "God Speaking" by Mandisa

- July 3, 2011
  "Someone Watching Over You" by Yolanda Adams

- July 4, 2011
  "Shackles" (Praise You) by Mary Mary

- July 27, 2011
  "Song of Restoration" by LeShawn Daniel

- August 1, 2011
  "Stronger" by Mandisa

- August 5, 2011
  "Cover Me" by 21:03
  "Holding on to You" by 21:03
  "Chozen" by 21:03
  "You" by 21:03
  "Love Song" by LeCrae

- August 7, 2011
  "Get Low" by LeCrae
  "Take Me As I Am" by LeCrae

- August 15, 2011
  "Beautiful Things" by Gungor

- August 18, 2011
  "The Light in Me" by Brandon Heath

- August 19, 2011
  "Yes" by John Waller
  "Commission My Soul" by Citipointe

- September 1, 2011
  "I Will Rise" (Live) by Chris Tomlin

- September 5, 2011
  "The Loving Proof" by Mary J. Blige
  "Crawl" by Superchick

- September 9, 2011
  "Everything Good" by Ashes Remain

- September 11, 2011
  "Times" by Tenth Avenue North

- September 12, 2011
  "Commission My Soul" by Citipointe
  "Still Here" by 21:03

- September 18, 2011
  "Beautiful Things" by Gungor

- October 4, 2011
  "Lean on Me" by Group 1 Crew

- October 6, 2011
  "Intimacy" by Trip Lee
  "Cling to You" by Trip Lee

- October 7, 2011
  "Courageous" by Casting Crowns

- October 14, 2011
  "What Love Really Means" by JJ Heller
  "Strong Enough" by Matthew West

- October 16, 2011
  "Rescue" by Newsong

- October 28, 2011
  "Miracle of the Moment" by Steven Curtis Chapman

- October 31, 2011
  "Times" by Tenth Avenue North
  "Let It Go" by Tenth Avenue North

- November 6, 2011
  "Battle" by Chris August

- November 8, 2011
  "Where I Belong" by Building 429
  "Everything I Need" by Kutless
  "That's What Faith Can Do" by Kutless
  "Lose My Soul" by Toby Mac

- November 16, 2011
  "All of Me" by Matt Hammitt
  "TRUST" by Matt Hammitt

- November 17, 2011
  "UNCONDITIONAL" by Tedashii
  "Beautiful Feet" by LeCrae

- November 20, 2011
  "Faithful" by Brooke Fraser

- November 22, 2011
  "More than a Friend" by Jeremy Riddle

- December 2, 2011
  "Bout Time Full" by Tedashii (feat. Cam)
  "Kingdom People" by Tedashii - He Cares Ft. Keynon Akers

- December 11, 2011
  "Broken by I'm Healed" by Byron Cage

- December 20, 2011
  "Boasting" by LeCrae (feat. Anthony Evans)

- December 22, 2011
  "Spoken For" by MercyMe

- December 30, 2011
  "I Believe" by James Fortune (FIYA)

- January 22, 2012
  "Loose Change" by Andrew Peterson

- January 24, 2012
  "Before the Morning" by Josh Wilson

- January 25, 2012
  "Forever Reign" by Hillsong